Have You Been to Delphi?

SUNY series in Western Esoteric Traditions

David Appelbaum, Editor

Have You Been to Delphi?

Tales of the Ancient Oracle for Modern Minds

Roger Lipsey

Including an Afterword
with Lobsang Lhalungpa on Tibetan Oracles

STATE UNIVERSITY OF NEW YORK PRESS

Cover photo appears courtesy of Ann Douglass Photography, © 2000

Published by
State University of New York Press, Albany

Printed in the United States of America

For information, contact State University of New York Press, Albany, NY
www.sunypress.edu

Production by Michael Haggett
Marketing by Dana E. Yanulavich

Library of Congress Cataloging-in-Publication Data

Lipsey, Roger, 1942–
Have you been to Delphi? : tales of the ancient oracle for modern minds / Roger Lipsey ; including an afterword with Lobsang Lhalungpa on Tibetan oracles.
p. cm. — (SUNY series in Western esoteric traditions)
Includes bibliographical references and index.
ISBN 0-7914-4781-2 (alk. paper) — ISBN 0-7914-4782-0 (pbk. : alk. paper)
1. Delphian oracle. 2. Apollo (Greek deity)—Cult—Greece—Delphi (Extinct city) 3. Delphi (Extinct city) I. Title. II. Series.

DF261.D35 L46 2001
938'.3—dc21 00-050956

10 9 8 7 6 5 4 3 2 1

For Dru

These are the men and women down to my own day who are said to have given oracles from the god. But in the long course of time there could still be as many again.

—Pausanias, second century C.E.

Contents

Acknowledgments

This book has few but deep debts. The staff of the Thesaurus Linguae Graecae at the University of California, Irvine, provided a database without which my research would have been incomparably more difficult. Lobsang Lhalungpa gave generously of his knowledge of the Chief State Oracle of Tibet. Among classicists, Charles Rowan Beye, Richard Geldard, Günter Kopcke, and Robin Waterfield were kind enough to read a near-final draft. They would be the first—and I the second—to point out that this book is a writer's exploration rather than a strictly conceived academic study. Katherine Roberts and Rebecca Tucker provided research assistance with good will and high intelligence.

Worth Bracken helped at later stages with permissions and other chores cheerfully assumed when my own cheer was in short supply. What a debt to him. I am grateful to my friend Prof. David Appelbaum, of the State University of New York at New Paltz, who cared for this book and introduced me to the University Press. Naturally, no colleague or friend is responsible for errors of fact or judgment that remain.

Portions of this book were first published in *Parabola*, the New York quarterly; for many years, its editors have generously opened its pages to work in progress.

I cannot complete this page without acknowledging again the influence of Ananda K. Coomaraswamy. His short essay, "The 'E' at Delphi" (*Selected Papers,* vol. 2), was a tap on the shoulder years ago. Later in life, one cannot wrap oneself in the mantle of a deceased master for protection—but surely one can, from time to time, for warmth.

No words can capture my gratitude to my wife Susan for her encouragement, insights, and patience during the writing of this book, during this life.

Permissions

PUBLICATIONS

The Knights and Other Plays, Aristophanes, translated by David Barrett and Alan H. Sommerstein (Harmondsworth, Penguin Classics, 1978), pp. 74, 134, 135, 136, copyright © David Barrett and Alan H. Sommerstein, 1978. Reproduced by permission of Penguin Books Ltd.

The Histories, Herodotus, translated by Aubrey de Sélincourt, revised edition by A. R. Burn (Harmondsworth, Penguin Classics, 1954, revised edition, 1972), pp. 50–53, 57–61, 67–69, 70–79, 481–490, 613–614, copyright © A. R. Burn, 1972. Reproduced by permission of Penguin Books Ltd.

Guide to Greece: Volume 1; Central Greece, Pausanius, translated by Peter Levi (Harmondsworth, Penguin Classics 1971, revised edition 1979), pp. 415, 428, 452, 455, copyright © Peter Levi, 1971. Reproduced by permission of Penguin Books Ltd.

Guide to Greece: Volume 2; Southern Greece, Pausanius, translated by Peter Levi (Harmondsworth, Penguin Classics, 1971), pp. 16, 292, copyright © Peter Levi, 1971. Reproduced by permission of Penguin Books Ltd.

Conversations of Socrates, Xenophon, translated by Hugh Tredennick and Robin Waterfield (New York: Penguin Classics, 1990), pp. 186–187, translation copyright © Hugh Tredennick, 1970. Revised translation copyright © Robin Waterfield, 1990. Reproduced by permission of Penguin Books Ltd.

Plato, *The Collected Dialogues of Plato*, edited by Edith Hamilton and Huntington Cairns, translated by Lane Cooper, R. Hackforth, Michael Joyce, Benjamin Jowett, Hugh Tredennick. Copyright © 1961, renewed 1989. Reprinted by permission of Princeton University Press.

Reprinted by permission of the publishers and the Loeb Classical Library from Cicero: *De Senectute, De Amicitia, De Divinatione*, vol. 20, translated by William Armistead Falconer, Cambridge, Mass.: Harvard University Press, 1923.

Reprinted by permission of the publishers and the Loeb Classical Library from Clement of Alexandria: *Exhortation to the Greeks*, translated by C. W. Butterworth, Cambridge, Mass.: Harvard University Press, 1953.

Reprinted by permission of the publishers and the Loeb Classical Library from Epictetus: *The Discourses as Reported by Arrian*, vol. 1, translated by W. A. Oldfather, Cambridge, Mass.: Harvard University Press, 1956.

Reprinted by permission of the publishers and the Loeb Classical Library from Epictetus: *The Discourses as Reported by Arrian*, vol. 2, translated by W. A. Oldfather, Cambridge, Mass.: Harvard University Press, 1960.

Reprinted by permission of the publishers and the Loeb Classical Library from Hesiod: *Homeric Hymns, Epic Cyle, Homerica*, translated by Hugh G. Evelyn-White, Cambridge, Mass.: Harvard University Press, 1974.

Reprinted by permission of the publishers and the Loeb Classical Library from Libanius: *Selected Works*, vol. 2, translated by A. F. Norman, Cambridge, Mass.: Harvard University Press, 1977.

Reprinted by permission of the publishers and the Loeb Classical Library from Lucian: *Alexander the False Prophet*, vol. 4, translated by A. M. Harmon, Cambridge, Mass.: Harvard University Press, 1925.

Reprinted by permission of the publishers and the Loeb Classical Library from Plutarch: *Plutarch's Lives*, vol. 1, translated by Bernadotte Perrin, Cambridge, Mass.: Harvard University Press, 1959.

Reprinted by permission of the publishers and the Loeb Classical Library from Plutarch: *Moralia*, vol. 1, translated by F. C. Babbitt, Cambridge, Mass.: Harvard University Press, 1927.

Reprinted by permission of the publishers and the Loeb Classical Library from Plutarch: *Moralia*, vol. 5, translated by F. C. Babbitt, Cambridge, Mass.: Harvard University Press, 1957.

Reprinted by permission of the publishers and the Loeb Classical Library from Xenophon: *Memorabilia*, vol. 4, translated by E. C. Marchant, Cambridge, Mass.: Harvard University Press, 1959.

Herodotus, *The History*, translated by David Grene, Chicago: The University of Chicago Press. Copyright © 1987 by the University of Chicago.

ILLUSTRATIONS

The Kodros Painter, *Aigios Consulting the Oracle*, Antikensammlung, Staatliche Museen zu Berlin—Preussischer Kulturbesitz, inv. no. 2538. Appears on p. 70.

"Herzsprung"-type Bronze Shield, The Ephorate of Prehistoric and Classical Antiquities, The Delphi Museum, inv. no. 7226. Appears on chapter opening pages.

Ann Douglass, *The Temple of Apollo at Delphi*, 1985. Appears on cover.

Preface

I asked my closest friend whether people today are interested in the Delphic oracle.

"No," was the reply, "but many are interested in things that can lead to the Delphic oracle."

The earliest inspiration for this book is the passage in Socrates' defense—Plato's version—where he recalls his service to the oracle. "Now gentlemen," he begins before a massive jury of fellow citizens, "please do not interrupt me. . . . I am going to refer you to an unimpeachable authority. I shall call as witness . . . the god at Delphi." Socrates reminds them of the oracle's assertion that no one is wiser than he and explains that this holy absurdity—for he knew himself to be ignorant—had prompted his long search. Only by finding a person wiser than himself could he hope to grasp the meaning of the oracle; hence his probing conversations.

Socrates' strategy was both ironic and devastatingly sincere. Delphi provided his mandate to pursue the philosophical life in the public forum where he believed it to belong. But behind his arguably cunning reliance on Delphi for institutional approval, the reader cannot help but recognize in his words and manner a quality of profound obedience to the oracle and fierce dedication to its service. Before all men, Socrates was a genial but ultimately implacable interrogator. Before the Delphic oracle he was vulnerable. "My service to the God," he admitted to the jurors, "has reduced me to extreme poverty."

That this man of unshakable independence depended so faithfully, even tenderly, on the Delphic oracle as the author of the guidelines of his life had the effect on me, some years ago, of a flare burning in the night: it indicated a direction, assured who knows what essential learning, were I to follow its lead.

My first steps in that direction, guided by an excess of curiosity and scant knowledge, soon led to the powerful novella embedded in Herodotus' *History of the Persian Wars,* the tale of King Croesus: Croesus who lavished gifts on the Delphic oracle, sought its advice on a matter of war and peace, and catastrophically misinterpreted the counsel he received. When disaster befell, he turned spitefully on the oracle, but in the end he proved able to acknowledge the precariousness of his own judgment. In the tale of Croesus, I detected both the grandeur of story at its best and a parable with many different thrusts. There was some compelling ritual of question and answer in Delphic material, some subtle etiquette governing human solicitation and divine disclosure that seemed both remote and intimately close. I felt encouraged to continue collecting Delphic tales from ancient literature, with increasing certainty that they were often beautiful and in some instances timelessly true.

Typically the tales were brief, more like anecdotes than proper short stories or folk tales. I found myself torn between perceptions of their vigor and weightiness and the disconcerting fact that they often occupy scarcely a paragraph or two in an ancient text. This was an embarrassment until I happened on a reflection of Elie Wiesel's concerning the same phenomenon in the Talmud: there, he writes, "a three-sentence legend often possesses the suggestive power of a lyrical poem."[1] I viewed the matter settled by this parallel in another ancient literature and could no longer feel isolated in my fascination with tales that amounted on occasion to three-sentence legends. On the other hand, I had begun to think of Plutarch's so-called *Pythian Dialogues*—lengthy discussions set at Delphi in the first century of our era—as tales of another sort, metaphysical tales that attempt to map enigmas.

Classical scholarship, properly speaking, is an exhaustive discipline that leaves no primary text or archaeological evidence unconsidered, no link unexplored, no prior scholarship unread in the search for truth. The footnotes of works in this field are, and must be, intricate mosaics of reference. This book is not of that kind. Its scholarship is pragmatic—thorough enough to encompass a topic that cannot be approached without learning, but scarcely virtuoso. Yet strange to say, the great scholarly studies of Delphi have inventoried the tales without especially befriending them, viewed them as documents without recognizing in them a dispersed but deeply appealing wisdom literature. There was, after all, room for a visitor in the bust-lined hall.

I am uncertain whether, in general, readers and writers are lately experiencing a classical revival—it seems to me that something of the kind is unfolding—but I can attest to my personal renaissance. Authors and personages who barely grazed me if I knew them at all as a young reader—Heraclitus, the Pythagoras of legend, Plato, Diogenes, Epictetus, Marcus Aurelius, Julian—now strike me as the soul of inquiry, persons of exceptional lucidity and seriousness who explored human experience with high concentration. The Delphic oracle was the creature of minds like theirs. From its legendary origin among goatherds, the oracle developed into a sophisticated religious manifestation within a profoundly intellectual culture.

The Greco-Roman world is a "world over there," a twin of our own and, because it ended, more measurable. Like anyone who has experienced the attraction of that world and explored some of its dimensions, I occasionally find its persistence, whole and rummaging, in my imagination. In that imagined landscape, Socrates still takes country walks with young Athenians, and their discussions continue; Heraclitus, surrounded by a handful of exceptionally hardy pupils, still fumes over the pettiness of human beings in a world which, could they but awaken, would awe them; Thucydides still gives grave attention to the struggle for world order; and embassies and pilgrims make their way to Delphi. But it is not only a landscape with philosophers: one cannot miss the movement of armies, the clash of ideas, the evolution of the "software" of complex societies—codes of law, forms of government—and the ceaseless measuring, by experienced persons of high intelligence, of their world and of themselves.

The question of how to tell, or retell, Delphic stories needed resolution as I brought them together from their resting places, some in high literature, others noted in passing by authors now little read. Herodotus' telling of the saga of Croesus, like Plato's rendering of Socrates' defense, is so superb that only direct translation could do justice; to retell would be to distort. On the other hand, many shorter tales in their original versions, even in Herodotus, are freighted with references to myth, place names, and other commonplaces of ancient knowledge that would only distract readers today from the tale as story, as human event. And then, the tales are often preserved in such abbreviated form that too little time passes from start to finish to establish an atmosphere. Gestures are implied but not described; wondering pauses can be surmised but they are rarely evoked; characterizations are schematic for an ancient audience that needed no introduction to many of the actors in these small dramas. The tales are often abstracts, reminding ancient readers of what they already know rather than providing immediate imaginative experience. Thus, there is often too little of one thing for us, too much of another.

I also recognized that, among the multiple versions of a tale in different authors, elements from some or all could be brought together to provide the richest version. On the other hand, the wealth of versions posed the danger of "variorum" storytelling, incorporating elements from so many different versions, where they exist, that the tale becomes a scholar's overview rather than a cry in the wilderness of our experience, which all good tales must be.

This was the puzzling situation. To resolve it, the storyteller had to prevail. Only the storyteller, responding with some freedom to Delphic tales, could hope to bring them to "modern minds." You will find in this book for the most part retellings of Delphic tales, pruned of references now lost on us unless they advance the tale in some way, with implied gestures and characterizations made a good deal more explicit. Yet the original story remains the central communication; there are no new shapes, only touches of new paint here and there to strengthen an outline, fill a gap. Only in this way, I believe, can tales of Delphi become a little more present to our imaginative and spiritual lives. Endnotes direct interested readers to the verbatim reality of the sources. The same reasoning, I should add, guided my renderings of the oracle's words. For the sake of clarity and directness I have often rephrased, but there is no change in essential meaning.

I have not retold the political and military history of Delphi, which readers will easily find in the first volume of H. W. Parke and D. E. W. Wormell's landmark study, *The Delphic Oracle*, and I have only occasionally selected tales that are deeply immersed in specific historical detail. That Apollo himself, so they say, protected Delphi from marauding Celtic troops by bringing down an avalanche on some and infecting the rest with self-destructive panic is a good tale, but not persuasively a wisdom tale through which we can gain a lively sense for what the Delphic oracle *meant* when it spoke, and how it worked with individuals and states, sometimes harshly, for their benefit.

"Have you ever been to Delphi?" asks Socrates. "What is Delphi?" we might ask in return. "And what can Delphi mean for us now?"

Historically, Delphi was a small city with a famed oracular temple where a priestess, the Pythia, periodically replied in Apollo's name and in his words to individual pilgrims and state embassies who journeyed there to inquire. From the Pythia's collected words and a long heritage of religious and philosophical inquiry at Delphi, there emerged a recognizably Delphic view of life, centered on the celebrated injunction, "Know thyself."

About inquirers at Delphi and their sometimes joyful, sometimes tragic destinies, there were many stories. Some have survived to our time in ancient literature. In addition, some stone has survived. As an archaeological site, Delphi is both deeply engaging and disappointing. One walks the temple precinct with a map: here *was*, there *were*. . . . Much more has vanished than survived. Yet the magnificent landscape is intact, the stones tell their story, and the museum at the edge of the temple precinct preserves some of the most beautiful sculpture of antiquity.

If this briefly responds to the question "What is Delphi?", it leaves untouched the further question of what Delphi might mean for us now. This book probes for that answer, and each reader will ultimately decide the question privately. It may be helpful, however, to formulate a preliminary answer that we can revise and enrich as we listen to tales of the oracle and understand what we can from Delphic prayers, poems, and aphorisms.

Delphi is the place of encounter with truth. It is both a specific place with its own history and customs, and a general metaphor for all such places, inner and outer, at that time and in our time. Delphi is rediscovered wherever human beings question intently and receive—from a helpful person, from inner resources, from on high—insights that suggest not just an immediate solution but a sense of the path ahead, of a destiny that invites or commands the inquirer to be all he can.

Characteristically, Delphic truth was not a finished recipe requiring only to be followed to yield its benefits. On the contrary, Delphic truth was often enigmatic—one could stay up nights trying to fathom it. Pilgrims had to *complete the oracle* through themselves, through their own thought, their own clarifications of feeling, their own action. The holy words were the beginning of a story, not the end. This characteristic incompleteness and ambiguity, and the call to intellectual and moral effort they implied, form a large part of the abiding appeal of Delphi. Some ancients resented or mocked this feature of Delphic truth; others could respect it as the wobble or uncertainty in the system that provided for human participation and transformed the imperious word of God into a challenge on our own scale. We shall encounter at Delphi a model of truth-seeking that places much responsibility on human beings—but not all. "The Lord whose oracle is at Delphi neither speaks nor conceals, but gives signs," said Heraclitus. This is a book of such signs and of the adventures to which they gave rise.

The Delphic oracle has vanished. Yet its memory has staying power, as if the Delphic model of truth seeking or dialogue with the divine is, if not perfect, then perfectly memorable. In the lost-wax technique of bronze casting, the wax original inside the mold must be melted off before the pour; nothing remains of it. Similarly, the oracle has long since disappeared, but its empty shape remains. That shape is provocative; it asks us about our own dialogue with the divine, our search for truth, our willingness to put ourselves at risk by questioning when we suspect that there can be no turning back from the answer.

Since my last book concerned the spiritual in twentieth-century art, while this book concerns an early stage of the Western effort to decipher experience and live well, readers can legitimately ask whether there is a sensible pattern in my activity as a writer. Perhaps I am too preoccupied with "first and last things," with *alpha* and *omega?* The pattern is this: to experience as fully as possible our troubled contemporary culture, especially in its uncertain religious and spiritual dimensions, and to venture where necessary for values and vitalities that shed light on, and envelop with warmth, our dilemmas. There is so much to remember as we grope toward a new, plural, but coherent vision of human possibility and obligation.

The afterword to this book is not an afterthought. As it has for me, the dialogue recorded there may complete the reader's concept of Delphi by exploring a better documented, essentially living oracular culture that implies many parallels with the Delphic oracle: the Chief State Oracle of Tibet, formerly resident in Tibet at Nechung Monastery, now resident in north India. The loss of comprehensive knowledge of Delphi over the many centuries since it flourished is not compensated by knowledge of Nechung. Gaps are gaps; they cannot be filled even with suggestively kindred material. On the other hand, the tension of experiencing—and accepting—the unalterably dark spots in our possible knowledge of Delphi is strangely released by this firsthand account of an oracle of our time which the people of Delphi would surely have found more than a little familiar.

Only when I had completed this book did it occur to me, like the slower heroes of Delphic tales, that I had not fully understood why Delphi mattered to me. I realized at last that the Delphic oracle models the uneasy interplay between wisdom and institutions dedicated to wisdom; between giving and withholding; between our obvious human limitations and our intuition of participating in a drama that reaches well past ourselves. And for all these reasons, in the narrative of ancient Delphi I had constructed, I perceived smiling—and, as always, gently ironical—the faces of my own mentors. The quest for knowledge of Delphi had begun with Socrates and ended as an oblique homage to men and women of our own time who embody Delphic values.

"Tell me, Euthydemos, have you ever been to Delphi?"

"Yes, certainly—twice."

"Then did you notice somewhere on the temple the inscription 'Know thyself'?"

"I did."

"And did you try to consider who you were?"

—from Xenophon's memoir on Socrates

A Word on the Endnotes

This book can be read without the endnotes, but some readers will be interested to consult sources from which the tales and other material are drawn. Endnote information is straightforward. At first citation, full bibliographical data are given. At first citation of a much-used source, an abbreviation is indicated for use in all subsequent references to the source. The Loeb Classical Library, a multivolume collection providing original text and facing translation, will be cited for convenience as LCL. A bibliographic overview at the end groups secondary studies of particular value and other resources.

I have ignored scholarly practice in two respects. Typically, scholarship requires the use of ellipses (. . .) to indicate deletions in quoted matter. The advantage of this practice is obvious. The disadvantage is that texts tend to read as if they were originally full of pauses, and their essential thought is often more difficult to grasp. Where texts with silent deletions are not in my view misleading, I have preferred to present them in that way so that the reader has uncluttered access to the material.

There is one further question: the spelling of ancient Greek names. Pure practice today renders all names in transliterated Greek spelling rather than in the Latinate forms which are often more familiar: thus we more easily recognize "Lycurgus" than "Lykourgos." I have thought it best to retain familiar Latinate forms and to transliterate more unfamiliar names—mixed practice, intended to merge the convenient with the evocative.

1

Introduction: A Bowl of Myths and Stories

"I am on my way to Delphi, Diogenes, to consult the oracle—but now my slave has run away and I'm searching for him."

These anxious words, spoken by a man from Corinth, are addressed to the famed Cynic philosopher whom he unexpectedly meets on the road. Always interested in confusion, Diogenes lures the man into conversation.

"Have you heard of the inscription at Delphi, 'Know thyself'?" he asks with the studied casualness of Socrates' heirs, who like their master tend to start toward the center from seemingly harmless inquiries.

"I have," responds the pilgrim.

"Would you agree," continues Diogenes, "that the god gives this command to us all in the certainty that we do not know ourselves?"

"It would seem so," answers the pilgrim, who must by now have laid down his bundle and taken a wary seat beside Diogenes.

"You, therefore, would be included in the 'all'?"

"I'm sure, Diogenes."

"So you also do not know yourself?" As Diogenes draws out this implication with the sticky meticulousness of his lineage, his deliberate face relaxes, for the end is already in sight.

"It follows," replies the pilgrim, "I admit that it follows."

"And not knowing yourself," Diogenes thrusts on, "you do not know Man. And not knowing Man, you are surely unable to make good use of a man. Yet despite this, you are going off to attempt to make good use of a god! Don't you see that this is a far more difficult enterprise?"

"Yes, Diogenes, but . . ."

Now the old sage is not to be stopped.

"Oracles are obscure, they have deceived many men. For Homer it was safe to go to Delphi—but for you? Aren't you afraid that when the god says one thing, you'll understand another? Apollo never asks those who consult him to commit dreadful acts, but men who are incapable of making good use of his oracle inquire, anyway, and then blame the god when they misunderstand completely and things go wrong!

"If you want my advice," concludes the sage, "first know yourself. If and when you find that much wisdom, you'll be free to consult the oracle at your good pleasure."[1]

This is not an historical encounter, it is a fiction written by Dio Chrysostom—Dio the Golden-Mouthed—in the first century C.E. But as in many ancient writings referring to Delphi, that the exchange did not occur at all or in quite the way described does not mean that it lacks truth. From the beginning there were two Delphis: the Delphi of fact and the Delphi of the mind. Throughout ancient times, the two followed generally parallel courses, linked to one another by pathways however slim, yet likely to diverge because Delphi lived richly in the minds of men and women, most of whom would never visit the holy city or enjoy the privilege of inquiring there. Delphi drew to itself, as if magnetically, both the refined inventions of poets, orators, and playwrights and the rough storytelling of common people. Even when historical figures about whom we know a great deal visited Delphi—for example, that model of Roman virtue, Cicero—the recorded results seem to swerve gaily from the verifiable realm of history to the imaginative realm of story, which may or may not be wholly "true."

Cicero's Question

After successfully defending a controversial client in Rome, Cicero—still a young man—feared for his safety and took refuge in Greece, where he was perfectly at home. No one was more confident than he that he would in time become a leader in the rough-and-tumble world of Roman politics, but his recent experience had shaken him. Like many Romans with an educated taste for things Greek, he decided to make the pilgrimage to Delphi.

At Delphi he did not hesitate to expose his heartfelt question to the unpredictable intelligence of the oracle. "What path must I take toward fame?" he asked. The oracle promptly advised him to make his own nature, not the opinion of the masses, his guide in life.

He found this challenge moving, he could not ignore it. When he returned to Rome he was far more cautious in seeking office than his political rivals had anticipated. Some belittled him, called him a "Greek," a "scholar"—they meant that he lacked the vigor of the true unspoiled Roman.

Yet his day, and his fame, arrived.[2]

Plutarch tells this story in the first century of our era; it is one of many we shall have from this dedicated priest of Delphi—for this he was—whose warmth, steady values, and tireless investigations of human affairs make him one of the most attractive authors of antiquity. Both Dio and Plutarch are latecomers to Delphic storytelling. By their moment in time, the oracle had been functioning for perhaps eight centuries, the earliest surviving testimonies predating them by some six hundred years. In consequence, both of them know how to tell Delphic stories perfectly, in the way that they always had been told. Dio knows that the pilgrimage to Delphi is not without risk: hadn't the great sixth-century king, Croesus of Lydia, misinterpreted the oracle's words to his catastrophic misfortune? To question God and receive an answer is an immensely charged occasion by which the questioner cannot expect to remain unchanged, although the impact of the holy words may be long in coming.

Dio gives Diogenes the task of reminding the agitated Corinthian that pilgrimage to the Delphic oracle is not even remotely a pleasure trip. Further, Dio knows that the Delphic commandment, Know Thyself, was always and remains the central message of the oracle. It was the great invitation and warning offered to all thinking Greeks: simple and concise, it haunted generation after generation. "I have searched myself,"[3] said Heraclitus at the beginning of the fifth century B.C.E. "Held bound," echoed Proclus antiphonally in the fifth century C.E., "by the forgetfulness incident to generation and sidetracked by the disorder of the irrational forms of life, we do not know ourselves."[4]

The Delphi of the mind survived the vicissitudes to which the Delphi of fact was subject: the Sacred Wars that disrupted its life and sacked its riches, the shifting loyalties of regional Realpolitik, the attacks of marauding Persians and Celts, the depradations of Roman emperors who regarded Delphi as an antique shop, the zeal of early Christians for whom Apollo was demon not god. The Delphi of the mind provided moral and spiritual guidance in centuries when the Delphi of fact had become a provincial backwater. Tales of Delphi traveled from the navel of the world—this was the ancient view of Delphi—to its farthermost fingertips and toes.

Plutarch was saturated both in the quotidian reality of first-century Delphi, where he often could be found, and in the sprawling tradition of Delphic myths, legends, historical narratives, wisdom tales, and racy anecdotes of which some small portion has survived to our day. His tale of Cicero is presented as biographical fact; it is nonetheless infused with the values of the Delphi of the mind. *If* Cicero called on the oracle, and *if* he came away with cogent advice, the event and the advice have been reduced by Plutarch to their essentials: a young, gifted man anxious to play a role in public life is warned to follow his inner promptings rather than heed or manipulate mass opinion. As a connoisseur of Delphic tradition, Plutarch knows that the oracle often assigned to individuals arduous or puzzling tasks. To fulfill the task was to fulfill—or at least safeguard—one's life. To ignore or misinterpret it was to risk catastrophe at once or in later generations vulnerable to the consequences of one's error. The oracle drew the inquirer into a momentous scenario, but it could not, and would not, assure the outcome.

As a Delphic storyteller, Plutarch is working within a tradition that agreed on certain grand fundamentals. Individuals are agents of choice in a field of forces that will tempt and challenge them; dispassionate penetration of the meaning of things and circumstances is indispensable; higher wisdom is available to human beings, although its availability implies nothing about our capacity to make good use of it. And to all of this should be added a fourth fundamental: the will of the gods and that of human beings interact in mysterious ways, the gods at times entangling us, like Oedipus, in fatality, but more often leaving us to work out our lives.

ANCIENT AUTHORS AND MODERN SCHOLARS

Ancient authors, and incomparably more so modern scholars, have gone to great lengths to distinguish the Delphi of fact from the Delphi of the mind. In ancient times, the degree of belief in the oracle as an authentic source of divine counsel was in part a generational marker—Herodotus in the early fifth century was a believer, Thucydides in the late fifth was a doubter—and in part a matter of temperament and training. Plutarch was accepting, but not carelessly so, of the rich aggregate of Delphic tradition. In a dialogue that unfolds as speakers tour the temple grounds, he includes this memorable sentiment, full of the joy in story that impelled his authorship: "There is set before us for general use a bowl of myths and stories combined, and where could one meet with more kindly listeners for testing these stories, just as one tests coins from foreign lands?"[5] Strabo, the geographer who preceded Plutarch by several generations, took a more critical view not only of Delphic lore, but also of tales associated with other oracular centers, such as the venerable oracle of Zeus at Dodona, where the rustling of leaves in a sacred oak was originally interpreted by legendary priestesses, the Doves: "As for the myths that are told about the oak tree and the Doves," he wrote firmly, "and other myths of the kind, like those told about Delphi, they are in part poetry."[6] True to his profession, he harbored the suspicion that the prestige of Delphi owed something not only to the generous presence of Apollo within the temple, but also to the city's smashingly beautiful setting beneath the height of Mount Parnassos: "The greatest share of honor was paid to this temple because of its oracle," he wrote, "since of all oracles in the world it was reputed to be the most truthful, yet the position of the place added something."[7]

Pausanias, author of a traveler's guide to Greece in the second century C.E., discovered that "there are a lot of different stories about Delphi, and even more about Apollo's oracle,"[8] and he was initially impatient with the obvious elements of fantasy in Greek tales: "I am bound to tell the stories that are told by the Greeks, but I am not bound to believe them all."[9] However, as time went on he softened: "When I began to write my history I thought these Greek stories were rather silly, but now I have decided to treat them from the point of view that the famous Greek wise men told their stories in riddles and not out of stupidity. In religious matters this is the principle we shall follow."[10] In his account of the Lesche at Delphi, an elegant clubhouse on the temple grounds where citizens and visitors could rest and converse, he accepted positively the meandering yet crucial exchange we call storytelling: "This is where people used to meet in ancient times both for old tales and for serious conversation."[11] The tales may not be quite serious, but they belong.

In modern times, Delphi was initially a French preoccupation, under excavation rights granted to French archaeologists. Over the decades, Greek scholars and those of other nations have made steady contributions to a vast increase in knowledge. More or less continuously conducted since 1892,[12] excavation at Delphi has revealed the site of Apollo's temple and its environs, provided masses of factual information, and set the pace for a critical reading of ancient literary references and carved inscriptions relating to Delphi and its oracle. The result of this century-long effort is curiously dual. On the one hand, Delphi is annually visited by a million or more tourists from around the world, who must be seeking contact, consciously or unconsciously, with a place and era of belief in which God spoke to man, and man to God. Many of these tourists, if confronted, would surely deny that a priestess could speak the words of a god in answer to inquirers' questions. On the other hand, the doubting tourists are *there*, advancing in the dry summer heat behind their polyglot guides, not to mock the ancient institution but to experience its magic. The painstaking archaeological effort to uncover Delphi has created an icon of popular culture, stationed just below the Athenian acropolis in its power to evoke rich imaginings.

On the other hand, within the scholarly world the religious prestige of the Delphic oracle has steadily eroded in the course of the same century that revealed the archaeological site and raised it to the level of a popular icon. Joseph Fontenrose's recent study of questions and answers at Delphi, of which some six hundred survive in ancient literature, relegates nearly all of the evocative material to the realm of fiction and typically takes to be authentic only those answers concerning ritual and religion which the priests at Delphi could formulate on the basis of practical knowledge. The Delphi of fact has been shrunk to the condition of a Holy See that saw nothing, while the Delphi of the mind, with its brimming "bowl of myths and stories combined," has been devalued because it is notoriously unreliable as history.[13]

This unsentimental critique was overdue. Delphi was a familiar point of reference to nineteenth-century readers and writers raised on Plato, Herodotus, and Plutarch, but the contradictory images of the oracle in ancient literature had not been sorted out, and the overall image was faint enough that writers could find in it what they wished. In the late nineteenth century, just a few years before archaeologists began persuading Greek villagers to move their homes from the rocky terrace that hid the ancient site, the widely read philosophical author, Edouard Schuré, rhapsodized about the oracle in a way that now seems religiously incontinent:

> The soul of Greece . . . shines at Delphi with Apollo, who dominates and penetrates all the temples with his light. This [was] the center of Hellenic life, the head and heart of Greece. . . . There processions of men, women and children coming from afar, ascended the sacred way to greet the god of light. . . . As in the great temples of Egypt, the divination practised at Delphi was composed of an art and a science.

> The art consisted in penetrating the past and future through clairvoyance or prophetic ecstasy; its science consisted in calculating the future according to the laws of universal evolution. Art and science controlled each other.[14]

Schuré's conversion of ancient Delphi into a model solution for the nineteenth-century problem of controlling the excesses of the Industrial Revolution had its echoes in mid-twentieth-century thought, despite the army of archaeologists and textual historians dedicated to replacing the romance of Delphi with stony reality.[15] Today the Delphi of nineteenth- and twentieth-century idealists feels uncomfortable, a little foolish, but the Delphi of some contemporary scholars is no less uncomfortable in its rigid lack of recognition of religious and other vital human values at work in "rocky Pytho," as Homer referred to Delphi. The project of this book is to stake a claim in rocky Pytho on behalf of modern minds for which *some* Delphic material—not all, by any means—can be uplifting and provocative, as it was for many ancient listeners and readers. As we cautiously sift and remove the soil at the site of our claim, we shall oddly enough find not fragmentary statues and potsherds but stories.

Among our near contemporaries, C. G. Jung had a keen ear for the Delphic message and more than enough scholarship to transcribe the message without distorting it. Above the doorway of his home and office at Kusnacht, near Zürich, was engraved in stately capitals a Delphic saying which he had copied out, early in life, from a Renaissance volume of adages. Its ultimate origin was Thucydides' history of the Peloponnesian War:

VOCATUS ATQUE NON VOCATUS DEUS ADERIT

—called or uncalled, the god will be present.[16] In context, these words answer an inquiry of the Spartans on the eve of war: could they hope for victory against the Athenian alliance? However, they are words of such compactness and electrifying certainty that they had long since transcended their immediate literary and historical context. Julian, the last "pagan" emperor who attempted to reconvert Rome from Christianity to the religion of the gods, remembered them when writing to a comrade about an impending campaign:

> God on His side will not fail us, but in the words of the oracle once given of old, "Invoked or uninvoked, God will be present with us."[17]

Questioned about why he had these words solemnly engraved above the doorway where patients regularly passed, Jung made clear that they still lived within him, evoking not only the promise of contact with the divine but also the risk of which Diogenes warned the Corinthian pilgrim. "It is a Delphic oracle," Jung wrote to his questioner,

> It says: yes, the god will be on the spot, but in what form and to what purpose? I have put the inscription there to remind my patients and myself: *Timor dei initium sapientiae* [Fear of the Lord is the beginning of wisdom]. Here another not less important road begins, not the approach to "Christianity" but to God himself and this seems to be the ultimate question.[18]

Jung's restoration to contemporary use of a fragment of Delphic wisdom provides a small but impressive model for this book as a whole. The Delphi for which we are going in search is neither the calculating priestly institution of some recent scholarship, nor the shiny ideal of an earlier generation of religious essayists. It is the Delphi of tales that informed, entertained, and aroused wonder in ancient listeners as they conveyed, by the undogmatic means of story, a vision of the promise, risks, and ambiguities of human life.

THE SIBYL'S MESSAGE

Tales are not philosophy, although they can incarnate philosophy. They are not statements of religious doctrine, although their patterns can illuminate and reassure. They answer the primordial question, "What happened?" They engage our attention at a fundamental level—perhaps that of the receptive child in us—where we know that "what happened" is terribly important. "What happened" is the flowing current of life, and as such more important than conclusions that might be drawn about it, although deductions and conclusions are not necessarily beside the point. "What happened" is still happening somewhere in some form, hence the almost instinctive scanning of tales for light on one's own life. Tales provide an efficient way of remembering; they arrange chunks of experience into sequences. Tales are resolutely democratic in the sense that they offer something for everyone: literal-minded listeners will enjoy a good yarn, while listeners attuned to symbolic pattern will enjoy the same material differently. Tales are often all that remains deeply appealing for thinkers who have exhausted their studies of principle and doctrine, and who are no longer moved by preaching even of the true faith. For such people, tales are the last resort but so vital that everything—philosophy, religion, preaching of the faith—can begin again on a renewed foundation. When a religious genius such as the twelfth-century Persian poet Rumi sets aside his reflections to tell a story, as he so often does, he is not interrupting the flow of teaching but releasing it. Storytelling is a way of thinking—perhaps the first way, the way of the Book of Genesis and the Tale of Gilgamesh. And in the encompassing word "story" we should feel free to include tales at all levels, from the grandest of myths and parables to legends and knee-socked folk tales.

Incomparably more has been lost of Delphic tradition, in all of its dimensions, than has survived at the temple site and in literature. As noted earlier, we know of some six hundred questions and answers—few when one considers that the oracle functioned for approximately one thousand years, from the era of Homer to a date approaching the late fourth century A.D., when the Christian emperor Theodosius closed all temples serving the ancient religion of the gods. We know of books, long since lost or surviving only in fragments, that amounted to a Delphic library—Plutarch's *Collected Oracles*, Porphyry's *On the Philosophy To Be Derived from Oracles*, Anaxandrides' *On the Oracle at Delphi*, Apellas' *Delphic History*, works by Philokoros and Ister and Theopompos, the latter described by Plutarch as the author "who has given more diligent study to the oracle than any one man."[19] To us his works are virtually unknown. A surviving fragment from the introduction to Porphyry's book, written toward the end of Delphic tradition, reflects beneath its formal rhetoric something of the pathos of the process of question and answer at Delphi, for people went there in search of solutions to real problems. They brought their pain.

> The utility which this collection possesses will be best known to as many as have ever been in travail with the truth, and prayed that by receiving the manifestation of it from the gods they might gain relief from their perplexity by virtue of the trustworthy teaching of the speakers.[20]

Two songs are still engraved on a wall at Delphi; how many others were sung? If, as scholars calculate, some 10 percent of ancient Greek literature has survived, we can surmise that some 10 percent of full knowledge of Delphi survived with it. True, the literature we have is stocked with references to Delphi, its oracle, and its celebrated athletic games and musical contests. Much can be understood from this fund of references; it is the stuff of this book. But the fact of loss cannot be underestimated.

"Hear the refrain from Delphi: PAIEON HIÉ!" The line is from a hymn to Apollo, written by the poet Callimachus in the third century B.C.E.[21] The refrain is so distant in time and muffled by intervening cultures that we cannot now experience the force of this once familiar Delphic cry of encouragement, as Apollo draws his bow to slay the Python or dragon[22] who dwelt at Delphi before his advent. From its origin in myth, the cry became in effect a way of saying, "Praise God!"

As it happens, the ancients had a tale about the loss of guiding knowledge, which can help us progress beyond this doubt on our way to Delphi. It is a Roman tale concerning an aged woman, a Sibyl, who arrived unannounced at the legendary court of the Tarquins, founders of Rome. This Sibyl, with her powerful message to an early king, had a sister at Delphi whom we shall come to know.

Reluctant Purchase of the Books

Once there arrived in the rustic court of Tarquinius Priscus, fifth of the kings of early Rome, an aged woman unknown to all. She was carrying a heavy bundle of nine books carefully wrapped in a skin.

"My Lord," she croaked to the king, "I shall sell you these books. I shall sell them to you for 20 pieces of gold—and you won't regret the price."

"What?" roared Tarquin. "You miserable creature from who knows what dark corner of our realm, *you* have books worth 20 pieces of gold? Away with you, stop joking with your king!"

The woman silently departed and burned three of the nine books. But the next day she reappeared.

"My Lord," she wheezed again, "I shall sell you these books. Now there are six, but I can sell them to you for 20 pieces of gold—and you won't regret the price."

"You again!" cried the king. "I'm surprised that my guards let you approach—they are too kind. Today you want to sell me only six books for the same price as before? And why, trembling mother, would I need these precious books? You must be mad. See her to the gate!"

The old woman slipped out, unprotesting as before, and burned another three books. On the following day, she deftly skirted the guards and presented herself at court with the three remaining books, which she offered to sell, as you might guess, for 20 pieces of gold. At this point, Tarquin's better nature whispered to him that he had passed the

> limits of a king's knowledge and stood on the threshold of mystery. He called in the court seers to advise him.
>
> Cradling the few remaining books, the aged woman stood impassively to one side while the augurs listened to Tarquin's explanation of the peculiar circumstance. Then they counseled in hushed voices with one another. At length, they turned to Tarquin.
>
> "My Lord," they said, "you must without fail buy the remaining books *at any price*. It is a misfortune that you did not buy them all, for we divine that these are books of unique wisdom which will guide Rome now and in the future at our moments of greatest need. Better to have had nine than three; better to have three than none."
>
> And so the bargain was struck. The woman turned over the books to the augurs with a solemn warning to care for them. Then she left, never to be seen again. These books of prophetic counsel, transcribed by the ancient Sibyls from their contacts with the gods, were safeguarded in a temple at Rome and interpreted for centuries to come.[23]

The tale is tinged with sadness; its legendary encounter in a faraway time strikes home. Many of us will perhaps recognize something of ourselves in Tarquin. But beyond this intimate dimension, the tale conveys an oblique metaphysical message concerning the degradation of knowledge as it makes its way down and into us. To convey the same thought, a Hindu tale speaks of the abridgment of knowledge. The legendary sage Manu Prajāpati first composed a book of 100,000 verses on all possible topics of importance to human beings. But Narada abridged this magnificent compendium to 12,000 verses, and again to 4,000 verses, "due to the shortening of human life and attention span in the later aeons."[24]

The Delphic oracle was there to overcome this estrangement from the gods and their wisdom. Classical scholars have often observed that the Greeks had no book occupying the central place of a Bible. Homer was reverently read and memorized by the young as a part of their education, but the epics were not regarded as Holy Writ. In facing the uncertainties of life, the Greeks found solace and a divinely inspired sense of direction in their mystery cults, which provided personal initiation into the enigmas of life and death, and in their oracles—from Dodona in the north to Delphi at the center, Klaros and Branchidae in the east, and the temple of Ammon in Libya, at the southern edge of the known world. There were still others, ranging from the solemn and frightening oracle at Lebadeia, near Delphi, to time-honored local oracles even in marketplaces. Among them all, Delphi was most prestigious, most storied, and, in its centuries of strength, most richly furnished both by the faithful and by city-states that valued the prestige of displaying elegant buildings and sculpture along the avenue leading to the temple at the Center of the World. Isocrates, an Athenian orator and teacher somewhat younger than Socrates, summed up Delphi's prestige in his era as "that oracle which all would acknowledge to be the most ancient, most widely accepted, and most trustworthy in existence."[25] Not infallible, then, but in the face of a world of uncertainty and unpredictable menace, a priceless resource.

THIS IS THE CENTER OF THE ENTIRE EARTH

To speak of Delphi as the Center of the World was not just naive geography. It was a statement of religious cosmology, an ordering of the world horizontally in terms of center and periphery, vertically in terms of high place and plain place, sacred and profane. Many peoples, not only Greeks, have identified the Center of the Earth in sites of overwhelming importance to them—among the ancient Jews, Jerusalem; among the Kogi people of the Andes, the vast mountain on which they still live; among Muslims, the Ka'aba at Mecca. Roman Catholics cannot forget the papal seat of St. Peter's in Rome, that artificial mountain with its world-embracing columned portico; it is the Center of their World.

The Center is the privileged place of contact and communication between "worlds," typically understood as heaven above, an underworld, and the world in which we live. Generally a high place—a mountain or mountainous edifice such as the ancient ziggurat—it is the *axis mundi*, the axis of the world around which all else turns, the vertical avenue along which the divine descends to address us and which permits us to contact beneficially the energies of the lower world. This structure is present at Delphi, the mountain site beneath the heights of Parnassos, where Apollo speaks from above, to us in our middle world, while a sacred *pneuma* or breath was thought to issue from the earth beneath the temple to inspire the Pythia.[26]

It was customary in ancient cultures to know where the Center is, just as it is customary now to know that we live on a small planet circling an average sun toward the edge of a galaxy like others—to know, in other words, that there is no Center and cannot be. Or is that so? There has been a contest for centuries in the West, originally pitting the Copernican view of the solar system against the traditional geocentric view, now pitting the magnificence of modern cosmology with its billions of galaxies against the stubborn conviction of otherwise reasonable people that there is, despite all physical evidence to the contrary, a Center. Its location is different for different people, but the question has not subsided; it still probes one's deepest convictions and intuitions. For this reason the ancients are worth hearing as they explain, or deny, that Delphi is the Center of the Entire Earth.[27]

They had their proofs. Plutarch, for example, cited myth:

> The story is told that certain eagles or swans, flying from the uttermost parts of the Earth toward its center, met in Delphi at the *omphalos*.[28]

This is the poet's version. The *omphalos* was the Navel of the Earth, given material form at Delphi by a stone carved to the shape of a half-egg and covered with an honorific net of woolen strands. Located near the Pythia's seat in the inner shrine of the temple where she spoke, it marked the very center of the Center. The *omphalos* was not just a topographic or abstract symbol but a vital one: here the world came to birth, here is the sign of the attachment of our world to what lies beyond it—and here, too, is the sign of our detachment, for the navel is our first scar. By returning to the Navel of the Earth we can resume, however briefly, our contact with the source from which we come. The fifth-century poet Pindar wrote of "the thunderous Earth's enshrined navel."[29] He was always one to put things in boldest terms, but we understand him: the *omphalos* was a powerful symbol and presence.

Strabo observed factually that Delphi occupied well-nigh the geographic center of Greece, and reported the tale of the eagles as a matter of duty:

> [Delphi] is almost in the center of Greece taken as a whole. It was also believed to be in the center of the inhabited world, and people called it the navel of the earth, in addition fabricating a myth that the two eagles (some say crows) which had been set free by Zeus met there, one coming from the west and the other from the east.[30]

To recall the endorsement of Zeus, a pair of golden eagles flanked the *omphalos* at Delphi in the centuries before armies and emperors began to rob the sanctuary. Plutarch adds to this particular bowl of myths and stories that a skeptic named Epimenides asked the oracle to confirm or deny that Delphi was the Center of the World. Receiving a "vague and ambiguous" reply, Epimenides triumphantly announced his conclusion:

> Now we know that there is no mid-center of earth or of ocean;
> Yet if there is, it is known to the gods, hidden from mortals.

But Plutarch was not taken in. "Very likely," he editorialized, "the god repulsed him from his attempt to investigate an ancient myth as though it were a painting to be tested by touch."[31] This is fun, but the sheer beauty of the image of eagles flying from the uttermost parts of the Earth toward its center does not escape us. Plutarch corroborates his evidence from myth by reference to a current event:

> A short time [ago], it happened that two revered men coming from opposite ends of the inhabited earth met together at Delphi.

Yet another stunning image: had the two men been of ordinary quality, it might not mean much, but these men were "revered," and their passage from the ends of the Earth to Delphi has the character of pilgrimage, a measuring out of sacred space.

Eagles and sages converged at Delphi. So too did all Greeks, to their benefit. Immensely competitive among each other, ever poised for war, the Greek cities nonetheless cherished the notion of "our common Greekness," as Herodotus put it: "We are one in blood and one in language . . . and there are our habits, bred of a common upbringing."[32] Delphi helped to nurture this very real, much violated sense of unity. Aelius Aristides, a literary man of the second century C.E., described Apollo at Delphi as "the common interpreter of the Greeks" and the sanctuary as "the common temple of the Greeks."[33] To acknowledge a Center of the World had positive political implications in the long centuries when Delphi's extended parish across the Greek world was routinely disrupted by war.

Where is the Center of the World for each of us? Delphi rather forces this odd question. Uniformity is not to be expected. A person might recognize, upon reflection, that the Center of the World is . . . the White House, a certain church or temple, a beloved person, the family circle in which so much of life is experienced, Yosemite Valley or another cherished place where Nature is strong, a business office or university laboratory where a great enterprise is shaped, a meditation hall or dance studio where life reaches highest intensity, a jazz club or concert stage where the power of music is revealed. From appropriate vantage points, all are possible Centers of the World. They have in common qualities of heightened intensity, of raised consciousness and significance: it is *here* that the most powerful and meaningful forces are most clearly experienced. The Center is the place of revelation. Perhaps one can only confess for oneself where the Center of the World is to be found and leave it at that.

When we come from opposite ends of the inhabited Earth to meet at Delphi, we must continue this conversation.

LET THE GAMES BEGIN

Our modern Olympics could have been Delphics: the quadrennial games at Delphi were scarcely less grand than those of Olympia.[34] However, the Olympic games were much older, and all Greece kept the calendar in terms of the four-year cycle of Olympiads; hence the legitimate priority of Olympia. Delphi was "on the circuit"; the games in different cities over the four-year cycle were not unlike the professional tennis circuit in our own day, with prominent venues and many lesser ones of local interest. The inscription from an athlete's tomb conveys where there was to compete and the dedication required:

> Here lies Dandes, the stadion racer, who gained honor by his victories for his fatherland, rich in pasture for horses. Twice did he conquer at Olympia, thrice at Delphi, twice at the Isthmus, and fifteen times at Nemea, and it is not easy to count his other victories.[35]

Such athletes were honored by their city-states, which generally saw to their material needs. However, a tale has come down to us in which an athlete's resentment of poor treatment at the hands of his fellow citizens required nothing short of an intervention from the Delphic oracle.

Honor the Achiever

> Oibotas was the first Achaian foot racer to win at Olympia, but for some reason his countrymen neglected to bestow on him the rewards he expected. Perhaps they had no customs concerning how to treat a victorious athlete: after all, he was the first. Oibotas was so upset by their indifference that he cursed the whole lot of them and petitioned the heavenly powers to prevent any future Achaian from winning at Olympia.

> Some god was impressed by his plea. Time passed—and the Achaians went from defeat to defeat in every Olympic event to which they fielded contestants. Finally they sent an embassy to the Delphic oracle. What is wrong? What must we do? And they learned that they would remain entangled by Oibotas' curse until they paid him full and proper honors. And so they did. Among other handsome gestures they dedicated a portrait of him at Olympia itself.
>
> To this day Achaians competing at Olympia make sacrifices to the spirit of Oibotas and, if they win, festoon his portrait with wreaths.[36]

Distinguishing the games at Delphi was an early and sustained emphasis on artistic as well as athletic competition. From the beginning, instrumental musicians and poets singing to the lyre or flute competed for recognition;[37] eventually, theatrical troupes, painters, and perhaps artists in other media had their competitions. Our Delphics today need be not athletic—the niche is occupied—but could well be international artistic competitions. Consider this a proposal.

The ancient name for the competitions was *agon*, in which we are not misled to hear the connotations of struggle and pain explicit in our word "agony." Antiphon, a sophist of the fifth century B.C.E., observed no less: "Olympic and Pythian victories and all pleasures are apt to be won by great pains."[38] Like the oracle, the competition manifested that elusive reality of "our common Greekness." The occasion was preceded by a truce and safe passage of unclear duration and dimension: did it mean only that the citizens of warring cities met in peace at Delphi, Olympia, and elsewhere for games, or did it mean that warriors lay down their arms for months at a time? In either case, there was a link between the fiercely competitive contests and the surcease of war.

The place of the arts at Delphi, both in the artistic competitions and in many other respects, is beautifully illustrated by legends associated with Pindar (518–438 B.C.E.), who in his era was virtually poet laureate of Delphi. They say that an iron throne was kept for him near the eternal hearth in Apollo's temple. When he came to Delphi—we glimpse here the archetype of the traveling bard, welcome everywhere—he occupied the throne to sing in Apollo's honor.[39]

The Bees' Seal

> Once, when Pindar was a very young man, he was traveling in the hot season. At mid-day, he found shelter beneath a roadside tree and fell into a deep sleep. While he slept, a swarm of bees approached him and

made wax on his lips. From this time, he began to compose his famous songs.

He was already celebrated throughout Greece when the Pythia conferred still more glory on him by telling the Delphians to grant Pindar an equal share in the wealth they gave Apollo.

In old age, they say, he had a vision while he slept: Persephone came to him from the world of the dead and said that she was the only god to whom Pindar had never addressed a song. But he would write her a song all the same, she said. On the tenth day after that vision he died.

There was an old woman in Thebes, a close relative of Pindar's, who over the years had learned most of his songs. Pindar appeared to her in a dream and sang a hymn to Persephone. As soon as she awakened, she wrote down what she had heard. It was the poet's last ode.[40]

The state of the arts at Delphi is reflected in another tale of an immortal poet:

Aeschylus' Dilemma

Once the city fathers of Delphi approached the great playwright, Aeschylus, to ask him to write a new hymn in praise of Apollo for use on special occasions. Aeschylus must have hesitated—his response was the soul of hesitation. "I cannot accept the commission," he replied, "although your kindness in offering it is not lost on me. Let me explain. Long ago, Tynnichos wrote a hymn for you—a much revered one that you still use. Were I to write a new hymn, it would suffer the same fate as a new statue of a god when it is placed alongside old and venerated statues. Old statues may be simple in their workmanship, but they are considered divine. No, I cannot write a new hymn for you—but I will gladly join you in singing the old ones!"[41]

Every artist who has felt not only the grandeur but the weight of tradition will know what he means.

2

A Code for Questioners

In an early hymn, Apollo surveys the beauty of the Delphic landscape and utters these vigorously reassuring words:

> In this place, I am of a mind to build a glorious temple as an oracle for men, and those who live in rich Peloponnesos and Europe and the wave-washed islands will bring perfect sacrifices when they come to question me. Answering from my rich temple, I will give them all counsel that cannot fail.[1]

When they come to question me. . . . At the Center of the World, where man could meet almost familiarly with God, was heard the murmur of questioning. Some of the finest minds of the ancient world, from Theognis in the sixth century B.C.E. to Epictetus in the high Roman Empire, thought through the issue of what questions could legitimately be brought to oracles and how the answers could best be received. In point of fact, individuals and even city-states on occasion asked frivolous, hypocritical, or massively inappropriate questions, and the Delphic oracle was not slow to respond sharply. But what emerges from surviving observations on appropriate questioning is a remarkable intellectual and emotional code, however much it may have been violated in practice. Like much else in Delphic tradition, this code is entirely of its own time and place, but richly suggestive for those today who are engaged in teacher/pupil relationships in any of the permutations that now exist in our society. We have no widely acknowledged oracles, but we continue to have questioners and sources of knowledge.

The most comprehensive view of appropriate questioning appears in Xenophon's memoir about Socrates, a work largely written some twenty years after the master's death in 399 B.C.E. Less read than Plato's Socratic dialogues, it is full of treasures. Xenophon was a man of striking breadth, a resourceful military leader, an historian, a theorist on education, a prolific author, a loyal pupil of Socrates. The following is his account of Socrates' reflections on the right question—and the wrong question—to bring to Delphi:

Socrates' Advice to His Pupils

> If there was no room for doubt, Socrates advised his intimates to act as they thought best, but if the consequences could not be foreseen, he sent them to the oracle to inquire whether the thing ought to be done. Those who intended to control a house or a city, he said, needed the help of divination. For the craft of carpenter, smith, farmer or ruler, and the theory of such crafts, and arithmetic and economics and generalship might be learned and mastered by the application of human powers, but the deepest secrets of these matters the gods reserved to themselves. They were dark to men.
>
> You may plant a field well, but you do not know who shall gather the fruits. You may build a house well, but you do not know who shall dwell in it. Able to command, you cannot know whether it is profitable to command. Versed in statecraft, you do not know whether it is profitable to guide the state. Though for your delight you marry a lovely woman, you cannot tell whether she will bring you sorrow. If any man thinks that these matters are wholly within the grasp of the human mind and nothing in them is beyond our reason, that man, he said, is irrational.
>
> But it is no less irrational to seek the guidance of heaven in matters which men are permitted by the gods to decide for themselves by study: To ask, for instance, is it better to get an experienced coachman to drive my carriage or an inexperienced hand? Is it better to get an experienced seaman to steer my ship or a man without experience? So too with what we may know by reckoning, measurement or weighing.
>
> To put such questions to the gods seemed to his mind profane. In short, what the gods have granted us to do by dint of learning, we must learn. What is hidden from mortals we should try to find out from the gods by divination: for to him that is in their grace the gods grant signs.[2]

Socrates' perspective is so reasonable and instinctively appealing that it scarcely requires commentary. He points insistently to a threshold *before* which we are entirely responsible for working out whatever answers we may need, *after* which we must take the risk of seeking divine counsel. This step is inherently risky because nothing guarantees that any one of us is "in the gods' grace" and therefore worthy of "signs." Socrates is in effect imposing a condition on the Heraclitan fragment quoted in the preface: "The Lord whose oracle is at Delphi neither speaks nor conceals, but gives signs." The Lord gives signs to those whom He accepts. Further, the idea of signs implies the need to interpret, and nothing guarantees sound interpretation.

Socrates' distinction between matters subject to measurement and those that surpass rational means echoes interestingly against the advice of Theognis, the aristocratic sixth-century poet from the city of Megara, between Athens and Delphi. Addressing much of his poetry to a young man, Kyrnos, Theognis lived out many roles in turn: crusty advisor, delighted lover, love's victim, high-born critic of the ordinary, connoisseur of those things—laughter, poetry, wine, and love—the Greeks enjoyed in their night-long symposia. Within this kaleidoscope of themes and attitudes, Theognis once offered his considered advice on the one and only way to receive an utterance from the god at Delphi:

Like a Carpenter

Kyrnos, the man who receives an oracle
From the priestess at the Pythian god's rich shrine
Must scrutinize the answer carefully
As if he were a carpenter, with rule,
Compass, and square. For if you add one word
You're lost; and if you take away, you'll find
There's no escaping guilt in the god's eyes.[3]

By his easygoing assumption that the youth would in time need this advice, we can deduce that inquiry at the Delphic oracle was not all that rare in his era—any citizen of adequate means might conceivably inquire there in the course of his life. In these lines, Theognis passes on what we might call respect for the text and a short version of the rules of interpretation. The Delphic pilgrim must not permit himself to alter the oracular words to suit his preferences. On the contrary, he must approach the interpretive challenge with a mind intent on accuracy. If, as Socrates says, the oracle begins where human knowledge and wisdom leave off, Theognis adds that a highly rational and disciplined approach to interpreting the oracle's words is essential. The Delphic oracle did not represent in ancient times the defeat of rationality or triumph of superstition but rather a border where rationality encountered the irrational—or a higher and richer rationality—in a fertile exchange.

Ancient authors were not particularly given to telling stories on themselves. In an exception to this rule, Xenophon recounts an exchange with Socrates in which the master was, to say the least, displeased with him.

Xenophon's Half-Hearted Inquiry

> At a fateful point in his earlier years, Xenophon was drawn to volunteer as a mercenary with the Persian armies of Cyrus the younger. At the time, Cyrus was preparing a military coup against his brother, who had recently ascended the throne. Xenophon sought Socrates' advice about his plan. Unsure of what would be best—there were good political arguments against an Athenian helping a Persian—Socrates advised him to consult the god at Delphi. Xenophon obediently trekked to the holy city and asked Apollo to which gods he should sacrifice and pray in order to succeed in the journey he had in mind and, after meeting with good fortune, return safely home. Apollo generously responded by telling him just what he had asked.
>
> When Xenophon returned from Delphi, he reported the details of the oracle to Socrates. After hearing out his pupil, Socrates upbraided him because he did not first ask the god whether it was better to go or stay. Instead, he had decided for himself that he would go and asked only how best to proceed.
>
> "However," added Socrates, "since you put the question that way, you must do what the god directed."[4]

The echo of this passage, like the one quoted earlier from Xenophon, can be heard intermittently in later centuries, most audibly in the transcribed lectures of Epictetus, the Stoic philosopher of Greek origin who taught in imperial Rome and the provinces in the later first and second centuries. Epictetus is yet another ancient thinker, known today primarily to academics and their students, who speaks with a freshness and impassioned love of truth quite out of keeping with the standard prejudice that ancient thinkers, like figures in a pale frieze, stood about stiffly orating to one another. To Socrates' meticulous reasoning about the content of questions appropriate to oracles, Epictetus adds insight about the emotional integrity of the questioner: is the questioner impelled by fear and desire, or by a detached wish for truth? Epictetus is thinking not of Delphi specifically but of the individual diviners, such as bird augurs, whom Romans more commonly consulted, although it is clear from a passage where he describes Delphic Apollo as "the greater diviner,"[5] that he conceived of means of prophecy along a curve that rises to Delphi.

Like a Traveler Asking Directions

> Because we resort to divination when there is no good reason for it, many of us neglect the duties of life. What induces us to use divination so constantly? Cowardice, fear of consequences. This is why we flatter diviners—we say, "Master, shall I inherit my father's property?" "Let us see," he replies sagely, "let us offer a sacrifice about that matter." "Yes, master, as fortune wills." And if the diviner says, "You will inherit the property," we thank him effusively—as though we had received the inheritance from *him*. Can we blame him for mocking us behind our backs?
>
> Well, what then? We ought to go to them with neither desire nor aversion, just as a traveler asks which of two roads leads to his destination, without any desire to have the right-hand road lead there any more than the left-hand road—for he does not care to travel one particular road of the two, but merely the one that leads to his destination. So also we ought to go to God as a guide, making use of Him as we make use of our eyes. We do not call on our eyes to show us one thing or another, we simply accept the impression of whatever they reveal to us.
>
> As we are, we tremble before the bird augur, lay hold on him, appeal to him as if he were a god, beg of him: "Master, have mercy, grant me what I wish." You slave![6]

In the *Encheiridion* or short manual of his ideas, Epictetus even more explicitly describes the encounter with a diviner as a classic exercise in Stoicism. A cool and sober mind must achieve dominion over the natural vacillations of the heart. Beyond this, he reopens Socrates' question concerning which inquiries are suitable and which should not be made because the answers are, theoretically, the common knowledge of any principled person. Xenophon's Socrates, concerned with intellectual honesty, leaves the issue of emotional honesty, or integrity, somewhat unspoken; Epictetus focuses almost entirely on the question of integrity, which he presents not as a "given" but as the result of searching self-recognition and self-control. Like Theognis, Epictetus also evokes a zone of experience that we shall explore in this book: the aftermath of inquiry at an oracle, when the questioner must assimilate the holy answer and act on it. Of this phase in the drama of inquiry, he writes with characteristic intensity, "Remember whom you have taken as counselor, and whom you will be disregarding if you disobey."

Remember Whom You Have Taken as Counselor

> Do not approach the diviner with desire or aversion, do not approach with trembling, but make up your mind that every possible outcome of your inquiry is indifferent and nothing to you. Whatever it may be, you will turn it to good use, and no one will prevent you from doing so. Go with confidence to the gods as to a counselor, and when their counsel has been given you, remember whom you have taken as counselor, and whom you will be disregarding if you disobey.
>
> Go to divination as Socrates thought men should go—that is, only in instances when neither reason nor technical knowledge are capable of uncovering the needed answer. Thus, when it is your duty to share the danger of a friend or of your country, do not ask the diviner whether you ought to share that danger. If he forewarns you that the omens of sacrifice are unfavorable, and death, injury, or exile is likely, reason still requires you to stand by your friend and share your country's danger.[7]

The code naturally excluded frivolous and vain questions. Inquirers who approached the oracle in search of flattery or the ancient equivalent of insider information were not necessarily well received. A pair of surviving tales reflects the severity of the oracle in these situations. The first concerns the city of Megara, home of Theognis.

The Megarians' Inquiry

> Dogged by self-doubt, the Megarians came to the oracle to confirm their respectability. "There are many great cities," they began, "some rank first among the Greeks, others just behind them. Where do we rank?"
>
> The oracle cannot have been pleased with this inquiry.
>
> "*Of all soils, Argos is the best,*" offered the Pythia as she began a tour of ancient municipalities.
>
> *Best are the horses of Thessaly,*
> *The women of Sparta,*
> *And the men who drink the waters*
> *of lovely Arthusa.*
> *Better even than these are the men*

Who live between Tiryns and Arkadia.
But you Megarians are neither third,
Nor fourth, nor twelfth. You do not appear
In any ranking.[8]

So much for the Megarians. Foolish questions were no more warmly received. In the following anecdote, ancient readers would have understood that Corinth and Sikyon were feuding neighbors, the region between them a disputed no man's land.

A Foolish Question

A fellow approached the oracle with a weighty question:
"How may I get rich, O son of Zeus and Letho?"
The Pythia replied gravely:
By acquiring the land between Corinth and Sikyon.

The transmitter of this tale could not resist adding: "Those who put foolish questions to the god are appropriately rebuked."[9]

It is, of course, impossible to measure how influential this composite code of conduct was over the centuries, as expressed and re-expressed by poets and philosophers from Theognis forward. Its call for intellectual and emotional integrity in approaching the oracle and for penetrating use of the mind, detached from personal preference, provides a steady background against which the whims and angers and thrashing self-interest of some inquirers can be more clearly seen. Obedience to this code of detached reflectiveness underlies the oddly plain, almost matter-of-fact attitude with which Dio Chrysostom encountered the oracle at a turning point in his life.

I Was Forced to Think

Exiled from Rome by the emperor Domitian in retaliation for his friendship with one of Domitian's political enemies, Dio took refuge in Athens. His thoughts were heavy as he reviewed his changed circumstances. As might be expected of a man trained in the Stoic view of life, he tried to attach some virtue to the prospect of long years in exile, but little by little he found himself sinking into despair. He remembered with the vividness of a through-and-through literary man the tales of many exiles—Ulysses first among them—who did everything in their power to return to their homes. He concluded that he, too, must find the way home, but he lacked all sense of how to get on with his life in the interval. In his dilemma, he turned to Delphi.

> He tells his own story from this point: "I decided to go to the god's temple myself and consult him, as a competent adviser, according to the ancient custom of the Greeks. For surely, I thought, if he gives competent advice about sickness and childlessness and harvests, he will not show any less ability in such a case as mine.
>
> "When I consulted him, he gave me a strange sort of reply, one not easy to interpret. For he encouraged me to continue single-mindedly pursuing the very thing I was already doing—namely, wandering the world—and qualified it as a most honorable and useful activity, '*until you come*,' said he, '*to the uttermost parts of the earth*.'
>
> "Lying is inconsistent even with a man's standards, to say nothing of a god's. Accordingly I reflected that Odysseus after all his wanderings did not hesitate to roam once more. Should I not follow his example if God so decreed? And so, after exhorting myself to be fearless and to set aside any thought that my decision was shameful, I put on a simple garment and took up the wanderer's life.
>
> "Those whom I met on my way would sometimes call me a tramp and sometimes a beggar—but others called me a philosopher. From this it came about gradually, and without planning or presumption on my part, that I acquired this name. Many would approach to ask my opinion about good and evil. I was forced to think."[10]

Dio's account of his experience brings more clearly to light a surprising feature of Delphic tales as they have come down to us: their characteristic indifference to the specifics of the ritual of inquiry at Delphi. Inquiry was a religious act in an era when religion was deeply embedded in ritual behavior, and scholars have ingeniously constructed from sources and the site itself a narrative, with gaps, of the ordered process through which the pilgrim passed—the purifications, the sacrifices, the payments—but the tales reflect almost nothing of all that (see chapter 4). Simple and direct, they focus narrowly on the identity of the questioner, his question and its answer, and the absorption or deflection of that answer as he continues on his way. This is true also when the questioner is not an individual but a state embassy, come perhaps to inquire about a life-or-death circumstance—war, plague, or famine.

Ancient authors seem to have valued and passed on what they experienced as the living core of these tales, and they did not regard Delphic ritual as especially colorful or interesting for their readers. Few narrative traditions in world literature are so strictly organized around questions and answers. On the other hand, we might ask whether the details of Delphic ritual were deliberately kept secret. To this day we know little about the Eleusinian Mysteries, the secret initiation regarded by generations of Athenians as more powerful and liberating than any other. Was Delphic ritual similarly protected?

It seems not. There are gaps in knowledge, as will become clear in chapter 4, but few appear to be deliberate. The reticence of the ancient narrator in front of secret knowledge is never subtle. "[The Egyptians] hold at night," wrote Herodotus, "an exhibition of the god's sufferings, a performance that the Egyptians call the Mysteries. I know more about these, but let me hold my peace. And again, about the rites of Demeter that the Greeks call the Thesmophoria, let me hold my peace."[11] Some seven hundred years later, Pausanias was equally cautious in his account of Eleusis. "I wanted to describe the contents of the sanctuary, but I was stopped by something I saw in a dream. I must turn to the things it is not irreligious to write for general readers."[12] There is little of this in Delphic tales. Scholars have speculated that the problem may be the opposite one: procedures for consulting the oracle were unremarkable in their era, hardly worth stopping the forward motion of a tale to report. Herodotus is again the best informant when, in the course of remarking briefly on another oracle, he draws a frustratingly offhand comparison with Delphi: "The well-known oracle of Dionysus is in the very highest mountains. The person who utters the prophecy is, as at Delphi, a priestess, and the procedure is no more complicated in the one place than the other."[13]

And so the tradition of Delphic tales is focused on question and answer, interpretation and consequence, not on the ritual that served as a vehicle for the encounter. To the code for questioners now assembled, we can add additional light from Iamblichus' biography of Pythagoras, written in the third century C.E. The passage in question is a blunt—and still liberating—warning from the great Pythagoras.

The Question Crowds Out the Answer

> Once when speaking with a gathering of pupils, as was his custom, Pythagoras gradually lost patience with a man who insisted on asking "Why? Why?" at every opportunity. Finally he turned on his tormenter: "And you," he said, "if Apollo were delivering an oracle to you, would you stop everything and ask him *why* he was doing so?"[14]

RIDDLING ORACLES, DARK AND BEYOND UNDERSTANDING

"Oracles are obscure," insisted Diogenes in his conversation with the naive pilgrim, "they have deceived many men." He might have added that this state of affairs cannot have entirely displeased the Greeks, who had a taste for riddles and enigmas. In their oracles, which represented an appearance of the "wholly Other" in their lives, there was more than a little of their own psyche, various and elusive, given to order yet disruptive, alternately serious and playful. The *Greek Anthology*, a rich collection of ancient literary fragments assembled by Byzantine scholars, actually drops a selection of Delphic responses into a chapter of riddles. From the cool distance of a later epoch and different religious moment, the structural similarity between Apollo's words and those of ancient thought-teasers was more noticeable than the vast difference in intent.

A marvelous tale in Herodotus illustrates the high value assigned by the Greeks to ingenious indirection.

The Scythian Riddle

> The Scythians, nomadic horsemen long familiar to the Greeks, were no match for the Persian army in set battles. But that is not how the Scythians chose to defend themselves when the Persians attacked. They relied instead on guerrilla tactics, and at length had so visibly exhausted the Persian troops that the Scythian kings decided to send a herald to Darius, the Persian king, with a quite special message. The herald arrived behind enemy lines with four gifts: a bird, a mouse, a frog, and five arrows.
>
> Naturally, the Persians asked the meaning of these enigmatic gifts. The herald replied that he had no instructions other than to present them and withdraw without delay. If the Persians were clever, he added, they would know their meaning.
>
> After his departure, the Persians plunged into debate. Darius held that the Scythians were in fact surrendering both themselves and the "earth and water" that figured in the traditional rite of surrender. He reasoned that the mouse is a creature of the earth, that the frog lives in water, that the bird in speedy flight is not unlike the Scythian war horse, and that the gift of arrows represented the Scythians' readiness to surrender. Such was his opinion. But one of his generals took a different view: "If you do not become birds and flee into the sky," he interpreted, "or become mice and burrow into the earth or become frogs and hide in the lakes, you shall never see your homes again, for we will overwhelm you with our arrows."[15]

Like the Scythian kings toying with their adversary, the Delphic oracle typically gave signs rather than absolute clarity. One of the names of

Apollo at Delphi was Loxias, the Oblique. Until later classical times this central trait seems by and large to have been accepted without prompting justification or ridicule: it was so, how could it be otherwise? Unquestionably, certain oracular answers within the mainstream of Delphic tradition seem designed to be misunderstood, but the ancients viewed the challenge of *completing the oracle* through one's own understanding and acts as a legitimate test. Consider, for example, the following pair of tales from Herodotus:

An Oven Full of Pots

When Arkesilas, the tough-minded king of Kyrene, was banished from his city, he found his way to the Delphic oracle. "*Reconquer your native land if you wish,*" said the Pythia, "*but live there quietly. And if you find an oven full of pots, do not bake them. Let them go downstream.*" Upon receiving this advice, Arkesilas gathered an army of mercenaries and battled his way back into the city. As soon as he was reestablished, he sought vengeance against his political enemies—some of whom took refuge in a tower. Arkesilas pursued them to the base of the tower. In the heat of passion, he ordered his men to pile wood against it and set a blazing fire. Soon his enemies were roasting.

And then he had a moment of thought. "I have baked the pots." Not long after, his surviving enemies found him.[16]

The Five Contests

Tisamenos was a seer who accompanied the Spartan army at Plataea, where the Greek allies defeated the Persians. Years ago, when he was a young husband, Tisamenos consulted the Delphic oracle about having children. His inquiry was one of many modest personal inquiries welcomed by the oracle. Whatever the god may have counseled Tisamenos concerning offspring, the Pythia enigmatically added that he should strive to win "*the five greatest contests.*" Quite naturally misreading the oracle's meaning, Tisamenos assumed that it referred to the greatest athletic contests of the Greek world. With this in mind, he neglected the gift of clairvoyance that since youth had been his and undertook a strict regimen of gymnastic training.

In time he was ready for the Olympic games. Competing in the pentathlon, widely considered "the greatest" and most challenging event, he came within a hair's breadth of winning—but didn't.

Strange. . . . His wiser friends began to rethink the meaning of the oracle that had launched Tisamenos on what now seemed a fruitless

> course. The oracle had not lied; the oracle did not lie. But then what had it meant by "*the five greatest contests*"? They realized in a flash that Delphi had attempted to guide Tisamenos not toward the contests of peace but those of war: he was destined to be their seer and holy guide in battle. His friends turned to him, pleaded with him, offered him substantial sums of money to assume this role. At last he was persuaded.
>
> His visionary foresight helped the Spartans win five great military contests.[17]

Tisamenos' misunderstanding prompted him to invest in efforts that were at best indirect preparation for his true calling. In the end his friends grasped the meaning of the oracle and helped him recognize his task. Arkesilas' misunderstanding was of another order: the oracle offered him a last chance to stay his hand before falling victim to his own violence. Had he been able to break through to a new kind of thinking—to the ability to see in the literal spectacle a hidden structure—he might have lived to fulfill his ambitions. Tisamenos was a seer who in effect refused to see, that is, to see beyond the obvious and at more than one level. Arkesilas was the farthest sort of man from a seer, but he missed the opportunity to see more. Both inquirers were led to the edge of their understanding; one, with help, found the way on. He completed the oracle.

"Riddling oracles, dark and beyond the power of understanding," wrote Aeschylus in *Prometheus Bound*.[18] The speaker, young Io, is referring to oracles from Delphi and the Zeus oracle at Dodona. But her tragic tone, suffused with the sense of human limitation, is less common in Delphic tales than vigorous intellectual response. Here is a holy riddle, an enigmatic description of reality—let us penetrate it. Plutarch speaks for this vigorous traditional attitude when he suggests that the enigmas of the oracle and the temple itself "act as a lure and an invitation to investigate, to read, and to talk about them."[19] In his era, some ancient Delphic customs and symbols were no longer fully understood; like the oracle's more mysterious sayings, they had become a focus of speculation among connoisseurs. Enigma was part of the fabric of Delphi, as were intellectual and moral effort in response to it.

Plutarch was willing to entertain the idea that in the centuries when state embassies regularly consulted at Delphi, Apollo looked after his own—the Pythia and priests in attendance—by obscuring his thought to avoid provoking violence against those serving the temple. In addition, Apollo had a perfect right to stage-manage human affairs. "I should not be surprised," he wrote, "if there were times when there was need of double entendre, indirect statement, and vagueness. There were naturally some things which it was well that despots should fail to understand and enemies should not learn beforehand."[20]

Yet Plutarch as apologist for the peculiarities of Delphi is less convincing than as a celebrant of the riches of its heritage. We are looking, with him, at a tradition whose modes of expression range from seemingly malicious indirection to the archaic pomp of epic verse, from stark confrontation that leaves nothing unclear to deeply puzzling advice that the recipient knows to be of utmost seriousness, however obscure it may seem. The Delphi of the mind was vast enough to encompass all of these characteristics, and honored enough by people in general to outlast its critics.

One of the most elaborate examples of Delphic metaphor, worth remembering for its style although its content is distant and archaic, occurs in a story told by Herodotus.

The Search for Orestes' Bones

"*There is a place in the Arkadian plain, Tegea its name,*"
intoned the Pythia,
With two winds breathing by hard necessity.
Blow upon blow is struck there, grief is piled upon grief,
And in that place the life-giving earth
Holds the bones of the son of Agamemnon.
Take them and you shall be master of Tegea.

The recipient of these high-flown words was a Spartan named Lichas, who participated in a state inquiry at Delphi at a time when Sparta was bound by uneasy truce with an adversary, the Arkadian city of Tegea. Were Sparta to find Orestes' relics and transfer them to Spartan soil, Tegea would be magically stripped of its power to resist Spartan arms. Lichas ventured out in search, with nothing more than these obscure words as his guide.

In time he came to an ironsmith's workshop on Tegean territory. It oddly arrested his attention. He stood to one side, lost in wonder, as the smith shaped red-hot metal while great bellows whooped life into the intense flames of the forge. Eventually, the sweat-wreathed artisan put down his tools and turned to him. "My friend, what I'm doing seems to fascinate you, but you would be more fascinated still by what I discovered just the other day. I was starting to dig a well here in my courtyard when I came upon a very ancient coffin, larger than any I have seen in my life . . ."

The smith continued reliving his experience, but Lichas could hardly listen further. Suddenly seized with the thought that the bones of the great hero, Orestes, lay within that massive coffin, his mind

> raced through the oracle's words and compared them point by point with the ironsmith's art that unaccountably had made him pause. "Two winds breathing by hard necessity—the bellows! Blow on blow is struck there—of course, of course! And 'grief laid upon grief'—what of that? Well, it's true enough that iron weapons have caused harm to mankind."
>
> With this line of thought reaching certainty, Lichas thanked the ironsmith for his time and tale and turned back toward Sparta.[21]

The tale fully exemplifies "the thrill of the chase" in the Delphic context, although the object of the chase in this particular tale is remote. The oracle offered Lichas an obscurely allusive map, but he knew enough to take it seriously. The odds were against making the right connections yet he succeeded, in part because he was willing to perceive common circumstances uncommonly.

In some other tales, the odds are so poor that a modern reader cannot help but detect a trace of *Schadenfreude*—of pleasure in others' failures—in the makeup of the ancient writers and readers who enjoyed them. For example, an anecdote about the great fourth-century Theban general, Epaminondas, seems tailored to reduce his heroic stature. The Pythia once warned Epimanondas to beware of the Sea. Not surprisingly, he was ever after cautious about commanding a fleet or even traveling in a merchant ship. Yet in the end, he met his death not on open water but in a deep oak forest known as the Sea. Our author, Pausanias, adds with analytical coolness: "Two places with the same name had tricked the Athenians in the past and tricked Hannibal of Carthage later."[22]

The ambiguous imagery and wordplay in some—by no means all—Delphic tales functions at several different levels of meaning. At the first and simplest level, Delphic ambiguity sponsors anecdotes, like that of Epaminondas and "the Sea," which compactly dramatize the uneven struggle to live securely and well. For example, legend holds that Herakles' descendants were instructed by the oracle to wait *for the third fruit* before returning home from a long campaign.[23] Believing that the oracle had advised them to wait three years, they delayed their departure accordingly and then fought their way out of the region where they had been trapped. Things did not go well for them, and their leader Aristomachos was killed. The oracle had in fact meant *the third generation*. Well, what is one to do?

Not every example at this first level of Delphic ambiguity is malicious, and not every inquirer fails to solve the riddle. In legendary times, Kephalos was banished from Athens after accidentally taking the life of his wife. He settled in a distant land. Ten generations later, his descendants Chalkinos and Daitos sailed to Delphi to ask the god's permission to return to Athens. The oracle gave them permission to do so but commanded them to make a sacrifice to Apollo wherever, as they approached the city, they saw a warship moving on dry ground. A warship on dry ground? We sense at once that we are again in the realm of riddles, perhaps divine sport, but Chalkinos and Daitos were equal to the challenge. When they reached the Painted Mountain, they caught sight of a magnificent snake dashing into its hole, and they were struck with the thought that here, if anywhere, they could credibly claim to have encountered "a warship moving on dry ground." They made their solemn sacrifice. A short time later, the Athenians welcomed them and restored their citizenship.[24]

Delphic ambiguity functioned at quite another level, where obscurity of word or image confronted inquirers, could they but see it, with themselves. As Epictetus counseled, would inquirers be capable of setting aside personal preference or obsession in order to examine circumstances objectively? Or would their minds be clouded by desire or prejudice, anger or fear? Delphi opened the field of choice but typically did not deprive inquirers of their opportunity to complete the oracle through their own decisions for good or ill. A rather grand and stark tale about events on the north Aegean island of Thasos illustrates the issue. It also demonstrates a trait of the oracle as recorded in literature, namely, that inquirers who failed the first time to interpret correctly had the option of returning for clarification. The second round of counsel was often mercifully straightforward.

Restore the Exiles

> Theagenes was an outstanding athlete from Thasos who competed for years on the tour that took athletes to the Olympic, Pythian, Nemean, and Isthmian games, not to mention others. The day finally dawned when Theagenes knew that age had caught up with him. He resumed permanent residence on Thasos, where he quickly rose to become a respected civic leader.
>
> Theagenes' record of success in everything to which he turned his hand provoked envy in just one of his peers. This powerful politician did him no harm in his lifetime, but he sought a bizarre satisfaction after Theagenes' death. According to custom, statues of the great men of Thasos were erected in the town center, and it was upon the statue

of Theagenes that this adversary unleashed his anger. Under cover of night, while the town slept, he would creep out to lash the statue with the kind of scourge used to punish common criminals. Again and again he would yield to his mad obsession—until the night came when he accidentally entangled the whip around the statue. As he drew it back for the next blow, the statue toppled over on him and he died instantly.

There was no doubt in anyone's mind. The legal code stated that if an inanimate object causes a person's death, it must be tried in court as if it were a person, found guilty when the facts warrant, and sunk in the sea. The dead man's relatives brought suit against the statue, and it was duly transported to a watery grave.

But the island did not fare well. A tremendous plague broke out. It threatened the entire population. At their wits' end, the city fathers sent a delegation to the Delphic oracle. "What are we to do?" they asked.

"*Restore the exiles,*" intoned the Pythia—this and nothing more.

Restore the exiles? Good, good, we have sent many men into exile with their families—the political life, you know, is not without its rough patches. But let us call them back, let us open our arms.

And so they did—but the pestilence raged on. A remnant of the community sailed again to Delphi. "What must we do?"

> *Him that you have forgotten in the ocean's deep sands,*
> *Theagenes, victor of many games: restore the exile!*[25]

Much beauty here lies in the relentless divine insistence on detail and in the shock of this complacent community's discovery that the one "exile" they had neglected—the abused statue—was most important of all. The tale in essence concerns a community's relation with its own ideals and history. Theagenes was the very model of the civilized, accomplished individual. While his adversary could not undo him in his lifetime, he succeeded—at unexpected personal cost—in damaging Theagenes' memory and subverting the history of the community. A plague descends sooner or later on all communities that betray their ideals and rewrite history. If we read the tale's meaning correctly, the remedy is to retrieve those ideals from exile and restore them to centrality. The initial vagueness of the oracle's words opened a field of choice in which the community was free to act as its collective wisdom prompted. Delphic vagueness sponsored self-confrontation and "a lesson learned" in a way that clarity in the first round of inquiry might not have achieved.

As this tale and others suggest, we need to be cautious about falling into step with those entertaining late classical authors and zealous early Christians who mocked the oracle's obscure turn of phrase. Lucian comes to mind, the brilliant Greek poet of the second century, who wrote for a cosmopolitan audience at the height of Roman power. In one of his comic dialogues, a character offers this remark immediately after Apollo speaks in praise of clarity:

> You were right, Apollo, to praise people who speak clearly, even though you yourself do not do it at all, for in your oracles you are ambiguous and riddling, and you unconcernedly toss most of them into debatable ground so that your hearers need another Apollo to interpret them.[26]

In another dialogue, Lucian has Hera, wife of Zeus and Queen of Heaven, berate Leto, mother of Apollo, for her son's shady commercial activities:

> Apollo pretends to know everything, be it archery, harping, medicine, or prophecy, and has set up prophecy factories in Delphi, Claros, Colophon, and Didyma, deceiving his customers by giving crooked replies, hedging between two possible answers, so there's no risk of a slip-up. He gets rich in this way, for there are plenty of willing victims of his quackery. However, the more intelligent people see through his mystery-mongering.[27]

If Lucian viewed the ambiguities of Delphic language in a comic light, others before and after him perceived quite another dimension, and their thoughts introduce us to a further level of meaning in Delphic ambiguity. For these philosophically minded authors, the difficulties served as a barrier to careless minds unprepared and perhaps unworthy to apprehend Truth. Further, the compactness of some of its statements should be viewed as a sacred shorthand that permitted the oracle to concentrate great meaning into few words. The image of the seed captured this ancient insight. Iamblichus, the third-century mystical philosopher and author of the marvelous legendary biography of Pythagoras, maintained that Pythagoras' condensed form of speech was very like Delphic sayings, and no less rich:

Potent Seeds

> Pythagoras was accustomed to pour forth sentences resembling oracles to his familiars in a symbolical manner, and which in the greatest brevity of words contained the most abundant and multifarious meaning, like the Pythian Apollo through certain oracles, or like nature herself through seeds small in bulk, the former exhibiting conceptions, and the latter effects, innumerable in multitude, and difficult to be understood.[28]

In another passage, Iamblichus gave succinct form to the concept that puzzling wordplay and images raised a necessary barrier against thoughtless people: "The entire Pythagoric discipline," he wrote, "was symbolic, resembling enigmas and riddles, just as the truly divine and Pythian oracles appear to be difficult to understand and explain to those who carelessly receive the answers."[29]

What, then, have we learned about the ambiguity of the words and images cast into the ancient world by the Delphic oracle? At one level, there is clearly an element of divine sport, indistinguishable on occasion from haughty malice or indifference. Heraclitus spoke from this essential Greek perception of the human condition when he said, "Time is a child moving counters in a game; the royal power is a child's."[30] The deep weariness blended with acceptance in these words reflects the tragic side of this perception, while the playful riddling of some Delphic responses reflects the comic side.

At a second level, Delphic ambiguity laid the groundwork for inquirers' confrontations with themselves and their illusions. Perhaps the finest and most memorable tales of the oracle fit into this category—for example, the saga of King Croesus (see chapter 6). At a third level, we cannot disregard the joint testimony of even-minded Plutarch in the first century C.E. and fiery Lucian in the second: the oracle occasionally hedged its bets. Protecting the pragmatic interests of the temple and the entire Delphic community, the oracle was willing to dress hard truth in such flowery language that powerful inquirers could confirm or deny their preferences at will. The Delphic institution was immersed in a warrior society, in which communal politics and diplomatic relations were never far from the sword. Unquestionably a civilizing force, the oracle can surely be forgiven for "hedging between two possible answers" when circumstances required.

At a fourth and perhaps final level, the compact and religiously rich messages that Delphi was reputed in ancient times to deliver—of which some few have survived—struck a number of sensitive contemporaries as the seed aspect of its teaching: much encompassed in few words, an outward hint of inner riches if one proved able to discover them. The thought is Porphyry's, in a surviving fragment from his lost book on oracles:

> These things I beg you to conceal as the most unutterable of secrets, for even the gods did not make a revelation concerning them openly, but by enigmas.[31]

A pair of tales captures the full range of the oracle's riddling style. The first, a tale of Homer, displays that disconcerting touch of divine malice, while the second displays the unexpected, momentous lucidity evident in the best of these tales.

A Little Tale of Homer

According to legend, the great Homer was unsure of his place of birth. Traveling once from city to city to recite his poems, he came to Delphi and naturally inquired about his birth. The Pythia answered:

> *The island of Ios is your mother's country,*
> *and it shall receive you dead.*
> *Beware of the children's riddle.*

Ever after, they say, he avoided Ios. But years later, now aged and universally admired, he nonetheless set sail to Ios and, weary of his travels, remained there for some time. As he was sitting by the sea one day, some boys beached their fishing boat nearby. Homer hailed them:

"Well, young ones, how was the catch today?"

They were in such good spirits that they replied with a riddle: "Everything we caught we left behind—but we have what we didn't catch."

The great man was puzzled. "What do you mean?" They explained that since the fish weren't biting, they had spent their time catching lice in their clothes and hair: the ones they caught they left behind, the ones they missed were still hidden on them somewhere! They laughed with pleasure.

At that moment Homer remembered the oracle and knew that his end of days had come. When he rose from the beach to be on his way, he slipped on wet clay and fell badly. It is said that he died three days later.

A trivial end to so great a man, and perhaps that is the message: death is the leveler. But Homer prevailed in the end, as the epitaph he wrote for himself, to which all would agree, bears witness:

> Here the earth covers the sacred head
> Of divine Homer, glorifier of heroes.[32]

The second tale does not have the blend of triviality and *gravitas* that makes this little tale of Homer so odd. On the contrary, it advances with mathematical precision toward an initially obscure but ultimately impressive goal.

The Delian Problem

> Devastated by a plague, the people of Delos sent an embassy to the Delphic oracle. "What must we do to halt this terrible plague?" they asked.
>
> *Double the size of your altar.*
>
> The instruction seemed straightforward. The embassy returned to Delos, gathered the city's surviving craftsmen, and explained the task.
>
> The craftsmen set to work. Their first impulse was to add a second altar of the same size to the existing one. They may well have done this—the sources are uncertain. What is certain is that the plague raged on. "The god," they concluded," must mean for us to replace the altar with one twice as large." They set to work again. Measuring each side of the existing altar, they doubled all of the measurements and began construction—only to realize after the first courses of marble had been laid that they were actually making an altar eight times as large as the previous one. There was something wrong with the calculations.
>
> The plague raged on. Hearing that Plato was returning from Egypt, they cheered up. Plato was one of the foremost geometers of their generation. They sent a delegation to overtake him at Karia. They explained their difficulty and the utter urgency of solving the problem. Smiling, the philosopher assured them that the answer was near at hand. Gathering the men around, he took a stick and sketched in the sand how to derive two mean proportionals from the existing dimensions of the altar. These lengths, and these alone, would permit them to double the altar.
>
> "You know," added Plato, "I cannot agree that the oracle was saying only 'do this thing, meet this challenge, and all will be well.' The message is larger than that. The god is telling you, and all Greeks, that if we cultivate geometry and all branches of learning we will have greater welfare. We will not be just warriors but students of the Muses, men of peace."[33]

Centuries after this legendary exchange, the participants in Plutarch's conversations at Delphi still remembered it. On one of those occasions, Theon related the Delian problem to the oracle's love of ambiguity: "That the god is a most logical reasoner," he said,

> the great majority of his oracles clearly show; for surely it is the function of the same person both to solve and to invent ambiguities. When they were told to double the size of the altar at Delos, it was not this that the god had in mind—he was urging the Greeks to study geometry. In the same way, when the god gives ambiguous oracles, he is promoting logical reasoning as indispensable to those who wish to grasp his meaning."[34]

3

Challenging Men to Gentleness: Apollo

A Greek friend took me aside several years ago, when I had just returned from Delphi, and confided with a blend of complicity and defiance that he privately worshipped the ancient gods. I did not imagine goat sacrifices in the suburbs or any absurdity whatever, and it was obvious that he had no such thing in mind. On the contrary, I sensed in him a devotion to certain ideals and, as well, the chaste metaphysical temperament of one who considers it his duty—and joy—to explore the many worlds emanating down from the divine *Nous* or Mind that shapes all.

The poet and novelist Robert Graves has retold the Greek myths for our time, just as venerable Bullfinch retold them for nineteenth-century readers of English;[1] we can conveniently explore these grand, obsessively detailed stories to our heart's content. Similarly, ancient Greek religion has been all but rediscovered by recent scholarship.[2] Absent from major scholarship, and rightly so, is the still, small voice of devotion that I was privileged to hear from my friend, and it is just this that we might hope to rediscover. From this point forward I suggest that we adopt the practice of capitalizing references to Apollo as if He were the focus of our own faith, in order to find the way back, if only a little, to the attitude of worship that so animated good and sensible men and women in ancient times. In an essay on the participation of senior citizens in public life, the elderly Plutarch made clear that nothing short of *force majeure* could prevent him from taking part in the religious life at Delphi. "Surely you know," he wrote, "that I have been serving the Pythian Apollo for many Pythiads, but you would not say, 'Plutarch, you have done enough sacrificing, marching in processions, and dancing in choruses, and now that you are older it is time to put off the garland and desert the oracle on account of your age.'"[3] In the first century of our era there was enough beauty in Delphic liturgy, and enough vigor in the philosophical and religious life of those close to the oracle, to keep an old man busy.

> *The number of sand grains I know, and also the measures of ocean;*
> *I understand him that is dumb, and can hearken to the voiceless.*[4]

Through the medium of His priestess, Pythian Apollo is speaking—in effect stating His divine credentials before delivering a message at a key moment in Herodotus' history of the Persian Wars. The voice is strikingly biblical as Apollo asserts His total knowledge of our world from its smallest particle to its largest unity, and beyond this reminds us of His communion with even the most frail and isolated human being. When listening to such warm language and sentiments, it is impossible to experience any trace of the Judeo-Christian-Islamic aversion to polytheism. Yet Pythian Apollo is only one among many gods, and must even be somewhat distinguished from manifestations of Apollo at other sacred sites. Is He not, then, a small fictive thing, a religious imagining that preceded the mature religious vision of monotheism? One is ready to answer yes, but the arresting voice of ancient hymns—the spoken I-Thou—makes itself heard again:

> You, Lord, who know
> The appointed end of all, and all paths:
> How many leaves in April the earth puts forth,
> How many grains of sand
> In the sea and in the rivers
> Are troubled by the waves and the swirling winds,
> And what shall be, and whence it shall come,
> You see with clear eyes.[5]

Apollo numbers and charts in a Heraclitan world of change that defies human understanding. Such eloquent language of vast reference, from a fifth-century song, continues to echo even when one sensibly consults *The Oxford Classical Dictionary*—an irreplaceable sourcebook—and reads that Apollo was the god of certain things but not others, the god of "music, archery, prophecy, medicine, and the care of flocks and herds, often associated with the higher developments of civilization, approving codes of law, inculcating high moral and religious principles, and favoring philosophy."[6] It is, of course, necessary to inventory knowledge in this way—if possible, without ignoring the song:

> His All-knowing Mind
> Holds no traffic with lies: no god, no man deceives it
> Either in word or in plan.[7]

Much as He could be merciless with inquirers who were foolish, insincere, or stained by evil acts, He was acknowledged as a source of comfort and renewal in times of misery. Pindar once evoked in song a pilgrim who

> made his way to Pytho
> To ask about the sorrows he could not bear.[8]

And if a pilgrim needed not just comfort but a verdict, for this, too, he could rely on Apollo:

> Come here and sing aloud
> Of holy Themis and Pytho
> And the straight justice of the navel of the world.[9]

Themis, daughter of Earth (Gaia), was among the first to give oracles at Delphi in the legendary epoch before Apollo's arrival, when Delphi was dedicated to Mother Earth. Strabo passed on a wonderfully rich concept of Pythian Apollo, derived from a fourth-century world history, now lost. "Historians take it for granted," he wrote,

> that Apollo, with Themis, devised the oracle because He wished to help our race; and [they say] that Apollo challenged men to gentleness and inculcated self-control by giving out oracles to some, commanding them to do certain things and forbidding them to do other things, and by absolutely refusing admittance to other consultants. Men believe that Apollo directs all this, some believing that the god himself assumes a bodily form, others that He transmits to human beings a knowledge of His own will.[10]

Challenging men to gentleness—what do our surviving tales of Delphi confirm or deny of this civilizing mission? A pair of oracular statements, detached from their tales and preserved in the *Greek Anthology*, offers a schematic sense of Delphic morality:

Come, Stranger

> Come, stranger, pure in mind, to the precinct of the pure god, after dipping your hand in the water of the nymphs. A drop is enough for the righteous, while the entire ocean cannot cleanse a wicked man with its streams.[11]

The Holy Places Are Open

> The holy places of the gods are open to the righteous, and they have no need to cleanse their bodies with water: no defilement touches virtue. But you who are evil at heart, leave this place. For by sprinkling your body you can never cleanse your soul.[12]

Diogenes, that impassioned observer of ancient life, converted these lofty sentiments into *ad hominem* attack in the streets of Athens. Once he came upon a fellow citizen performing the simple ritual of sprinkling his body with holy water to establish purity. "Unhappy man," said Diogenes, "don't you realize that you can no more get rid of errors of conduct by sprinkling yourself with water than you can mistakes of grammar?"[13]

As a working priest, Plutarch was well placed to give us a pragmatic sense of what it meant to inculcate Delphic values in a crowd that ranged from pilgrims to tourists and gawkers—to sports fans, for we should keep in mind that not every person cheering on his city's athletes from the bleachers was a philosopher. As usual, Plutarch is quite high-minded in his comment, but his disillusionment shows through:

> No aspect of man is more divine than reasoning, especially reasoning about the gods, and nothing has greater influence toward happiness. Consequently, we give instructions to anyone who comes down to the oracle to think holy thoughts and speak pious words. But the mass of men act ridiculously in the processions and festivals. At first they vow to speak piously, but later say and think the most unholy thoughts even about the gods.[14]

For his part, Epictetus did not miss the distance between the steadfast purity of Apollo's mission to humankind and the wavering responses of His parish. In a passage from his recorded oral teaching, Epictetus depicts Apollo at Delphi nearly in tragic guise, as One who persists. His initial point of reference is the familiar legend of Oedipus, who unknowingly murdered his father Laius. Laius had received a warning from the oracle, but:

Although No One Pays Attention

> Did Laius obey Apollo? Did he not go away and get drunk and say good-by to the oracle? What then? Did that keep Apollo from telling him the truth? Apollo knew perfectly well that Laius would not obey, and yet He spoke. But why did He speak? And why is He Apollo? And why does He give out oracles? And why has He placed Himself in this position, to be a prophet and a fountain of truth, and for the inhabitants of the civilized world to come to Him? And why are the words "Know Thyself" carved on the front of His temple, although no one pays attention to them? Did Socrates succeed in prevailing upon all his visitors to keep watch over their own characters? No, not one in a thousand. Nevertheless, once he had been assigned this post, as he himself says, by the ordinance of the Deity, he never abandoned it.[15]

Who would not like to have known this Epictetus? Here he is in the second century of our era, taking up ancient materials and discovering entirely fresh inspiration in them. Apollo becomes for him the very model of Stoic insistence on respecting the truth despite the difficulties or disappointments this may occasion.

In His civilizing mission, Apollo at Delphi is not only a patron and inspirer of the arts—one of His names was "Leader of the Muses"—but also a source of swift insight into justice: the range is from sensuous beauty to the harsh arrow of judgment. In an early hymn, Apollo's words at birth assert His dedication to these unlike values and to His oracular mission:

> Thy lyre and the curved bow shall ever be dear to me, and I will declare to men the unfailing will of Zeus.[16]

Elsewhere in the early hymns, Apollo is described as a musician of literally divine powers and a youth of extraordinary beauty. But his eternal youth and his command of the arts did not blunt the hard ambiguity with which on occasion he confronted those who questioned Him. Like so many tales of Delphi, the following episode is no doubt legendary, but it captures in few words the Delphic conviction that we human beings would know more of the future, were we willing at key moments to rise to an objective view of our own affairs.

Wreathed Is the Bull

> Philip of Macedon, warrior father of Alexander the Great, came to Delphi seeking Apollo's blessing on his imminent campaign to liberate

> the Greek cities of Asia Minor from the Persian yoke—and thereby advance his imperial ambitions. The Pythia's words to him were chillingly brief:
>
> *Wreathed is the bull. All is done.*
> *There is also one to strike it down.*
>
> Philip could not help but find this response ambiguous. On the other hand, he took it in a sense favorable to himself. He reasoned that the oracle foresaw the slaughter of the Persians like a sacrificial victim.
>
> It was not to be so. The day dawned when Philip, garlanded for a festival, was stabbed to death by his enemies. He was like a bull at the altar.[17]

"I will remember and not forget Apollo the Far-Shooter,"[18] sings the ancient, anonymous psalmist—impressive words, drawing a mysteriously satisfying distinction between remembering and not forgetting. Through these words can be detected again the *felt* reality of Apollo, in relation to Whom men and women ages ago experienced an authentic link with the divine.

Yet that reality and the human experience of it remain elusive. Some quality of direct address continues to escape us. In searching through the composite memory of Delphi in ancient sources, I instinctively sought a remedy for this distancing, and perhaps discovered it in the legend of Jason and the Argonauts. You probably remember that the Argonauts set out to sea under Jason's leadership to find and return with the magical Golden Fleece. Intended as a voyage to their deaths, this all but impossible task was assigned to Jason by his uncle, who had usurped his father on the throne of Iolkos. The uncle hoped to dispose of the nephew without openly refusing him the throne he had come to reclaim. In the version by Apollonius of Rhodes, the legend has only one passing reference to Delphi: Jason sought and received the blessing of the oracle before setting out. The oracle added to its blessing the gift of a pair of sacred symbols—small tripods—which, wherever Jason set them on the ground, would magically call forth peace.

But there is something more in the legend, a strangely touching detail hinting again at the feeling that linked the precarious lives of men and women with the steady wisdom and unsentimental compassion of ancient oracles. Jason's longship, the *Argo*, possessed a voice. Designed and built with divine Athena's help, *Argo* had a unique keel carved in oak taken from a tree sacred to Zeus at the oracle of Dodona, where He "gave signs" through the rustling of leaves. Toward the beginning of Apollonius' retelling, this timber in the depths of the ship cries out for Jason to leave harbor and get underway. Later *Argo* is blown off course by a dangerous storm sent by Zeus,

> and suddenly there called to them in the midst of their course, speaking with a human voice, the beam of the hollow ship, which Athena had set in the center of the stem, made of Dodonian oak. And deadly fear seized them as they heard a voice that told them of the grievous wrath of Zeus. *Argo* cried through the darkness.[19]

The passage locates the voice of the oracle where it belongs: at the center, hidden yet vigilant. For those in ancient times who approached Apollo as One willing to be questioned and to share the problems of life, His words settled somewhere at the center of their persons, often enough forgotten or neglected until the moment arrived when the inquirer suddenly recognized their truth. The configuration of the good ship *Argo* with its special keel resembles other, more familiar configurations in the history of religious imagery, for example, Muhammad's teaching that Allah is "closer to us than the vein in our neck" and Jesus' teaching that "the Kingdom of Heaven is within you." Challenging men to gentleness, the Delphic oracle operated ultimately not from outside but within, where its words either settled firmly or—to the inquirer's sorrow—found nowhere to rest.

> He grants to men and women
> Healing from grievous sicknesses;
> His is the harp. He gives to whom he will
> The Muse, and brings into the heart
> Law, that thinks not of battle:
> In the Cave of Prophecy he is to be found.[20]

WHY DOES HE GIVE OUT ORACLES?

This strident but lively question was voiced a few pages earlier by Epictetus and implicitly answered with the thought that Apollo's wisdom mission to humanity is unconditional. We may listen, we may not; notwithstanding, He remains at His post. The question can be answered in another way by considering the ancients' view of how Delphi became an oracular center. They told several different origin tales ranging from folk story to high myth. Diodorus Siculus, author of a world history in the first century C.E., offers a folk version that provides glimpses of the legendary predecessors of the Pythia at work:

Origins I: The Folktale

> Long ago, it is said, goats discovered the oracle. That is why the Delphians today still chiefly sacrifice goats when they question it. The discovery occurred in the following way. There was a hole in the ground where the adyton of the sanctuary [*the innermost shrine where the Pythia spoke*] is found today. Goats were grazing in the vicinity, for Delphi at that time was not yet inhabited. Whenever an animal approached the hole and leaned over it, it began to leap about in a strange way and to emit strange bleats. The goatherd, puzzled by this, went up to the hole, peered into it, and experienced the same symptoms as the goats; he behaved as though possessed; the man predicted the future. When the people of the region heard of the effects that the hole produced on whoever came near, they flocked there and, intrigued by the phenomenon, all wished to experience it. Whoever approached the hole fell into a trance. That is why the oracle was revered and considered to be the Earth's prophetic sanctuary. For a time, moreover, those who wished to consult it were content to approach the hole and deliver oracles to one another. Since many people in a state of possession leapt into the hole and vanished, the inhabitants of the area, in order to cope with the danger, chose a single woman to serve as prophetess for all, and subsequently the consultation was carried on through her. They fabricated an object upon which she could sit in complete safety while entering into a trance and delivering oracles to anyone who might consult her. This object had three supports, which is why it was called a tripod.[21]

This charming tale, with its cast of Shakespearean rustics reveling in a supernatural force, is incorporated in a stately—although rather sulkily narrated—version of Delphic origins preserved by Pausanias.[22] More interesting for our purpose is a much earlier account found among the Homeric Hymns, works of the eighth through sixth centuries B.C.E. The *Hymn to Pythian Apollo* conveys Apollo's advent at Delphi in terms with which the ancients were thoroughly familiar: the statement of divine purpose, the long search, the meeting with a deceptive nymph, the recognition of Delphi's rightness, the battle for possession, the establishment of a priestly tradition. For readers today the hymn moves at what may seem an annoyingly deliberate pace with frequent repetition and florid forms of naming. Yet it would be a mistake to ignore it. Myths of origin encode and preserve the values that make things what they are.

Origins II: The Great Myth

Shall I sing how you went about the Earth seeking a place of oracle for men, O far-shooting Apollo? To Pieria first you went down from Olympus and passed by sandy Lektos and Enienae and through the land of. . . . [*A travelogue ensues, reflecting the ancient love of the land and its place names. In time, Apollo* . . .] went toward Telphusa, and there the pleasant place seemed right for a temple and grove. You came near and spoke to the nymph of that place: "Telphusa, here I have in mind to make a glorious temple, an oracle for men, and here they will always bring perfect sacrifices, both those who live in rich Peloponnesos and those of Europe and all the wave-washed isles, coming to seek oracles. And I will deliver to them all counsel that cannot fail, giving answer in my rich temple."

So said Phoebus Apollo, and laid out the foundations wide and long. But when Telphusa saw this, she grew angry and spoke as follows: "Lord Phoebus, worker from afar, I will speak a word of counsel; I ask you to take it to heart. The trampling of swift horses and the sound of mules watering at my sacred springs will irk you, and men will prefer to gaze at the well-made chariots and stamping horses than at your great temple and its treasures. But if you will be moved by me—for you, lord, are mightier than I—your strength is great: build at Krisa below the forests of Parnassos. There no bright chariot will resound, there will be no noise of swift horses near your altar. The glorious tribes of men will bring gifts to you, and you will receive their rich sacrifices with delight." So said Telphusa—so that she alone, and not the Far-Shooter, should dwell at that lovely place. And she persuaded him.

You went on, far-shooting Apollo, to Krisa beneath snowy Parnassos. A cliff overhangs it, and a rugged glade runs below. There Lord Phoebus Apollo, resolving to make his temple, said: "In this place I have in mind to build a glorious temple to be an oracle for men, and here they will always bring perfect sacrifices, both those who dwell in rich Peloponnesos and the men of Europe and from all the wave-washed isles, coming to question me. And I will deliver to them all counsel that cannot fail, answering them in my rich temple."

When he had said this, Phoebus Apollo laid out the foundations wide and long, and upon these Trophonios and Agamedes, dear to the deathless gods, laid a footing of stone. And the countless tribes of men raised a temple of wrought stone. We must sing of it forever.

> But nearby was a sweet spring, and there with his strong bow the lord killed a bloated she-dragon, a fierce monster who did great harm to men and to their thin-shanked sheep. Whoever met the dragon doom swept away until Lord Apollo, who delivers death from the distance, shot a mighty arrow into her. Then she, torn with bitter pangs, lay drawing great gasps and rolling about. An awful noise welled up as she writhed on the forest floor. So she left her life, breathing it out in blood. And Phoebus Apollo boasted over her:
>
> "Now rot here upon the soil that feeds man. You shall live no more to plague men who eat the fruit of the all-nourishing Earth, and who will bring here perfect sacrifices. Here shall Earth and the shining sun make you rot."
>
> Darkness covered her eyes. And the holy strength of the sun made her rot away.[23]

As the Great Myth continues, Apollo abruptly realized that Telphusa had fooled him, and He returned to her dwelling place to settle His score with her. Not one to take half-measures, He irreversibly changed her lovely waterway by releasing an avalanche down the slopes that sheltered it, and He erected an altar to His own manifestation there as Telphusian Apollo. So much for trifling with a god. At that point he turned to the larger issue of what men should be his ministers in rocky Pytho. While considering this, He became aware of a swift ship upon the wine-like sea in which were many men, Cretans, sailing on a business venture to Pylos. Phoebus Apollo met them: in the open sea He sprang onto their ship in the form of a great dolphin. For a long moment, He lay quietly on the deck. The crew tried to throw Him back into the sea, but He made the ship shake and its timbers quiver.

> They huddled together silent and terrified, and though they did nothing to change the set of their sails, a rushing south wind hurried the swift ship forward. [*There ensues a maritime travelogue as Apollo magically propels the vessel past familiar coastal landmarks.*] Lord Apollo led them on until they reached far-seen Krisa, land of vines, and there the sea-coursing ship grounded on the sands.
>
> Then, like a star at noonday, Lord Apollo leaped from the ship: flashes of fire flew thick from him and their brightness reached heaven. Entering his shrine, he made a flame spring up so brightly that its radiance filled all Krisa far below at the water's edge, and the wives and daughters of the city cried out, for he cast great fear upon them all. From his shrine he sprang forth again, swift as a thought, to speed again to the ship, now taking the form of a man, brisk and sturdy, in

the prime of his youth, with hair cascading over his broad shoulders. And he spoke winged words to the Cretans, [*asking who they were and whether they needed food and rest,*] until he had put courage in their hearts, in answer to which the master of the Cretans briefly recounted their adventure and concluded: "One of the deathless gods has brought us here against our will."

Then far-working Apollo said: "Strangers who once dwelt at wooded Knossos but now shall return no more each to his beloved city and fair house and dear wife: here shall you keep my rich temple that is honored by many men. I am the son of Zeus, Apollo is my name. I brought you over the wide gulf of the sea, meaning you no harm. For here you shall keep my temple, and you shall be honored for all time."

Under the circumstances, this seemed a reasonable offer to the Cretan mariners. After prayers and preparations and the good meal that Apollo recommended to his new staff, they set off for the temple. Apollo played heartening melodies on the lyre as they made their way up the steep slope from Krisa to the high shelf of land where the temple stood. As they marched, the mariners chanted a hymn.

Arriving at the temple, they lost heart again when they saw the rocky, unforgiving soil of Delphi. Turning to Apollo, they asked him how they could grow enough food in such a place and pasture large enough herds to satisfy their needs. He answered:

"I will tell you a word, and you must set it in your hearts. Though each of you with knife in hand should slaughter sheep continually, you would always have abundant food from the gifts brought here by the glorious tribes of men. But you must guard my temple and receive those who assemble here, and above all you must show mortal men my will and keep righteousness in your heart. If any of you disregards my warning, or if you give yourselves over to idle words or acts or outrages such as occur among ordinary people, then other men shall become your masters and with a strong hand shall subjugate you forever. All has been told: do you keep it in your hearts."[24]

APOLLO AND DIONYSUS AT DELPHI

Within the *adyton*, the innermost shrine of the temple where the Pythia spoke, lay the tomb of the god Dionysus. Of course, it was the tomb only of the body he abandoned after his passage on Earth in mythic time. To rephrase this mysterious religious design: in the temple of Apollo lay the tomb of Dionysus. This cannot help but strike fairly furiously on the ears of everyone who has been impressed, even at second hand or years ago, by the unforgettable pairing of Apollo and Dionysus in Nietzsche's first book, *The Birth of Tragedy*. As Nietzsche well knew, Plutarch had anticipated him in drawing the double portrait of Delphic Apollo as the god of reason and order and Dionysus as the god who inspires ecstasy and unconstraint. Apollo helped to create the bonds of civilization; Dionysus saw to it that they were periodically loosened. Plutarch could read these things out of the temple itself where he spent so much time. During the three coldest months of the year, Apollo was traditionally thought to leave the temple to return to his northern homeland, and Dionysus reigned supreme at Delphi. For this reason, Plutarch could write of "Dionysus, whose share in Delphi is no less than that of Apollo," and go on to compare their profoundly unlike natures:

> To [Dionysus] they sing the dithyrambic strains laden with emotion and with a transformation that includes a certain wandering and dispersion. But to Apollo they sing the paean, music regulated and chaste. Apollo the artists represent in paintings and sculpture as ever ageless and young, but Dionysus they depict in many guises and forms; and they attribute to Apollo in general a uniformity, orderliness, and unadulterated seriousness, but to Dionysus a certain variability combined with playfulness, wantonness, seriousness, and frenzy.[25]

To investigate in depth the coexistence at Delphi of Apollo and Dionysus would need another book. However, this much should be said: it is a sign of religious genius that two primary aspects of human nature, so often set against one another, were harmoniously joined at Delphi and recognized as equally rooted in the divine order of things. That Dionysus was contained within Apollo's house may imply for Delphic tradition a stronger allegiance to the disciplines of reason than to the inspirations of feeling or the sensuous life of the body. On the other hand Apollo, divine sponsor of the sometimes wracking experience of divination, was responsible for a quite special kind of inspiration, the *enthousiasmos* of the Pythia.

4

Unfolded Into Light Through a Woman: The Pythia

She *should* be like Diotima, the priestess from whom Socrates learned the philosophy of love.[1]

"Deeply versed in this and many other fields of knowledge," he recalled, she instructed him through informal dialogue—as he would instruct others in later years. He credited her with postponing a plague in Athens through the power of a sacrifice she conducted. Diotima will have something of importance to say to us.

She should be like Diotima, but there is no evidence of connection between Diotima and Delphi; no evidence, in fact, for Diotima herself apart from the luminous passage in Plato's *Symposium* where we meet her. However, among the contradictory signs in ancient literature some point to qualities in the Pythia much like those of Diotima: maturity, wisdom, clarity, firmness. Other signs point elsewhere, for example, toward a woman deranged in the oracular session although normal at other times, and, quite differently, toward a simple peasant woman not given to dramatics. We must search for the Pythia. We cannot help but find many, not just one.

This is to be expected. The Delphic institution endured for more than a thousand years of vast change in Greek culture, and the name "Pythia" designates an office held by many, many women over the centuries. They cannot all have been alike, although the office required certain capabilities of all who held it, and the long survival of the institution implies some continuity in its more intimate dimensions. We cannot reasonably expect the Pythia of Socrates' age to be identical with the Pythia of Plutarch's age, any more than we can expect a woman of the medieval era to resemble in education and aspiration a woman today. As a priest of Delphi and historian of its traditions, Plutarch was acutely, even uncomfortably aware of signs of change over the centuries in the person and style of the Pythia. As we shall see, he gave a good deal of thought to the question of change because he wished to grasp—and defend against skeptics—the essential reality of the oracle abiding beneath changing appearances.

"Unfolded into light through a woman"—the words are from Pythagoras, or at least Pythagorean tradition, in Thomas Taylor's sparkling early-nineteenth-century translation. Pythagoras offered the observation that women are "better adapted to piety" than men; hence the oracle at Delphi, and at Dodona as well, was "unfolded into light through a woman."[2] The gender configuration is sure to give us pause: as Plutarch reports, no women were permitted to consult the oracle in his era,[3] although the oracle was wholly dependent upon a woman. At the center of the Center of the Earth was a woman. There have been few higher pedestals, but pedestals are narrow places. She in turn offered the transparency through which the word of God could be conveyed. How total was that transparency, to what degree did her own person and the interventions of the Delphic corps of priests alter the form or substance of the divine message? These are questions which Plutarch was moved to raise, and later we shall join that conversation.

To speak of the Pythia takes us into the realm of "states," nonordinary states of mind or of the whole person. This is not a realm which many of us are well prepared to understand. Mainstream Western culture has no great interest in states apart from psychotherapeutic concerns, nor are states integral to our cultures of worship, dance, direction finding, or wisdom sharing. In every instance, states are matters of experience about which explanation, if not well conceived, can seem weak or talky. However, shared experience in recent decades has encouraged better understanding than in the past. The counterculture of the 1960s initiated numbers of people in the West into two very different experiences of altered states, and the consequences of these initiations continue to flow into mainstream culture. In homage both to Nietzsche and to Delphi, we could say that the first initiation was Dionysiac: the experience of drug-induced "trips" that "open the gates of perception," exposing the individual to vivid psychic scenarios and heightened perceptions of physical reality. The second was Apollonian: the disciplined experience of meditation typically guided by trained priests and adepts of Eastern religions, which tends in the opposite direction, toward the release of psychic scenarios and discovery of the undisturbed, fertile ground of consciousness. In addition, anthropological data once locked away in marvelous but little known publications of natural history museums and research institutes have become something more like public knowledge through televised films documenting non-Western cultural experiences such as trance dancing in Bali and shamanic trance in Siberian cultures. Further, in fundamentalist churches across the United States a form of wisdom sharing is widespread in which congregants speak as if under the inspiration of the Holy Spirit, typically supported by strong communal validation.

These points of reference in overlapping circles of our culture should persuade us not to regard the oracular experience at Delphi as necessarily an exercise in sanctioned deception or self-delusion. They encourage suspension of judgment and good listening to what the ancients had to say about matters they themselves found puzzling, for their own theories, like ours, reached only so far into the heart of the matter. Ancient efforts to understand the oracular process were not narrow, stingy little affairs; on the contrary, from the Center of the World at Delphi, the ancients drew increasingly vast circumferences within which they accumulated views of divinity, speculations on the mechanics of communication with the divine, a chapter or two of eschatology (the theory of "last things," of life after death), some abnormal psychology, and wondering guesses about chthonic influence—that is, the powers of the Earth itself at specially endowed places.

MADNESS AND ANGELS

Just as we come to the Delphic oracle as outsiders, so all of the ancients who tell us about it came to it long after its structure, personnel, customs, and rituals had been fixed. They, too, sought to understand "after the fact." Among thoughtful people in the era of Socrates and Plato, the understanding of the Pythia's activity—and of prophecy in general—was organized reasonably firmly around two concepts: madness and angels. However, by the time of Plutarch many centuries later the relative simplicity of the Socratic conception had yielded to a series of alternative explanations, none of which must have seemed independently strong enough to account for the oracle. Pursuing a satisfactory understanding, Plutarch pondered the capacity of the soul constrained within the mortal body to receive messages from souls that roam freely and know more when released from the body. He also explored, among other inviting concepts, the traditional Delphic notion of a "prophetic current" that issues from the earth, flows with streams, circulates in the air. His essentially conservative goal, like that of St. Thomas Aquinas in another era, was to "seek for explanation of such matters as seem to stand in the way, and not relinquish the reverent faith of our fathers."[4] That something exceptional occurred at Delphi was evident to him and others—although not to skeptics who argued that duplicity was the best name for it. The mechanism of the oracular event was a matter of conjecture even for Plutarch, an avuncular and communicative temple official who would have told us exactly, had he known exactly.

I ask scholars to forgive me for initially translating *daimon* as "angel"; only an approximation, with irrelevant Christian connotations, it nonetheless conveys the notion of an intermediary, messenger spirit moving freely and invisibly between Heaven and Earth on missions of goodness—and this is the meaning we need. No one will object to translating *manía* as madness; it is, visibly, the source word for modern English "mania."

The key early discussions of madness in the sense of divine possession occur in three Platonic dialogues. In the *Phaedrus*, Socrates speaks as follows:

> [Some argue that] madness is an evil, but in reality, the greatest blessings come by way of madness . . . that is heaven-sent. It was when they were mad that the prophetess at Delphi and the priestesses at Dodona achieved so much for which both states and individuals in Greece are thankful; when sane they did little or nothing. As for the Sibyl and others who by the power of inspired prophecy have so often foretold the future to so many, and guided them aright, I need not dwell on what is obvious to everyone. Yet it is in place to appeal to the fact that madness was accounted no shame nor disgrace by the men of old who gave things their names; otherwise they would not have connected that greatest of arts, whereby the future is discerned, with this very word "madness," and named it accordingly. No, it was because they held madness to be a valuable gift, when due to divine dispensation, that they named that art as they did, though the men of today, having no sense of values, have put in an extra letter, making it not *manic* but *mantic*. That is borne out by the name they gave to the art of those

> sane prophets who inquire into the future by means of birds and other signs, [which] by its components indicated that the prophet attained understanding and information by a purely human activity of thought belonging to his own intelligence.[5]

From this passage we can collect a notion of the Pythia as stepping voluntarily into an inner territory that struck others as unknown, charged, and irrational to the point of madness. For the ancients, the concept of inspiration was conveyed by the word *enthousiasmos*, instantly recognizable although only people with a special interest in language hear in our word "enthusiasm" the echo of the Greek roots *en theos*, meaning "with god." The temporary madness of the Pythia was caused by some internal wrenching associated with the advent of Apollo within her.

A related passage in another Platonic dialogue underscores these ideas and begins to describe mantic madness or enthusiasm as an agitated state: Socrates uses words such as distemper, dementia, and possession, none implying meditative calm. He is speaking generally, and his frame of reference includes both inspired dreams and the activities of male seers, but it all applies to the Pythia:

> God has given the art of divination not to the wisdom, but to the foolishness of man. No man, when in his wits, attains prophetic truth and inspiration, but when he receives the inspired word, either his intelligence is enthralled in sleep or he is demented by some distemper or possession. And he who would understand what he remembers to have been said, whether in a dream or when he was awake, by the prophetic and inspired nature, or would determine by reason the meaning of the apparitions which he has seen, and what indications they afford to this man or that, of past, present, or future good and evil, must first recover his wits. But, while he continues demented, he cannot judge of the visions which he sees or the words which he utters; the ancient saying is very true—that "only a man who has his wits can act or judge about himself and his own affairs." And for this reason it is customary to appoint interpreters to be judges of the true inspiration. Some persons call themselves prophets, being blind to the fact that they are only the expositors of the dark sayings and visions, and are not to be called prophets at all, but only interpreters of prophecy.[6]

His last comment seems to take a whack at the arrogance of priests, perhaps even some serving at Delphi, who attributed to themselves the light which, in reality, they borrowed. From this passage we can collect a clearer sense of the Socratic concept of *mantiké* as dementia of a special kind, in which the workmanlike rational mind cedes to an unfathomable, suprarational intelligence:[7] the window opens upward. Socrates holds that the assertions of this presumed higher intelligence need to be tested by rational means and may not always meet that test, but interpretive analysis is a later stage in the process. The configuration at Delphi—the Pythia at the center, a corps of priests working closely with her—finds some of its rationale in Socrates' comment on the necessity for partnership between inspired seer and analytical interpreter.

There is another source for Socratic or Platonic views of inspiration: their view, not through-and-through friendly, of poets and the art of poetic composition. Plato's *Ion,* a little masterpiece, narrates Socrates' search for the truth about poets' knowledge—and for a few shreds of modesty among the celebrated practitioners of that art.

> A poet is a light and winged thing, and holy, and never able to compose until he has become inspired, and is beside himself, and reason is no longer in him. So long as he has this in his possession, no man is able to make poetry or to chant in prophecy. . . . Not by art do they utter [their poems], but by power divine. . . . Herein lies the reason why the deity has bereft them of their senses, and uses them as ministers, along with soothsayers and godly seers; it is in order that we listeners may know that it is not they who utter these precious revelations while their mind is not within them, but that it is the god himself who speaks, and through them becomes articulate to us.[8]

Had the poet Ion, whom Socrates questioned to reach these views, shown a little more modesty in discussing his *oeuvre*, Socrates might never have been driven to such an extreme. He saw a fool before him, yet a fool who had written great poetry. What else could he conclude? The conclusions are relevant to our own inquiry. However, Socrates does not seem to have been fully satisfied with a concept that implies the total, albeit temporary replacement of human nature by divine presence. About this we can consult Diotima, as Socrates recalled her teachings, and it is also time to remember that Socrates described himself as "a seer, not a very good one, it's true, but, like a poor scholar, good enough for my own purposes."[9] His beautiful modesty underplays the fact that a *daimon* customarily alerted him when he was on the point of committing a serious error; this was, he said, his "familiar divine sign." He never speaks of it as displacing his ordinary person, never attributes shape to it; yet we can derive from what he says of his experience that inwardly and unexpectedly he encountered Another, a totally reliable intelligence from elsewhere. Such "others," according to Diotima, are *daimons*, translated as "spirits" in the following passage from her lessons to Socrates:

> Spirits, you know, are half-way between god and man. . . . They are the envoys and interpreters that ply between heaven and earth, flying upward with our worship and our prayers, and descending with the heavenly answers and commandments, and since they are between the two estates they weld both sides together and merge them into one great whole. They form the medium of the prophetic arts, of the priestly rites of sacrifice, initiation, and incantation, of divination and sorcery, for the divine will not mingle directly with the human, and it is only through the mediation of the spirit world that man can have any intercourse, whether waking or sleeping, with the gods. And the man who is versed in such matters is said to have spiritual powers, as opposed to the mechanical powers of the man who is expert in the more mundane arts.[10]

We have now encountered the key Socratic/Platonic texts, and the understanding they assemble feels, not surprisingly, like a satisfactory whole. However, it is a poetic and broadly stated whole, and for this reason it left room for later speculation, particularly on the nature of daimons and their intimate communication with us. Further, it disregards the important Delphic tradition concerning the mysterious power of place, and it gives scant attention to the question of the language and purity of Apollo's oracle: does the Pythia voice the very words of God, or does she offer an approximation, dimmed further if and when priests convert her spontaneous words into formal verse? These are central topics of Plutarch's so called Pythian Dialogues, set at Delphi, conducted by a group of inquiring visitors and local authorities.[11]

Concerning prophetic madness, Plutarch left a mixed message. On the one hand, certain passages in the Pythian Dialogues (as well as his *Dialogue on Love*) leave no doubt that the Pythia spoke from an altered state of high intensity. "The god of this place," he wrote,

> reveals his own thoughts through the medium of a mortal body and a soul that is unable to keep quiet or, as it yields to the One that moves it, to remain unmoved and tranquil, but, as though tossed amid billows and enmeshed in the stirrings and emotions within itself, it [becomes] more and more restless. As eddies exercise no sure control over bodies

> carried round in them—bodies are carried round and round by a compelling force while they naturally tend to sink—and there results a confused and erratic circular movement, so, in like manner, what is called *enthousiasmos* seems to be a combination of two impulses, the soul being simultaneously impelled through one of these by some external influence, and through the other by its own nature.[12]

Whirling and sinking, tossed and enmeshed—these are not words that imply calm and detached mediumship. In the *Dialogue on Love*, Plutarch prompts one of his speakers to observe that "the Pythia regains calm and tranquillity once she has left her tripod and its exhalations,"[13] and in the same work he permits himself to draw a simile, quite popular among writers who did not have his good Delphic credentials, between the agitation of love and that of the Pythia in trance. "Recite for us the ode," begs one of his characters, "in which fair Sappho describes how her voice is lost and her body burns; how she turns pale, reels, and grows giddy when her beloved appears." "In Heaven's name," comments one of those present when the ode has duly been recited, "is this not a plain case of divine possession? Is it not a supernatural agitation of the soul? Is the disturbance of the Pythia grasping her tripod so great?"[14] If reports of the Pythia's agitation in trance were sensationalist gossip, it seems unlikely that Plutarch, as a Delphic insider protective of the oracle, would perpetuate the misunderstanding even in the fictional context of his *Dialogue on Love.*

There is a fragment of evidence in his writings that recent scholarship has offered to support the notion that the Pythia's agitation was a literary convention, intriguing to ancient audiences but untrue. The evidence is a tale told by one of Plutarch's local authorities to illustrate the sensitivity of the Pythia and of seers generally. It turns on a preparatory ritual of the temple. To ascertain whether the god welcomed oracular activity on a particular day and for a particular client, the priests would douse a sacrificial goat with water. If the creature shivered fully upon sudden contact with the water, the day and the inquiry were deemed suitable. If it failed to shiver or scarcely shivered, the oracle was closed either for the day or for the luckless inquirer whom the god refused.

The Death of a Pythia

> When the prophetic faculty is in the proper state to attune itself to the spirit, *enthousiasmos* is bound to come. But when conditions are unfa-

> vorable, it is bound not to come—or when it does come to be misleading, abnormal, and confusing, as we know from the case of the priestess who died not so long ago.
>
> A deputation from abroad had arrived to consult the oracle. However, the sacrificial goat remained indifferent to the first libations. In their eagerness to please, the priests persevered beyond their normal practice, and only after the creature had nearly drowned did it at last give in.
>
> The Pythia was aware of this departure from norm. She went down into the place of prophecy unwillingly, half-heartedly. As soon as she spoke it was clear from the harshness of her voice that she was not responding properly: she was like a laboring ship, filled with a mighty and baleful spirit. Finally she became hysterical and with a frightful shriek rushed toward the exit and threw herself down. At this, not only the members of the deputation fled but also the officiating priest Nikander and the holy men who were present with him. After a little while they rallied their spirits, returned to the temple, and transported the Pythia to her quarters. But she lived on for only a few days.[15]

This sober tale sets a limit on the dementia or distemper, as Socrates put it, to which the Pythia, at least of Plutarch's era, was subject when she met her lord Apollo and gave Him voice. Taken together with the others, the passage invites us to imagine the Pythia performing her role even under normal circumstances in a state of high intensity. In the ancient construction of the meeting between divine and human in the person of the Pythia, there was an unmistakable element of *strain*: that Greatness and our finitude could not draw near one another without tension. The Pythia received on our behalf, but not without cost; in her person humanness stretched to its limit. We begin to understand existentially why the oracle typically functioned, apart from special requests from weighty inquirers,[16] just one day each month during the nine months of Apollo's "residence" at Delphi. At the center of the Center of the World, there was not only the murmur of conversation between God and man, there was an enactment of the *difficulty* of blending with that which is above us. The predictable rituals of Delphic inquiry encased this spiritual drama in a steady order. To the stately idea of the axis and center of the world where the divine and human touch on one another, we can add from Delphic sources: the communication of God and humankind is strained, intrinsically difficult, never to be assumed, yet possible and necessary.

If we adopt this general view of the Pythia's *enthousiasmos*, we are disagreeing both with much modern scholarship, which discredits ancient descriptions of her agitation, and with many later classical authors who played up the dramatics. The Pythia was a celebrity of the ancient world, Delphi a glamorous gathering place by virtue not only of its religious aura but also its athletic and musical competitions and handsome theater. To pass on and on a wild image of the Pythia made a satisfyingly provocative story—as, for example, in this passage from the poet Lucan, a Roman contemporary of Plutarch's:

> Apollo never more abundantly invaded his priestess's body. He expelled her former mind and bade her human nature yield her breast wholly to him. She rages madly about the cave . . . and Phoebus' bands and garlands loose in her bristling hair, her head shaking, she circles about the temple's empty spaces and scatters the tripods in her way; she seethes with great fury, bearing you, Phoebus, in her rage. . . . Then mad frenzy flows through her foaming lips, groans and loud panting cries; and then when the maiden was at last subdued a dismal wail and finally words sounded in the vast caves.[17]

This is soap opera, presumably originating not in direct experience of Delphi but in a literary tradition of exaggeration that had roots, improbably, in the quiet truths—I take them as such—we first encountered in Plato.

Certain fragments of ancient knowledge still need to be set in place, among them the tradition of the sibyl, "the first woman to sing oracles"[18] at Delphi and other temples across the ancient world. Every visitor to Delphi is shown, still today, a raw boulder a little below the temple, beside which a sibyl is said to have prophecied long before the advent of Apollo and His Pythia. This is a parallel tradition of seership—mythic, therefore unlike the flesh and blood reality of the Pythia, but powerfully present in the minds of those who cared about such things in ancient times. No statement of the sibyl's power surpasses that of Heraclitus, the darkly poetic philosopher:

> The sibyl with raving mouth utters solemn, unadorned, unlovely words, but she reaches out over a thousand years with her voice because of the god within her.[19]

Something of the flavor of this mythic sibyl attaches to the historical Pythia; they are not the same, not wholly different. Scholars have proposed that the literary tradition exemplified by Lucan's wild account of the Pythia has a root in lore of the raving sibyl. Be that as it may, to imagine Delphi well we need to join the ancients in seeing with the mind's eye the first sibyl, Herophile, traveling from temple to temple, periodically "standing by this rock to sing,"[20] and ending her days somewhere in the region of Troy beneath this uncompromising epitaph:

> I Sibylla, Phoebus' wise woman,
> am hidden under a stone monument:
> I was a speaking virgin but voiceless
> in this manacle by the strength of fate.
> I lie close to the Nymphs and to Hermes:
> I have not lost my sovereignty.[21]

I have not lost my sovereignty. . . . Some part of the message of this book is captured in these strong words, which claim sovereignty not for the sibyl's form—it disappeared in death—but for the hiddenness of worthwhile knowledge and for the seership which discloses it.

IF NOT APOLLO, THEN A *DAIMON* OR A BREEZE

Socrates' remarkable mentor, Diotima, taught that "spirits are half-way between god and man. . . . They are the envoys and interpreters that ply between heaven and earth. . . . The divine will not mingle directly with the human, and it is only through the mediation of the spirit world that man can have any intercourse, whether waking or sleeping, with the gods." This conception acquired the weight of authority over the centuries; that Apollo himself enters into the Pythia, as if He were a divine ventriloquist, seemed to Plutarch's people a notion "foolish and childish in the extreme"; to their minds, such an "entanglement" in human affairs is beneath His dignity.[22] On the other hand, they realize that discarding the notion of direct intervention—"let us not imagine that the god goes in and out and is present at these ceremonies and helps to conduct them"—must not lead them into "making the relations of gods and men remote and alien."[23] Here the theory of daimons makes its reappearance. But Plutarch's is a different era than Socrates'; if there are mysteries in Plutarch's era, there is also a science of mysteries. His discussants push toward a reasonably analytic understanding of the nature of daimons and their affinity with us.

They are "a force to draw together and to unite [the] common fellowship" between God and man.[24] Apollo is not a direct participant but, they agree, "let us commit [oracular] matters to those ministers of the gods to whom it is right to commit them, as to servants and clerks, and let us believe that daimons are guardians of sacred rites of the gods."[25] So far they recapitulate the Socratic view, adding only as the discussion continues that some daimons are beneficent, others troublemakers. The discussants push on, feeling the need to identify, in good Aristotelian fashion, the "causative means and power" by which the daimons play upon an oracle as if it were a musical instrument, which "lies idle and inarticulate"[26] in their absence.

The nature of daimons is by no means obvious to them. One Ammonios ventures the theory that they are human souls, released from the body and "making their rounds": "It is not at all unreasonable or even marvelous that souls meeting souls should create in them impressions of the future, exactly as we do not convey all our information to one another through the spoken word, but by writing also, or merely by a touch or glance."[27] Lamprias finds this notion generally acceptable, but he is uncomfortable with the idea that souls released from the body acquire powers they lacked while in the body. No, he argues, it must be a matter of degree:

> It is not likely that any power[s] accrue to souls when they have left the body, if they did not possess them before, only they possess them to a slight degree while joined with the body. Just as the sun does not become bright when it bursts through the clouds, but is bright always, and yet in a fog appears to us indistinct and dim, even so the soul does not acquire the prophetic power when it goes forth from the body as from a cloud; it possesses that power even now, but is blinded.[28]

As proof of his proposition, Lamprias refers to the prophetic power of dreams and to the sometimes acute insights of those near death who are freer to "range amid the irrational and imaginative realms of the future" and report back to us.

Nothing is permanently settled in Plutarch's Pythian Dialogues; the participants never offer a unanimous "hear! hear!" as if they were gathered around a table in an English tavern several thousand years later. The topic of conversation glides on to other aspects or issues—as in this instance, when Lamprias begins to question how the body participates in prophecy. Withdrawal from the present and receptivity to the future are "brought about by a disposition of the body as it is subject to a change we call *enthousiasmos*," he ventures, and immediately adds that the body's sensitivity to subtle environmental factors is such that it is capable of actually initiating the shift into *enthousiasmos*; it need not invariably follow, it can lead. "The earth sends forth streams of potencies, some of them producing derangements, diseases, or deaths; others helpful, benign, and beneficial, as is plain from the experience of persons who have come upon them. But the prophetic current (*hreuma*) and breath is most divine and holy, whether it issue by itself through the air or come in the company of running waters; for when it is instilled into the body, it creates in souls an unusual temperament, hard to describe with exactness."[29] It is worth noting again the modesty of Plutarch's inquirers: they are simply not sure of the truth but keenly interested in exploring toward something more like truth.

Lamprias speculates that the *hreuma* operates somewhat like wine, "by warmth and diffusion [opening] up certain passages through which impressions of the future are transmitted." On the other hand, he is not uncomfortable with the idea that it might operate in a completely different way—for example, through a "dryness engendered within the heart," which releases the spirit of prophecy, or by "a sort of chilling and compacting" as when hot steel is dipped in cold water to temper it. None of these arguments is taken to be binding, all are possible versions of a phenomenon that ultimately surpasses the range of reason.

Agreed among the gentlemen is the presence of power in the place itself, embodied in the folkloric legend of Delphic origins as the mind-altering vapor rising from the chasm into which goats and peasants fell. Lamprias draws an engaging analogy: as light is to the eye, so the *hreuma* is to the prophetic powers of the human soul. The eye can see, but it requires light to see. Similarly, the soul can foresee, but it requires a special influence—the subtle material of the *hreuma*—to do so.[30] Lamprias is willing to connect Earth's special exhalations with the sun, and therefore with Apollo, because the sun's heat and light nurture the generation of *hreuma* within the Earth. And because his line of thought is moving now in the midzone between spirit and matter, he finds it unsurprising that *hreuma* of the Earth and atmosphere comes and goes like any other physical substance. A plague in the city of Orchomenos, he relates, closed down an oracle of Teiresias, not, he implies, because the temple officials were stricken, but because the beneficent *hreuma* was choked off in the plague-ridden air.[31]

At this point Ammonios complains that the exchange has slipped down a perilously reductive path: first, in our arguments, we replaced the gods with daimons; next, we replaced daimons with earthly vapors; and now we are acting as if anyone at all, under the requisite influence, can see as much as a Pythia.[32] If this last point is really so, he asks, why do we make such a fuss at the temple? Why do we pour libations over sacrificial goats and eagerly observe whether they shiver in just the right way? Why do we "employ one woman alone for the purpose of oracles and give her trouble by watching her to keep her pure and chaste all her life?" There is a clear conflict between reasonable explanation and the liturgical life of the temple, which is based on faith that Apollo Himself or His daimon appointees, are constant invisible participants, and audible at the proper moment through the Pythia.

Plutarch gives the role of conciliator to Lamprias, who now tries to assemble the elements of their discussion into a continuous whole.[33] He affirms that searching for a reasoned understanding of the oracle and its mechanism is no error; however, the company does err by emphasizing one point at the expense of others that may be no less important. It seems to him that to describe the human soul as an instrument upon which subtle prophetic influences play, as if it were a musical instrument, is very fitting. And to adopt this image is not to overemphasize the material aspect of the oracular process because, after all, the Earth and Sun from which these influences proceed are, "by the usage of our fathers, gods for us." Second, he is content to leave the daimon concept intact; the daimons become, in his culminating version, vigilant tuners of the harmony of the oracular institution, "slackening here and tightening there on occasion, taking from it distracting and disturbing elements and incorporating those that are painless and harmless." As to periodic changes in the strength of the *hreuma* that inspires the Pythia, he considers it a matter of common knowledge that the open booth in which inquirers sit "is filled, not frequently or with any regularity, but as it may chance from time to time, with a delightful fragrance coming on a current of air which bears it towards the worshippers, as if its source were in the [*adyton*]." This seems to him empirical evidence that the special vapors influencing the Pythia vary in strength. At this point in his conciliatory summary, he focuses quite closely on the Pythia:

> You will at least all agree that the [Pythia] herself is subject to differing influences, and that she does not always keep one temperament, unchanged on every occasion. For many annoyances and disturbances of which she is conscious, and many more unperceived, lay hold on her body and filter into her soul; and [on occasion] it is better that she forego surrendering to the control of the god when she is not completely unhampered (as if she were a musical instrument, well strung and well tuned), but is in a state of emotion and instability.

> It is for these reasons that they guard the chastity of the priestess, and keep her life free from all association and contact with strangers, and take the omens before the oracle, thinking that it is clear to the god when she has the disposition suitable to submit to *enthousiasmos* without harm to herself.

At this point Lamprias has nearly concluded, but he wants to be certain that recognition of the special role and capabilities of the Pythia is preserved; he feels compelled to remember that even the holy institution of the oracle is subject to time's depradations. "The power of the spirit," he points out,

> does not affect all persons nor the same persons always in the same way. It only supplies an enkindling and an inception for those who are in a proper state to undergo the change. The power comes from the gods and the daimons, but, for all that, it is not unfailing nor imperishable nor ageless.

Lamprias concludes his speech, and Plutarch his dialogue, with the surprising suggestion that much of what they have said could after all be reconsidered and even sensibly contradicted. We, Plutarch's readers—hungry for certain, steady information about the Pythia and the oracular process—are left, like his inquirers, better informed but with questions still tugging at us.

THE SIMPLE, SHORT ANSWERS OF OUR TIME

Plutarch's interrogation of the Delphic oracle is not yet complete. There is another set of troubling questions having to do with the linguistics of the sacred. Why, in former times, did the Pythia deliver her messages by and large in formal verse of Homeric cast, whereas today she generally speaks in plain prose? To what extent is it true that we hear *her* voice, not His—not Lord Apollo's? What sort of blending occurs? How does God relate to His prophet? How does God relate to *us*? The seemingly academic question of poetry versus prose leads relentlessly toward the largest question: the authenticity of the oracle.

The exploration begins with what amounts to aesthetic reflections: a young visitor to Delphi, Diogenianos, expresses surprise that the Pythia's responses, even centuries ago, were often delivered in commonplace verse, at times marred by glaring technical errors.[34] How could this be, since Apollo is the Leader of the Muses, capable of effortlessly outsinging

Homer, should He choose to do so? The company briefly entertains the idea that our standards of excellence are flawed: God's "style" is necessarily superior to our own, however blind we have been to think otherwise. But this thought is quickly demolished by Sarapion, a skilled poet, who suggests a more convincing point of view, ethical rather than aesthetic. "We have a sickness of ear and eye," he says,

> we have grown accustomed through luxury and comfortable living to regard pleasure and beauty as identical. We shall soon be blaming the Pythia for not making sweeter sounds than the lyre-singer Glauke, and for not using perfume or putting on a purple dress before going down to the oracle, or burning incense of cassia or laudanum or frankincense instead of bay and barley meal. Pindar says that Kadmos heard the god performing "right music"—not sweet, or voluptuous, or effeminate in its tunes, but "right." The pure and passionless gives no place to pleasure.[35]

Since one could still take Sarapion to mean that Apollo Himself is the author of these unadorned but "right" words, another participant steps in to state what he believes to be a more reasonable view. "Whether these lines are inferior to Homer or not," Theon interjects,

> let us not believe that the god composed them, but only that he initiates the movement, and each of the prophetesses is moved according to her nature. If they had to write the oracles instead of speaking them, I don't imagine that we should complain that the handwriting was not as good as that of royal documents! Voice and sound, diction and metre, belong not to the god but to the woman. He merely puts the concepts into her mind, and gives her soul light to view the future; that is what *enthousiasmos* means.[36]

At a later stage of the conversation, Theon return to these thoughts to put a finer philosophical finish on them.[37] Our body uses instruments, he notes, and our soul uses the body as an instrument, and God uses our soul as his instrument. But the thought of God, impressed upon us as if a seal were pressed into wax or gold, cannot be entirely "pure and free of passion or error, as it was in its creator . . . for the thought is in itself not accessible to our view, and when it appears in another object or through another medium it is inevitably imbued with the nature of that medium." There will be distortions, as when an imperfect mirror distorts an image; there will be diminutions, as when the light of the sun, reflected in the moon, weakens. "Think of the god here," he suggests, "as using the Pythia in the world of hearing as the sun uses the moon in the world of sight. He reveals and discloses his thoughts, but only as they are mixed in a mortal body and a human soul."[38]

Theon's view seems to prevail with the company. Even in our own era, some thoughtful "mediums"—or "channels," as we now call them—do not claim to capture the entire message mysteriously initiated within them; they allow a margin for error. The analogy of sun and moon, of seal and wax, retains its pragmatic validity. Theon illustrates this in the terms of his own era and experience by recalling the simplicity of the current Pythia: she is not a person who could be expected to hold forth in heroic verse. But this "deficiency" does not undo the sacredness of the messages she delivers. "An uneducated person," he says,

> who has never heard verses cannot speak poetically. The present servant of the god is a case in point. She has lived from birth as lawful, honorable, and orderly a life as anyone in Delphi, but she was brought up in the house of poor peasants, and when she goes down into the [oracle] she takes with her no resources of art or experience or capacity. Like the bride whom Xenophon thinks ought to go to her husband's house "having seen very little and heard very little," she is, for all practical purposes, totally ignorant and inexperienced; she goes to the god truly with the soul of a virgin.

No, he says, we should not "expect the god to make the Pythia's language a sort of tragic performance, with flute accompaniment."[39]

Plutarch's discussants come finally to an ironic reflection: in ancient times, people often complained about the ambiguity and elusiveness of the Pythia's high-flown verse, and now they complain about the simplicity and absence of artistic ambiguity in her messages. Then, they feared that the interventions of professional poets, parasitically clustered about the temple, obscured what God wished to say; now, they resent that God does not speak with enough flourish. In Theon's opinion this is all foolishness. "The Pythia's language," he asserts, "has the characteristic that mathematicians attribute to a straight line: it is the shortest line between two points. Her words have no twists or curves, no double sense or ambiguity. They go straight to the truth."[40]

WE GIVE HER TROUBLE

The Pythia lived a militantly sheltered life: one of Plutarch's people acknowledged that "we give her trouble" by guarding her against stray contact with strangers and watching over her chastity and purity. Was she already a mature person, or young, when she began her dedicated life? Diodorus of Sicily tells the tale of a young Pythia long ago with whom an inquirer fell in love: the result was so devastating for the general order of the temple that the officials decided thereafter to employ only women of mature age.[41] How long this prohibition lasted is unclear; it may have been rescinded at some point.[42] If the Pythia was an older woman, there seems to have been no prohibition against marriage and children in earlier life, although when she entered the temple she became celibate. Be she old or young, the Pythia dressed as if she were a young woman.

References in the Greek playwrights point consistently toward a woman of years. She might well have been selected from among the older women who tended the eternal fire at the temple; in this service, she would be well known, and she in turn would know the temple.[43] Sheltered as she was and subject to a male hierarchy, the Pythia was nonetheless mistress of mysteries about which even Plutarch could only speculate uncertainly. This was her domain. In her *enthousiasmos* dwelt a divine secret. Male reasoning about her special role and abilities tended to focus on her transformation from the status of an incapable woman into a powerful seer. Aelius Aristides, a literary man and frequenter of medicine temples in the second century C.E., struck this note:

> What art do these priestesses know, who are incapable of preserving and memorizing anything? Medicine is feeble, I think, in contrast to the cures from Delphi, which privately and publicly have been revealed to men for all diseases and sufferings. What of your proud legislation? It will yield, I think, or rather it long ago yielded to the women on the tripod. Men go to Delphi and inquire about constitutions. Yet these women neither have any deeper knowledge than other men, nor, if they do know anything, do they speak from training and prescience. But as they are moved each time by the god, they dispatch men to the ends of the world. At the very moment when they are ignorant even of the affairs of their neighbors, suddenly they know those of all men.[44]

This image of a woman wise only by virtue of the wisdom passing through her from on high must be partial. Inscriptions at Delphi indicate that for some centuries the Pythia was selected from among priestly families, and we have warm evidence from Plutarch that at least in his era a priestess at Delphi could be his intellectual peer. He addressed several works to a cultivated woman named Klea, seemingly still young, clearly someone with whom he enjoyed conversation on philosophical and religious matters. Like the Pythia of her era, Klea was deeply involved in the religious life of Delphi, but in another branch: she was the leader of the female worshipers of Dionysus, joined annually by their Athenian counterparts for ritual activities at Delphi and in the uplands of Parnassos. Klea also had been "consecrated," as Plutarch writes, by her father and mother to the holy rites of Osiris, and "that Osiris is identical with Dionysus who could more fittingly know than yourself, Klea?" he asked.[45] It seems unlikely that the Pythia would be, always, an empty vessel for the god when women such as Klea were at Delphi.

In the dramas of Aeschylus and Euripides, the Pythia is hardly a peasant, as she was in Plutarch's time; on the contrary, she is well-spoken and thoughtful, respected not just for her role but for her person. It seems fair to assume that this characterization did not shock the playwrights' audiences; it must have made sense. In Aeschylus' *Eumenides*, set at Delphi and Athens, the Pythia opens the drama with an immensely dignified prayer of remembrance and self-dedication as she stands on the temple porch at daybreak.[46] In Euripides' *Ion*, which unfolds before the temple at Delphi, the Pythia is again represented not only as a person of sophistication and dignity, but also of a will independent from Apollo's, although freely coordinated with His wishes. Toward the end of the play, she reveals to young Ion parts of his background which she had long withheld from him. She concludes her revelations with these words:

> Now you have heard
> All that we have to say—Apollo, who had
> An interest in your fate, and I myself.[47]

The Pythia is again anything but the empty-headed creature imagined by Aelius Aristides. She is an independently thoughtful protagonist in a drama, who comes before us as an agent, not merely a passive vehicle of divine messages.

By an accident of survival, there exists a vase painting of the mid fifth century (*fig. 1*), depicting the legendary encounter of the Athenian leader Aigios with a priestess of the oracle, not a Pythia but her divine predecessor Themis, daughter of Earth. This is the only image we have of a Delphic priestess seated upon the tripod to convey the words of Apollo. In her right hand the strikingly graceful figure holds a branch of laurel, sacred to Pythian Apollo, while in her left she holds a shallow bowl of water, perhaps drawn from the sacred spring Kassotis, from which in ancient times she was said to drink as an additional means of entering the state of *enthousiasmos*.[48] Aigios stands before her in a state of

Figure 1. The Kodros Painter, *Aigios Consulting the Oracle*, Antikensammlung, Staatliche Museen zu Berlin—Preussischer Kulturbesitz, inv. no. 2538.

expectancy. The column tells us we are in the temple, and by its position between them notifies us that Themis and Aigios occupy different worlds. She is enfolded in the world of the gods, he stands outside of that world yet, as his posture makes clear, insistently awaits an answer from it. A single painted image of a moment from legend on a domestic bowl hardly constitutes definitive proof of anything at all, but it tells us at very least that the Delphic priestess received, in the popular imagery of her era, a dignified representation not out of keeping with the dramatic representations of Aeschylus and Euripides.

"How can we know the dancer from the dance?" asked W. B. Yeats in a justly famous poem. His question echoes against the Delphic tales. There is no relentless distinction in the tales themselves between God and His vehicle, between Apollo and the Pythia: His words are hers, hers His—at least in practice and as inquirers perceived them. The divine is Other than any of us, including the priestess who conveys its messages. The Pythia was not "deified." But in the sharp encounters between her and inquirers, there may not always have been time or taste for fine distinctions. Once, memorably, a pilgrim came to her with a question.

"*Too late you have come*," she replied.[49]

Who was speaking?

ENTER

> All these victors from the Tyrrhenian wars
> were on their way to Apollo at Delphi
> with the first plunder
> when they found their grave
> on one night, in one ship, in one deep sea.[50]

It remains difficult to sense that Delphi was real—that somewhere between the richly colored Delphi of the mind and the often more bleached scholarly reality, there was a circumstance that people lived fully and as a matter of course: it was what there was to do, and it was worth doing. Perhaps this short but vivid poem of Simonides, from the later sixth or early fifth century, can convey, as more words might not, the material reality of the Delphic oracle.

In the Hellenistic era, when the various kingdoms carved out of Alexander's empire competed bitterly with one another, King Eumenes of Pergamon made the journey to Delphi by sea. Disembarking at the port below, he and his men started the long climb to the holy city high on its shelf of land against Parnassos—and fell victim to a Macedonian ambush somewhere along the trail.[51]

Had these victors and this king arrived, they would have passed through a not especially difficult sequence of rituals and payments, and come under simple behavioral injunctions, in order to gain their turn as questioners at the oracle. "Enter, as the custom is," said Aeschylus' Pythia from the temple steps, as she invited the inquirers to draw lots to establish the sequence in which they would present themselves. Other sources tell us that the privilege of moving to the head of the queue was commonly issued to major donors, favored corporations, and prominent city-states.

In his *Ion*, Euripides offers a direct impression, as if taken from life, through the young temple servant for whom the play is named. Ion sweeps the temple steps at sunrise, delights in the freshness of the morning, and starchily reminds his fellow temple attendants of their duties. "The smoke of unwatered myrrh drifts/To the top of the temple," he observes.

> The Delphian priestess sits on the
> Sacred tripod chanting to the Greeks
> Echoes of Apollo's voice.
> You Delphians, attendants of Phoebus,
> Go down to Castalia's silvery eddies:
> When you have bathed in its holy dews
> Return to the temple.
> Let your mouths utter no words
> Of ill-omen, may your tongues
> Be gracious and gentle to those who
> Come to the oracle.[52]

Centuries later, Plutarch was no less concerned as a priest of Delphi with what must have been a practice of guarded speech: questioners approaching the temple were asked to think only kind and holy thoughts and to avoid harsh language.

Euripides gives Ion another admonition, in this instance to a group of young women untutored in the ways of the temple and fluttering like tourists:

> If you have offered sacrificial food
> In front of the temple, and you have a question
> For Apollo to answer, come to the altar steps.
> But do not pass into the inner shrine
> Unless you have slaughtered a sheep.[53]

From Ion's words, even without additional sources, we can assemble an impression of the early stages of the process. One was required to bathe in the waters of the stream, Kastalia, which flows to this day from a rocky gorge a few minutes' distance from the temple. A masonry bathing pool, still extant, now dry, captured the water and made it conveniently available. At that time one came under what appears to have been the inner requirement of the sacred place: to strive to calm one's thoughts and words.

Scholars have worked with remarkable ingenuity to assemble an understanding of the process of inquiry, which is not thoroughly described by any surviving text. Georges Roux has been particularly successful in reconstructing, often from minute fragments, a lively and persuasive account of the Delphic process.[54]

Inquiry was expensive, although on a sliding scale for cities, individuals, and favored cities or groups. Cities with no special claim on Delphian friendship paid the highest monetary fee. At the other extreme, the medical guild to which Hippocrates belonged paid no monetary fee at all. A person with meager resources was better off whispering his question into the ear of the oracular statue of a god or goddess in his hometown marketplace; it cost only a small coin or two, plus a little oil for the holy lamps.[55] At Delphi the first payment was made in silver coin. The second payment, purchase and sacrifice outside the temple of a sheep or other animal, was made by the Delphians themselves on behalf of all foreigners or could be required of individual or state questioners, depending on circumstance. The goat used to determine whether the day was suitable for oracular activity may have been "tested" in the *adyton*, the innermost shrine, and later sacrificed outside the temple.[56] Questioners were also expected to leave an offering of meat on a table within the temple itself, and they may have been required to make a sacrifice to Athena at her precinct not far from the Apollo temple. These multiple sacrifices represented further payments, fulfilling Apollo's ancient promise that the Delphians need not rely on their rocky soil as long as they served Him with integrity. There was a marvelous festival in Delphi to which people brought the very best leek they could, to compete with other leeks. We have to assume that these vegetables, like much else brought to honor the god, did not return unmolested to the farm; they must have been dropped into a big vichyssoise for everyone to enjoy.

With the smoke of so many sacrifices rising above their temple and so many payments in coin on deposit in their treasury during the centuries of abundance, the Delphians could not escape a reputation for greed. A proverb was candidly transmitted by Plutarch: "Who offers sacrifice at Delphi must buy meat for himself."[57] In other words, don't count on the usual division of the sacrifice that gave equitable shares to the god, the priests, the officiating cooks, and the donor. Callimachus, the normally elegant poet of the third century B.C.E., was unsparing of Delphi when he wrote of

> . . . wasps that at a Delphic feast
> Swarm around the butcher-priest.[58]

The sequence of ablution, fee, and sacrifice, and the need to order the day's inquiries and preserve peace in what must sometimes have been a crowd of questioners, imply a substantial administrative staff. The patchy record confirms this commonsense conclusion. At the summit of the hierarchy was the Pythia herself—three such women, according to Plutarch, in the era when the oracle was most in demand. In the period for which there is evidence, she was assisted by a pair of priests, and they in turn were assisted by perhaps two *prophetes*, whose responsibilities seem to have been like those of a deacon: one may have been responsible for the good order of events just outside the temple, while the other was charged with restating for questioners, orally or in writing, the Pythia's message. The prophets had their own corps of assistants known as the Consecrated, five in number. It may have been among their duties to judge whether the sacrificial animal provided the auspicious sign necessary to begin an oracular session. There were also cooks, as we have seen, regarded by Roux as professional sacrificers and preparers of the meat and offerings. The older women of Delphi looked after the eternal fire within the temple and perhaps assisted the Pythia. It is difficult to imagine the institution functioning properly without a professional archive unit, as well as secretaries, janitors, and gardeners. Young Ion seems to have been responsible for many of these caretaking roles. Finally, there existed associations functioning as what we would today call "Friends of the Delphic Oracle," one of which is known to have seen to the sacrifice made on behalf of all foreigners. Questioners met nearly all of these temple officials and servants as they made their way through the pattern and reached their moment of truth.

The temple precinct was not rigidly hushed with reverence during the daylong oracular session on the seventh of the month.[59] A pilgrim steadily mounting the Sacred Way to the temple would no doubt also be distracted by the overwhelming beauty, scale, and number of works of sculpture, painting, and architecture pressing in on him. Some of the war monuments would remind him of his city's defeats, others would remind him of victory. Statues honoring great athletes of his own time and centuries past would stir his blood. Were he to allow all of these memories and evocations and the presence of crowds to affect him, the questioner could easily arrive at the temple in fairly ragged condition. The contrast of animation, even provocation, outside the temple and increasing quiet as one approaches the inmost shrine can be confirmed from other sacred places, even those of our own time, particularly in Asia. Plutarch was aware of it. Speaking of a gathering of friends in the Lesche or clubhouse within the temple precinct, he writes that the "many activities and distractions occurring because it was a day for oracles and sacrifice made our conversation desultory and disconnected."[60]

Accompanied by an attendant, the questioner would pass through the columned western façade into an open anteroom in which the Delphic commandments were inscribed on the walls or on freestanding pillars. *Know thyself. Nothing too much*—fundamental reminders offered to the questioner approaching the Center of the World. Passing through another portal, the questioner entered the lofty *megaron*, the central chamber of the temple, divided by two ranks of columns, where another assault on his calm awaited him, for in its era it was anything but the whitely empty space suggested by our collective image of the Greek temple. Apollo's temple housed His wealth.

Sources help us imagine the accumulated centuries of pious offerings and sports souvenirs that confronted the questioner when he raised his eyes from the neutral paving stones: lyres, tripods, victors' chariots (some suspended as if in flight), the iron throne of the poet Pindar, weapons taken from the vanquished and given in gratitude, tables fashioned from precious metals, decorated vessels, bronze cauldrons, elegant wine-mixing bowls, jewelry, wall paintings, solemn statuary. And everywhere along the walls, it seems, colorful headbands and victory wreathes donated by athletes and artists who had triumphed in the Pythian Games. In Aeschylus' words, this was "the wreathe-hung recess."[61]

Somewhere in the *megaron*, perhaps in the south aisle, the questioner would see an altar to Poseidon, one of the early proprietors of the oracle before the advent of Apollo. One would undoubtedly pass by and acknowledge the eternal fire, sacred to Hestia, goddess of the hearth. It was from this universally respected hearth that the fires across Greece were renewed after the invading Persians had been repulsed.

At last one descended into the *adyton*, the innermost part of the temple where the Pythia awaited questioners. It seems safe to assume a short flight of stairs leading to what appears to have been a roofless rectangular space, perhaps with an earthen floor, certainly with its own special relics and furnishings. As every visitor to Delphi will testify, the *adyton* today, after painstaking archaeological effort, is surprisingly mute. The masonry fragments do not spontaneously rebuild in one's mind into what this place was; for that, one must turn to Roux and other scholars. Why such destruction? The *adyton* may, in fact, have been twice destroyed in the mid or late fourth century C.E., when "pagan" temples were being progressively closed—voluntarily destroyed by temple officials who did not wish this most sacred place to be vandalized, and further destroyed by Christians wishing to nullify the "pagan" past. To these causes of obliteration, one can add centuries of earthquakes and the borrowings of local masons for whom the precut stone of the temple represented a convenient quarry.

Yet literature, inscriptions, and a fine reading of the site have yielded reasonable understanding of what was there. Remember the folktale concerning peasants' discovery of an opening in the earth and their speaking in tongues of prophecy when they breathed the vapor rising from it. That opening in the earth may have still been present beneath the *adyton*; Roux suggests that the temple can be viewed as a reliquary sheltering it.

Descending directly into what may well have been a curtained booth furnished with a bench, the questioner might have caught a glimpse in passing of the Pythia seated upon the sacred tripod, poised to begin the session in the company of temple officials. He might also have glimpsed some of the sacred objects housed in the *adyton*: a laurel tree, the tomb of Dionysus, a golden Apollo, an ancient Apollo in cypress wood, and—beneath a small freestanding chapel—the *omphalos* covered by a woollen net and flanked by golden eagles, marking the very Center of the World. This was a place of intensity, the extreme point of our own world and the beginning of another. The deep strangeness of the Pythia's actions here must have maintained its power over the centuries. Questioners unaccustomed to it may not have been "quite themselves"—and this was probably all to the good.

What became of the opening in the earth that gave rise to all of this activity? Roux suggests that we take literally, for the most part, the description offered by the geographer Strabo:

> They say that the seat of the oracle is a cave hollowed out deep down in the earth, with a rather narrow mouth, from which arises a *pneuma* that inspires a divine frenzy; and that over the mouth is placed a high

> tripod, mounting which the Pythian priestess receives the *pneuma* and then utters oracles.[62]

Archaeologists would have liked very much at the turn of the century to confirm this description on site, but they found only slight indications that a small underground cell may have existed: there is no surviving cave, no "narrow mouth," no geological feature that suggests even the possibility of a natural fumerole. Beneath the *adyton* today lie about five meters of soil, impenetrable bedrock thereafter. Yet this temple was repeatedly called "the hollow of God" by the poets and playwrights. Roux joins what little evidence there is at Delphi and other oracular temples to the literary record to assert speculatively that there was indeed a hollow in the earth here, perhaps formed up by masons into a beehive-shaped space beneath the *adyton* and terminating in a narrow circular masonry "mouth" over which the Pythia's seat, the tripod, was firmly cemented in place. There cannot have been a visible *pneuma* released from the opening, although nothing excludes the use of incense to endow the metaphysical reality of the sacred vapor with a physical analogue.

It was in this setting that God spoke to man. His vehicle, the Pythia, had prepared herself no less carefully than the questioners joining her in the session. As for the Pythia in Aeschylus, prayer must have been a part of her preparation. We know that, like the temple officiants and questioners, she bathed privately in Kastalia's water: simple water, touching and cleansing the whole body, was a collective signal at Delphi to put ordinary concerns aside. We suspect that she drank water from a spring named Kassotis that may have been channeled into the *adyton* itself at some early point in the temple's history but in Plutarch's time welled up in a fountain outside. There is a suggestion, late and dubious, that she chewed laurel leaves to facilitate her transition into trance; however, a dedicated nineteenth-century scholar once chewed laurel leaves and, to his chagrin, remained just what he was. Plutarch tells us that she donned the simple garment of a girl, and she may well have worn a laurel wreath. Moving through the temple, she placed some barley grains and laurel leaves on the eternal hearth.

> *Hestia, you who tend the holy house of Lord Apollo, the*
> *Far-Shooter*
> *at goodly Pytho, with soft oil dripping ever from your*
> *locks. . . .* [63]

She may have briefly joined in song the company of women tending the fire. In any event, she must have entered the *adyton* fully prepared for trance—provided that the signs from the sacrificial animals were positive.

When she took her seat on the tripod, the evidence argues that she at once began to enter trance and recovered her normal state only when she dismounted from this strange enthronement. In no other setting was a tripod pressed into service as a seat. At normal size and in normal use, it was a cooking utensil, placed over the fire with a covered cauldron nested in a ring at the top. Owing to the prestige of the Delphic tripod, small tripods were awarded as trophies in athletic and artistic competitions, and tripods in precious metal served as votive offerings at holy places. As we shall hear, tripods make their way into tales of Delphi in interesting ways. The ancients described the unvarnished truth about a situation as "spoken from the tripod," as if the Pythia herself had proclaimed it.[64] But the use of the tripod as an oracular seat goes unexplained in surviving writings, and we are much on our own in attempting to understand it. M. L. West has suggested an intriguing parallel with Siberian shamanic practice: in one initiatory vision, the apprentice shaman experiences himself as butchered and boiled in a cauldron, after which his body is returned to him renewed and spiritually charged.[65]

Roux urges us to take the fifth-century cup painting (fig. 1) literally. If this is so, the Pythia seated upon the tripod would have held a branch of laurel in her right hand and a shallow bowl of holy water, perhaps from Kassotis, in her left. He believes that she would have shaken the laurel branch as she officiated. If she did indeed hold the bowl of water, its precariousness must have had a stabilizing influence. But nothing in ancient texts or images sheds indisputable light on how the session was conducted. Piecing together what little evidence exists with reasonable speculation, Roux believes that the questioner seated in the curtained booth could hear but not see the Pythia. His question may have been conveyed to her orally or in written form by the attending prophet—perhaps both means were used, depending on circumstance. It is certain that her answer was voiced aloud and later transcribed for the questioner, typically on a sealed tablet for a state embassy charged with delivering the answer unchanged to their city's leadership. The prophet—or a street poet—could work up the Pythia's words into better verse or convert prose into verse, but there appears to have been a "control" on these elaborations, owing to the strong likelihood that the questioner heard her initial statement. The Pythia could also be asked, according to well-established custom, to draw lots to decide an issue with the god's authority, to choose a white bean or a black one or a silver vessel or a gold one in order to yield simple yes/no decisions, or to select a name or names from a list of candidates. But the great majority of recorded episodes, be they historical or fictitious, depict her speaking for Apollo in response to specific questions.

Only on rare occasions did she answer a question before it had been asked, but Plutarch wants us to know that this, too, was within the realm of the possible when one entered the *adyton*:

> The Pythia is accustomed to deliver some oracles at once, even before the question is put, for the god whom she serves
> *understands the dumb and hears when no man speaks.*[66]

"MY LORD, YOU ARE INVINCIBLE!" TALES OF COERCION AND CORRUPTION

The Delphic oracle was a natural target. It offered more than one vulnerable point. Persons seeking their own advantage could attempt to corrupt the Pythia herself; failing that, priests might be persuaded to influence the divine message in less than divine ways; sacred ambassadors plying back and forth between the oracle and home cities with sealed tablets enclosing state messages also might be drawn into conspiracy. There was little to prevent turbulent questioners from attempting to coerce desired answers from the oracle if they were not freely offered. The ancients were aware of all this, and tales of Delphi reflect it. By the evidence of the tales, attempting to coerce the oracle was a far less grave offence than attempting to corrupt it. Coercion could have an open, bravura quality that the ancients, immersed in their warrior culture and fond of the sparks of competition, rather prized. The oracle could always resist and a lot of excitement would be generated. However, the tales are all but unforgiving of insidious attacks on the integrity of the oracle and broadcast a dire warning throughout the Greek world about the consequences.

The two most memorable tales of coercion concern heroes for whom many Greeks had warm feelings: the Herakles of myth, the Alexander of history.

Herakles and the Tripod

> Few of us now remember all that much of the saga of Herakles: we may recall that there were Twelve Labors—but just what were they? Something about a stable . . . Among the adventures in Herakles' strenuous

mortal life, for which he was eventually raised to the semidivine status of a hero, one episode brought him, temperamental but penitent, to the Delphic oracle.

Herakles won an archery contest for the hand of Iole, daughter of a man whom he thought to be his friend. But Iole's father, convinced that Herakles would not care properly for his daughter, deliberately insulted him and drove him away. Herakles vowed to avenge this wrong but went his way without violence. Meanwhile, a famed master thief named Autolykos, ancestor of Odysseus, happened by the palace one day and stole a precious herd of mares with their offspring. One of the sons of the palace, Iphitos, set off after the herd, and found that the trail led to Tiryns, home of Herakles. Alone among his family, Iphitos had sympathized with Herakles after the archery contest. Now he regretted that Herakles might have sought revenge through common thievery.

Iphitos soon encountered Herakles at the palace. Disguising his suspicion, he asked Herakles' advice about recovering the herd. But Herakles, sensing Iphitos' suspicion, was deeply offended. He too concealed his feelings.

After a hospitable meal together, Herakles invited Iphitos to join him on a high platform. They looked out over the landscape. "Tell me," asked Herakles, "do you see your herd anywhere?" "No," replied the other, "it is nowhere to be seen." Then Herakles unmasked: "But you thought me a thief, did you not? You thought me a petty thief!" With these words, he seized Iphitos, who was no match for him, and flung him from the platform to his death below.

Some say that Herakles grew ill with a vile disease as punishment from the gods for this senseless murder. Others say that he suffered nightmares, that his friends shunned him. Those with the authority to purify him of his crime refused to do so. Desperate for relief, he journeyed to the Delphic oracle. There too he was refused: Xenokleia, the Pythia of his era, remained silent despite his repeated requests for assignment of a penance that would free him from misery.

Herakles was not one to be refused. "Well, then," he roared, "if you will not answer me, I will take what I need to make an oracle of my own—perhaps there I will receive an answer!" Wherupon he unseated the Pythia, wrenched the sacred tripod from its place, and rushed out of the temple.

Instantly aware of the challenge to his oracle, Apollo descended from heaven to wrestle the tripod from Herakles' grip. The two struggled until father Zeus threw a thunderbolt between them and called a halt to the chaos. The tripod was restored, and the Pythia resumed her role. Now she consented to voice the penance that Herakles must pay: he would be sold into slavery and his purchase price would be given to the

> orphaned children of Iphitos. He would serve his owner faithfully for three years.[67]

The combat of Herakles and Apollo for the tripod was appealing to the ancients. Poets, sculptors, painters appreciated the theme and at Delphi itself there survives an eroded but impressive archaic relief carving of the incident. It pitted the most powerful human being against the gods, represented a disruption of the communication between the divine and ourselves. Although Herakles ultimately had to stand back, he did himself proud before the Father of the Gods intervened to set things right. Underlying resentment of the gods' power—and of our human weakness—may have prompted the ancients to cheer Herakles on, although everyone knew that he had to be defeated. Herakles' audacity was a common point of reference, nearly a proverb.

Why are epochal struggles associated with the oracle? "In the beginning" Apollo had to slay the Python to establish His oracle at Delphi. And now, well after the beginning, He must rescue the oracle from a hothead. In the language of story, aren't we being told that the place of truth, the center, must be earned away from denying forces and is never fully secure? Pindar once sang of the Apollo temple: "Its porch, in the pure light . . ."[68] The ancients knew that such beauty and the voice of truth at Delphi would endure only so long as they were willing to spring to their defense.

Such was the mythic antecedent: coercion on the scale of gods and heroes, resolved only by the Ultimate Power. The earthly counterpart involved Alexander the Great, mid-fourth-century conqueror of Greece and of all Asia to the northern reaches of India.

"You are invincible, my son!"

> A general assembly of the Greeks voted to make an expedition against Persia under the leadership of Alexander. Wishing to consult Apollo about the wisdom of the expedition, Alexander went to Delphi, where he arrived on one of the inauspicious days when it is unlawful to deliver oracles. He nonetheless summoned the Pythia to her place on the tripod. Invoking the iron-clad law governing oracular activity, she refused to obey. Upon hearing this, Alexander went to her private quarters, demanded her immediate services, seized her and began dragging her off to the temple. Overwhelmed by this rough treatment, she cried out: "You are invincible, my son!"
>
> At once Alexander released her. "I need no other prophecy," said he.[69]

Alexander was forgiven by chroniclers for this surreptitiously humorous incident; it was not counted among his sins. The tales, however, draw a line at attempts to corrupt the oracle; no one who did so evaded at least temporary retribution. There is again a mythic prototype.

Corrupting the Oracle: The Jealousy of Ino

> In legendary times, Athamas ruled a large kingdom. Blessed with a son and daughter by his wife Nephele, he took Ino as his second wife. She also gave him two children. As time went on, Ino became secretly embittered over the certainty that Nephele's son, Phrixos, would succeed to the kingship. Wishing at any cost for her own children to rise to power, she hatched a plot with the women who cared for the wheat. "Parch the wheat!" she commanded—and so they did. They secretly roasted it, killed its goodness. When winter passed and the fields were sown with the parched wheat, there were no crops. The people of the region wailed that a curse had descended on them.
>
> As Ino expected, Athamas sent a sacred embassy to the Delphic oracle to ask what must be done. She had already spread her web of deceit over the emissaries. "Lord Apollo," they lied upon their return, "has said that our king must sacrifice his son, Phrixos, to father Zeus if the fields are to be fruitful again."
>
> The people forced Athamas to obey what they took to be the divine will. Phrixos was brought to the altar. Now, Nephele had witnessed all of these hard events in silence, but the time had come for her to reveal resources of her own. She took her children aside and gave them a ram with a golden fleece which she had received from the god Hermes. When they leaped astride the ram, it flew them to safety across land and sea.[70]

Ino fared rather well in the aftermath of this plot. Although she was driven mad (as was her husband—some blamed him for complicity), she had divine connections and eventually became an obscure sea goddess known to Homer. But the plot was foiled; the gods protected their own.

The penalties are heavier in tales of historical figures who attacked the integrity of the oracle.

Corrupting the Oracle: The Plot of Kleomenes

> From earliest days there were two kings in Sparta, each descended from a different family. In the period around 500 B.C., one of those kings was Kleomenes, a cruel but efficient warrior. The other was Demaratos.

There was no love between them. When Kleomenes was away on campaign, Demaratos tried to undermine his reputation at home—and when Kleomenes returned, he conceived an elaborate plot to depose his rival. It is this plot that our tale preserves. Working secretly, Kleomenes bribed the Pythia to give the Spartans certain messages that suited his purpose. At the same time, he persuaded a member of Demaratos' family to make a claim to the throne based on words uttered by Demaratos' father at the time of the child's birth—to the effect that he was not absolutely sure of being Demaratos' father. Foolish words. Now they rose up against his son.

The Spartans were confused by the claims and counterclaims. Naturally, they turned to the Delphic oracle. But the Pythia said only what Kleomenes wished. On the basis of her words, Demaratos was soon deprived of his throne and Kleomenes' ally in the other royal line was installed as king.

Demaratos went into exile at the Persian court. Hoping to regain his throne, he assisted the Persian armies in their ultimately failed campaign against the Greeks. However, he managed to find pleasant employment as a ruler in Asia Minor and gave up his aspiration to one of the dual thrones of Sparta.

Things did not go so well for Kleomenes. He went mad, took up his sword, hacked at his own body, died raving and miserable. Everyone wronged by Kleomenes had his own explanation for this horrid end. The Delphians say it was a simple matter: he was punished for bribing the Pythia. "As for corrupting the oracle," adds Pausanias, "we know of absolutely no one but Kleomenes who ever dared to do it."[71]

Strange that Pausanias chose not to tell the tale of Lysander, another famous and ambitious Spartan who did, indeed, dare:

Apollo's Child: A Tale of Corruption

The Spartan general Lysander was a hero of the Peloponnesian War who longed to convert military into political leadership. There was one great obstacle: he was not a member of the royal houses of Sparta. In his own eyes, he was condemned merely to be respected, to be showered with honors, but never to be king. This did not please him.

He conceived the idea of a peaceful revolution, in effect a constitutional change. Why shouldn't the rule of Sparta be assigned on the basis of merit rather than lineage? Were the citizens incapable of recognizing those among them who best deserved to guide them? He decided to present arguments for this innovation in a carefully memo-

> rized speech. He also recognized that his proposal was so extreme that his countrymen would need to be moved to adopt it by supernatural influence, if such a thing could be arranged.
>
> The Spartans were deeply attached to the Delphic oracle and trusting of its counsel. In this Lysander found much to cheer him. Going in secret to Delphi, he attempted to persuade the Pythia that the good would be served, and she herself would earn a fine sum of money, if she were to give certain messages to the Spartans when the time was ripe. She resisted, refused. Not to be stopped, our villain went to the venerable oracle of Zeus at Dodona—only to find the officials there as resistant as the Pythia.
>
> There was one more possibility: the distant oracle of Ammon in the Libyan desert. There too he met with refusal. Outraged, the priests sent messengers to Sparta to denounce Lysander. He managed to escape the charges, and resumed his quest for power.
>
> At this point, a truly feverish imagination enters to direct the plot. Lysander heard of a woman in a distant city of Asia Minor who had recently given birth to a son. She claimed that the boy's father was none other than Lord Apollo. Some believed her, others did not, but wealthy citizens took an interest in the boy and saw to his education. These facts were enough to excite the interest of our villain. With the help of well-placed friends, he circulated the news that certain secret messages for the citizens of Sparta, deposited on ancient tablets at Delphi, could only be revealed to a child of Apollo. While this story was gaining credibility among the worthies of Sparta, Lysander once again went prospecting for allies at Delphi, and this time found priests who were willing to forge these ancient tablets and hand them over to the boy, were he to appear at Delphi with proper tokens of his birth. Lysander also made contact with this young son of Apollo and his family, and persuaded them to participate in the conspiracy. The boy Silenos was to go to Delphi, prove his legitimacy to the receptive priests, and obtain the unopened tablets. He was then to read them aloud—and, lo, they would support the notion that the Spartans must choose kings on the basis of merit.
>
> Luckily, all of this international activity ground to a halt. One of the conspirators could no longer stomach the affair. He withdrew. The plot was discovered only some years later, after Lysander had died on the field of battle—so say the sources. Perhaps it is truer to say that Lysander's friends protected him from himself.[72]

The Delphic oracle had once again proved to be vulnerable, but Lysander's stature as a military leader seems to have spared him becoming the target of divine vengeance. Not so for Heraklides, a fourth-century philosopher whose thirst for honor led to a hellish end.

Corrupting the Oracle: A Philosopher's Plot

> A terrible famine came over the region of Heraklea. The people sent to Delphi for help. There was among them a philosopher, Heraklides, who nursed bitter feelings because he had never received the honors due him, so he thought, for his intellectual accomplishments. In the misery of all, he perceived an opportunity for himself. Travelling with the sacred embassy to Delphi, he managed to bribe the Pythia and the oracle-bearers to announce the following: If Heraklides, son of Euthyphro, were crowned with a crown of gold in his lifetime and received the honors due a hero after his death, the fields would become fertile again.
>
> The people of Heraklea had no reason to doubt this seemingly holy counsel. The day of the ceremony dawned. Heraklides came to the theater where, witnessed by the entire community, the great honor was to be conferred. But as soon as the crown pressed down upon his head, he was seized with violent convulsions. A moment later he fell dead. The people were not slow to grasp that they had been deceived. Rising up, they stoned to death the envoys who had brought the false message, who had mocked their misery.
>
> At that moment, entering the *adyton* at Delphi to take her seat on the tripod, the false Pythia was bitten by a snake and instantly died.[73]

The tale is harsh, but tales such as this put the world on notice that the Delphic oracle was not to be tampered with.

5

Socrates Impoverished and Enriched

I think of Socrates as more than a man, much as the followers of Pythagoras used to say of their teacher that there are three kinds of biped—human beings, birds, "and a third thing."[1] One can almost see them pointing surreptitiously toward the odd person—the third thing—who had changed their lives. The key Delphic narratives are a long passage from Socrates' defense before the people of Athens and the saga of King Croesus. The first is modest in scope and intimate in means: Socrates scarcely leaves the city, and he does nothing more than engage his fellow men in conversation. The second is on quite another scale: it involves world-historical events, the movement of great armies across Asia, the rise and fall of empires. Yet as the saga of Croesus unfolds, it becomes little less personal and inward than Socrates' defense. We are offered not just the colorful portrait of a cunning ruler but the psychological drama of his conversion from arrogance to another condition of mind and heart, schooled by the oracle and by circumstance, humbled but now wise, genuinely touching in his humanity. This chapter and the next explore these great narratives.

Socrates was brought before an Athenian jury in the year 399 B.C.E. on charges of introducing strange gods into Athens and corrupting the youth of the city. The jury that he faced in his effort not so much to acquit himself as to unveil his motives in a valedictory statement, was nothing like the "twelve men strong and true" of American courtroom tradition; it was composed of some six hundred male citizens, among whom the strong and true were surely outnumbered. As reconstructed with magnificent art by Plato, the passage in Socrates' defense that bears on Delphi does not directly address the formal charges against him but speaks to what he took to be the real complaint: he had repeatedly humiliated the citizens of Athens through probing conversations that left them feeling foolish, uncertain, reduced.

Socrates' narrative begins with his report of a message from the Delphic oracle that he had not personally sought but could not ignore when it was made known to him. He speaks familiarly, as if without style, but one is riveted by his words at every new reading. Plato's version of Socrates' defense, like the Book of Ecclesiastes and a handful of other ancient texts, addresses us with a simple eloquence that makes so much else seem overdressed—as if literature is essentially conversation, and the best of it, no matter how grand in theme, retains that flavor.[2]

Socrates' Call

> I have gained [my] reputation, gentlemen, from nothing more or less than a kind of wisdom. What kind of wisdom do I mean? Human wisdom, I suppose. It seems that I really am wise in this limited sense. . . . Now, gentlemen, please do not interrupt me if I seem to make an extravagant claim, for what I am going to tell you is not my own opinion. I am going to refer you to an unimpeachable authority. I shall call as witness to my wisdom, such as it is, the god at Delphi.
>
> You know Chaerophon, of course. He was a friend of mine from boyhood. . . . And you know what he was like, how enthusiastic he was over anything that he had once undertaken. Well, one day he actually went to Delphi and asked this question of the god—as I said before, gentlemen, please do not interrupt—he asked whether there was anyone wiser than myself. The priestess replied that there was no one. As Chaerophon is dead, the evidence for my statement will be supplied by his brother, who is here in court.
>
> Please consider my object in telling you this. I want to explain to you how the attack upon my reputation first started. When I heard about the oracle's answer, I said to myself, What does the god mean? Why does he not use plain language? I am only too conscious that I have no claim to wisdom, great or small. So what can he mean by asserting that I am the wisest man in the world? He cannot be telling a lie, that would not be right for him.
>
> After puzzling about it for some time, I set myself at last with considerable reluctance to check the truth of it in the following way.

I went to interview a man with a high reputation for wisdom, because I felt that here if anywhere I should succeed in disproving the oracle and pointing out to my divine authority, You said that I was the wisest of men, but here is a man who is wiser than I am.

Well, I gave a thorough examination to this person—I need not mention his name, but it was one of our politicians that I was studying when I had this experience—and in conversation with him I formed the impression that although in many people's opinions, and especially in his own, he appeared to be wise, in fact he was not.

Then when I began to try to show him that he only thought he was wise and was not really so, my efforts were resented both by him and by many of the other people present. However, I reflected as I walked away, Well, I am certainly wiser than this man. It is only too likely that neither of us has any knowledge to boast of, but he thinks that he knows something which he does not know, whereas I am quite conscious of my ignorance. At any rate it seems that I am wiser than he is to this small extent, that I do not think that I know what I do not know.

After this I went on to interview a man with an even greater reputation for wisdom, and I formed the same impression again, and here too I incurred the resentment of the man himself and a number of others.

From that time on I interviewed one person after another. I realized with distress and alarm that I was making myself unpopular, but I felt compelled to put my religious duty first. Since I was trying to find out the meaning of the oracle, I was bound to interview everyone who had a reputation for knowledge. And . . . gentlemen, for I must be frank with you, my honest impression was this. It seemed to me, as I pursued my investigation at the god's command, that the people with the greatest reputations were almost entirely deficient, while others who were supposed to be their inferiors were much better qualified in practical intelligence.

I want you to think of my adventures as a sort of pilgrimage undertaken to establish the truth of the oracle once for all. After I had finished with the politicians I turned to the poets, dramatic, lyric, and all the rest, in the belief that here I should expose myself as a comparative ignoramus. I used to pick up what I thought were some of their most perfect works and question them closely about the meaning of what they had written, in the hope of incidentally enlarging my own knowledge. Well, gentlemen, I hesitate to tell you the truth, but it must be told. It is hardly an exaggeration to say that any of the bystanders could have explained those poems better than their actual authors. So I soon made up my mind about the poets too. I decided that it was not wisdom that enabled them to write their poetry, but a kind of instinct

> or inspiration, such as you find in seers and prophets who deliver all their sublime messages without knowing in the least what they mean. It seemed clear to me that the poets were in much the same case, and I also observed that the very fact that they were poets made them think that they had a perfect understanding of all other subjects, of which they were totally ignorant. So I left that line of inquiry too with the same sense of advantage that I had felt in the case of the politicians.
>
> Last of all I turned to the skilled craftsmen. I knew quite well that I had practically no technical qualifications myself, and I was sure that I should find them full of impressive knowledge. In this I was not disappointed. They understood things which I did not, and to that extent they were wiser than I was. But, gentlemen, these professional experts seemed to share the same failing which I had noticed in the poets. I mean that on the strength of their technical proficiency they claimed a perfect understanding of every other subject, however important, and I felt that this error more than outweighed their positive wisdom. So I made myself spokesman for the oracle, and asked myself whether I would rather be as I was—neither wise with their wisdom nor stupid with their stupidity—or possess both qualities as they did. I replied through myself to the oracle that it was best for me to be as I was.
>
> The effect of these investigations of mine, gentlemen, has been to arouse against me a great deal of hostility, and hostility of a particularly bitter and persistent kind, which has resulted in various malicious suggestions, including the description of me as a professor of wisdom. This is due to the fact that whenever I succeed in disproving another person's claim to wisdom in a given subject, the bystanders assume that I know everything about that subject myself. But the truth of the matter, gentlemen, is pretty certainly this, that real wisdom is the property of God, and this oracle is his way of telling us that human wisdom has little or no value. It seems to me that he is not referring literally to Socrates, but has merely taken my name as an example, as if he would say to us, The wisest of you men is he who has realized, like Socrates, that in respect of wisdom he is really worthless.
>
> That is why I still go about seeking and searching in obedience to the divine command, if I think that anyone is wise, whether citizen or stranger, and when I think that any person is not wise, I try to help the cause of God by proving that he is not. This occupation has kept me too busy to do much either in politics or in my own affairs. In fact, my service to the God has reduced me to extreme poverty.

Socrates speaks mightily for himself, with clarity that requires no interpretation, but it is often by searching back through a text—by holding it directly in our hands, so to speak, and sensing its texture—that we can best grasp its meaning. For example, we have discussed in general and observed in Delphic tales that the oracle's message is often enigmatic to the one for whom it is intended: he must interpret and act on the message in such a way that it yields fruit, not destruction. Even great Socrates was not exempt from confusion when confronted with "his" Delphic message. "When I heard about the oracle's answer, I said to myself, What does the god mean? Why does he not use plain language?" Of course, the language *was* plain, nothing like the high-flown verse we have already come across in some tales. But in another sense, Socrates was right: its meaning was anything but plain and necessarily prompted him "to puzzle about it for some time." He began, in other words, to work toward an interpretation.

His first act, as an interpreter of Delphi, was to eliminate the possibility that the oracle was lying. He did so really as a person of faith: "[The god] cannot be telling a lie, that would not be right for him." However, this assent put Socrates in a difficult position; he could not bring himself to agree with such an outrageous statement about his own person, nor could he deny that the oracle spoke the truth. To resolve the dilemma, one side or the other had to give a little. Thus, Socrates decided "with considerable reluctance" to put the truth of the oracle's words to the test. It is impossible to judge whether his reluctance had to do with the audacity of questioning the oracle's truthfulness or with an intimation of the difficulties that lay ahead.

Whichever it was—perhaps both—his initial program to check the truth of the oracle was not especially ambitious. He decided to interview just one well-chosen individual who was widely admired for wisdom. If Socrates could establish to his own satisfaction that this fellow was wiser than himself, he would in one stroke eliminate a literal interpretation of the oracle's words. Briefly drawing on his consummate sense of theater, Socrates mimed for his audience the exchange that he had hoped to have, virtually man to man, with the "divine authority" at Delphi in which he would "point out" with tutorial pleasure that the message praising his wisdom had, after all, been mistaken.

Socrates goes on, with a studied naiveté that surely fooled no one, to recount that the political leader he had chosen for this experiment unfortunately proved to be unwise, "although in many people's opinion, and especially his own, he appeared to be wise." And when Socrates tried to show him the true state of affairs, not only the man himself, but also witnesses to the conversation became upset. In another writing, Plato vividly describes the difficulty of conversations with Socrates, of which this was the first, in the years after he received the message from Delphi:

> Anyone who is close to Socrates and enters into conversation with him is liable to be drawn into an argument, and whatever subject he may start, he will be continually carried round and round by him, until at last he finds that he has to give an account both of his present and his past life, and when he is once entangled, Socrates will not let him go until he has completely and thoroughly sifted him.[3]

This sifting was, for many, a powerfully unpleasant experience. Continuing his recitation, Socrates described himself as walking away from this first effort to resolve his problem and muttering that he was clearly wiser than the politician "to this small extent, that I do not think that I know what I do not know." Here entered Western thought, with touching modesty, the concept of unknowing. Expressed earlier by Heraclitus in a grand abstraction,[4] it now comes fully to life in the person of a man no longer young, muttering.

He decided to try again, by interviewing "a man with an even greater reputation for wisdom," and of course he was again disappointed and aware of the irritation of bystanders witnessing the conversation. At this point Socrates' preliminary efforts to resolve his dilemma blossomed into a full-blown program constrained by no particular limits. "From that time on I interviewed one person after another." He realized "with distress and alarm" that he was seriously offending people, but he had come to regard these conversations as his "religious duty," a "sort of pilgrimage" undertaken "at the god's command." In truth, this bold idea of pilgrimage and religious duty represents his second interpretation of the Delphic message and a way of acting on it that someone else might not have conceived. Delphi had said nothing about launching a philosophical project among the people of Athens and with distinguished visitors whom he felt drawn to sift—or had all this, after all, been implied? "Since I was trying to find out the meaning of the oracle, I had to interview everyone who had a reputation for knowledge." There is no clearer example of *completing the oracle* through interpretations and actions that bear one's own stamp and serve to intensify either strengths or weaknesses.

Socrates started at the top of society, according to his account, and worked his way down the ladder of prestige by first interviewing political leaders, then poets and playwrights, then craftsmen. One result of structuring his investigation in this way was to turn his perception of the social hierarchy upside down: he found that "the people with the greatest reputations were almost entirely deficient, while others who were supposed to be their inferiors were much better qualified." But the situation among artists and craftsmen was scarcely more satisfactory. As evoked more fully in Plato's short dialogue, *Ion*, Socrates discovered that the poets and playwrights must have composed their works in a state of inspiration much like that of a prophet or seer because later, by the clear light of day, they proved unable to "explain" their works—and, like the politicians, were conceited enough to think that they understood "all other subjects," although Socrates satisfied himself that this was not in the least true. Among craftsmen, Socrates found impressive technical knowledge but, again, the erroneous assumption that their technical knowledge fitted them to "claim a perfect understanding of every other subject." "I felt that this error more than outweighed their positive wisdom."

Having illuminated all this for the jurors, Socrates then reported a daring moment of role play that conveys an almost inexpressible trait of his character: a blend of humor, detachment, and relaxed intimacy with the divine. "So I made myself spokesman for the oracle, and asked myself whether I would rather be as I was—neither wise with their wisdom nor stupid with their stupidity—or possess both qualities as they did. I replied through myself to the oracle that it was best for me to be as I was." One is tempted to imagine Socrates rushing from chair to chair to carry out this conversation between himself as a solemn temple official and himself as Socrates "replying through himself," in the manner of an oracle, in response to the oracle. What an irrepressible mind, playing deliciously when his life hung in the balance.

Socrates' account of his relation with Delphi and its impact on him was now moving toward conclusion—and, curiously enough, he concluded with two fresh interpretations of the Delphic message that had set so much in motion. "The truth of the matter, gentlemen, is pretty certainly this, that real wisdom is the property of God, and this oracle is his way of telling us that human wisdom has little or no value. It seems to me that he is not referring literally to Socrates, but has merely taken my name as an example, as if he would say to us, The wisest of you men is he who has realized, like Socrates, that in respect of wisdom he is really worthless." Through this interpretation, Socrates distanced the message and shucked the burden of taking it personally. Even the message itself he now described as addressed to "us" rather than to himself.

But that is not quite the end. He went on to describe himself as permanently engaged in trying "to help the cause of God" by unmasking those who pass for wise in society but are not so. "That is why I still go about seeking and searching in obedience to the divine command." The oracle's message may have been depersonalized, but Socrates' service to "the cause of God" called for total engagement of his person, even to the point of courting death at trial by apologizing for nothing and, instead, insisting on the piety and goodness of his enterprise. Helping the cause of God represented the final interpretation and action called forth by the Delphic message.

Readers who turn back to the full text of the defense and to the *Phaedo*, Plato's account of Socrates' last hours, may experience—for the first time or again—that a space hollows out inside where something of Socrates thereafter dwells; soon forgotten, of course, but not altogether. One becomes, if only a little and from time to time, "of the party of Socrates."

And Socrates was of the party of the Delphic oracle. One could argue that Socrates' professed dedication was merely or mainly a ruse to legitimize, in the eyes of his conventionally pious fellow citizens, the philosophical project in which he would in any event have engaged. But his tone throughout the defense argues otherwise. As in the Bible, the prophet is called into action, he does not call himself; and he is sustained in his prophetic task by a sense of intimacy with the divine source that first summoned him and now oversees his fulfillment of the task. That great irrational temple at Delphi was Socrates' partner in bringing to his community, and thereafter to all, a special sort of rationality—relentlessly logical, filled with goodness, ready at the appropriate moment to yield to prayer or silence.

6

Croesus, King of Lydia: A Tale from the Age of Belief

After Dunkirk there was a brief period when Hitler sought a negotiated end to hostilities with Britain. He had everything to gain by British withdrawal from the war. Churchill, of course, had other plans. Hitler attempted a last appeal in mid-1940 from the Reichstag podium. "Mr. Churchill," he said, "ought perhaps, for once, to believe me when I prophesy that a great empire will be destroyed—an empire that it was never my intention to destroy or even to harm."[1] With these words the history of our own era recapitulated with unerring irony the legendary history of Croesus, King of Lydia, whose tale as Herodotus shaped it was an enduring influence on Delphic tradition. His story has all of the "required" elements of a proper Delphic tale presented at length and with consummate narrative art, so much so that it would not be surprising if the ancient idea of a proper Delphic tale owed its definition to Herodotus. We shall find in the saga of Croesus the weighty question, the ambiguous divine reply, the moment of interpretation—hasty, insouciant in the case of Croesus—then recourse to action based on the oracle's message and the concluding epiphany in which the meaning of the oracle comes clear. To all of this, the Herodotan tale of Croesus adds a marvelously measured philosophical framework that opens with a grave conversation on the meaning of happiness and concludes with Apollo's defense of the oracle's role in the collapse of Croesus' empire.

First recited at gatherings across Greece in the later fifth century, Herodotus' history—of the Persian War and much else besides—was a permanent "best seller." An inexhaustible ocean of story, it begins with accounts of early encounters between Greeks and foreigners to the East, notably Croesus, "the first foreigner so far as we know to come into direct contact with the Greeks."[2] Reigning in the second quarter of the sixth century until about the year 550, Croesus is one of very few figures from ancient times whose memory vestigially survives in common expressions: "rich as Croesus," we say (as a boy I had no idea that the renown of this name rippled well past our neighborhood across ancient seas).

The Croesus of history and legend, rather than of childhood guesswork, was king over Lydia, in Asia Minor. He was fifth in a dynasty founded by Gyges, a common soldier of the king's bodyguard, who usurped the throne by murdering his king and taking the queen for his own wife. This *Hamlet*-like background is worth knowing because the Delphic oracle in Gyges' era confirmed his kingship but warned that his sins would be paid for in the fifth generation. By Croesus' time, the heavy destiny awaiting the line of Gyges appears to have been forgotten or discounted: it nowhere constrained Croesus' actions or entered his thoughts as Herodotus conveys them, yet the play of events in the saga of Croesus was secretly impelled by this debt. His tale follows, in de Sélincourt's fluent translation, to which have been added brief titles to clarify the flow of the narrative. Our own discussion can resume after listening to the tale.

The Interview with Solon

In the course of time Croesus subdued all the peoples west of the river Halys, except the Cilicians and the Lycians. The rest he kept in subjection—Lydians, Phrygians, Mysians, Mariandynians, Chalybians, Paphlagonians, Thracians (both Thynian and Bithynian), Carians, Ionians, Dorians, Aeolians, and Pamphylians. When all these nations had been added to the Lydian empire, and Sardis was at the height of her wealth and prosperity, all the great Greek teachers of that epoch, one after another, paid visits to the capital. Much the most distinguished of them was Solon the Athenian, the man who at the request of his countrymen had made a code of laws for Athens. Croesus entertained him hospitably in the palace, and three or four days after his arrival instructed some servants to take him on a tour of the royal treasuries and point out the richness and magnificence of everything.

When Solon had made as thorough an inspection as opportunity allowed, Croesus said: "Well, my Athenian friend, I have heard a great deal about your wisdom, and how widely you have travelled in the pursuit of knowledge. I cannot resist my desire to ask you a question: who is the happiest man you have ever seen?"

The point of the question was that Croesus supposed himself to be the happiest of men. Solon, however, refused to flatter, and answered in strict accordance with his view of the truth. "An Athenian," he said, "called Tellus."

Croesus was taken aback. "And what," he asked sharply, "is your reason for this choice?"

"There are two good reasons," said Solon, "first, his city was prosperous, and he had fine sons, and lived to see children born to each of them, and all these children surviving; and, secondly, after a life which by our standards was a good one, he had a glorious death. In a battle with the neighboring town of Eleusis, he fought for his countrymen, routed the enemy, and died like a soldier; and the Athenians paid him the high honor of a public funeral on the spot where he fell."

All these details about the happiness of Tellus, Solon doubtless intended as a moral lesson for the king; Croesus, however, thinking he would at least be awarded second prize, asked who was the next happiest person whom Solon had seen.

"Two young men of Argos," was the reply; "Cleobis and Biton. They had enough to live on comfortably; and their physical strength is proved not merely by their success in athletics, but much more by the following incident. The Argives were celebrating the festival of Hera, and it was most important that the mother of the two young men should drive to the temple in her ox-cart; but it so happened that the oxen were late in coming back from the fields. Her two sons therefore, as there was no time to lose, harnessed themselves to the cart and dragged it along, with their mother inside, for a distance of nearly six miles, until they reached the temple. After this exploit, which was witnessed by the assembled crowd, they had a most enviable death—a heaven-sent proof of how much better it is to be dead than alive. Men kept crowding round them and congratulating them on their strength, and women kept telling the mother how lucky she was to have such sons, when, in sheer pleasure at this public recognition of her sons' act, she prayed the goddess Hera, before whose shrine she stood, to grant Cleobis and Biton, who had brought her such honor, the greatest blessing that can fall to mortal man.

"After her prayer came the ceremonies of sacrificing and feasting; and the two lads, when all was over, fell asleep in the temple—and that was the end of them, for they never woke again.

"The Argives had statues made of them, which they sent to Delphi, as a mark of their particular respect."

Croesus was vexed with Solon for giving the second prize for happiness to the two young Argives, and snapped out: "That's all very well, my Athenian friend; but what of my own happiness? Is it so utterly contemptible that you won't even compare me with mere common folk like those you have mentioned?"

"My lord," replied Solon, "I know God is envious of human prosperity and likes to trouble us; and you question me about the lot of man. Listen then: as the years lengthen out, there is much both to see and to suffer which one would wish otherwise. Take seventy years as the span of a man's life: those seventy years contain 25,200 days, without counting intercalary months. Add a month every other year, to make the seasons come round with proper regularity, and you will have thirty-five additional months, which will make 1050 additional days. Thus the total of days for your seventy years is 26,250, and not a single one of them is like the next in what it brings. You can see from that, Croesus, what a chancy thing life is. You are very rich, and you rule a numerous people; but the question you asked me I will not answer, until I know that you have died happily. Mark this: until [a man] is dead, keep the word 'happy' in reserve. Till then, he is not happy, but only lucky. No man is ever self-sufficient—there is sure to be something missing. But whoever has the greatest number of good things and keeps them to the end, and dies a peaceful death, that man, my lord Croesus, deserves in my opinion to be called happy.

"Look to the end, no matter what it is you are considering. Often enough God gives a man a glimpse of happiness, and then utterly ruins him."

These sentiments were not of the sort to give Croesus any pleasure; he let Solon go with cold indifference, firmly convinced that he was a fool. For what could be more stupid than to keep telling him to look at the "end" of everything, without any regard to present prosperity?

The Trial of Oracles

Cyrus, son of Cambyses, had destroyed the empire of Astyages, and the power of Persia was steadily increasing. This gave Croesus food for thought, and he wondered if he might be able to check Persian expansion before it had gone too far. With this purpose in view he at once prepared to try his luck with the oracles, and sent to Delphi, to Abae in Phocis, to Dodona, to the oracles of Amphiarius and Trophonius, and to Branchidae in Milesia. These were the Greek ones which he consulted, but, not content with them, he sent also to the oracle of Ammon in Libya. His object was to test the knowledge of the oracles, so that if they should prove to be in possession of the truth he might send a second time and ask if he should undertake a campaign against Persia.

The Lydians whom Croesus sent to make the test were given the following orders: on the hundredth day, reckoning from the day on which they left Sardis, they were to consult the oracles, and inquire what Croesus, son of Alyattes and king of Lydia, was doing at that moment. The answer of each oracle was to be taken down in writing and brought back to Sardis. No one has recorded the answer of any of the oracles except that of Delphi; here, however, immediately the Lydians entered the shrine for their consultation, and almost before the question they had been told to ask was out of their mouths, the Priestess gave them, in hexameter verse, the following reply:

I count the grains of sand on the beach and measure the sea;
I understand the speech of the dumb and hear the
voiceless.
The smell has come to my sense of a hard-shelled tortoise
Boiling and bubbling with lamb's flesh in a brazen pot:
The cauldron underneath is of bronze, and of bronze
the lid.

The Lydians took down the Priestess' answer and returned with it to Sardis.

When the other messengers came back with the answers they had received, Croesus opened all the rolls and read what they contained. None had the least effect upon him except the one which contained the answer from Delphi. But no sooner had this one been read to him than he accepted it with profound reverence, declaring that the oracle at Delphi was the only genuine one in the world, because it had succeeded in finding out what he had been doing. And indeed it had; for after sending off the messengers, Croesus had thought of something which no one would be likely to guess, and with his own hands, keeping carefully to the prearranged date, had cut up a tortoise and a lamb and boiled them together in a bronze cauldron with a bronze lid.

So much for the answer from Delphi. As to the oracle of Amphiarius, there is no record of what answer the Lydians received when they had performed the customary rite in the temple; all I can say is that Croesus believed this oracle too to be in possession of the truth.

Croesus now attempted to win the favor of the Delphian Apollo by a magnificent sacrifice. Of every kind of appropriate animal he slaughtered three thousand; he burnt in a huge pile a number of precious objects—couches overlaid with gold or silver, golden cups, tunics, and other richly colored garments—in the hope of binding the god more closely to his interest; and he issued a command that every Lydian was also to offer a sacrifice according to his means. After this ceremony he melted down an enormous quantity of gold into one hundred seventeen ingots about eighteen inches long, nine inches wide, and three inches thick; four of the ingots were of refined gold weighing approximately a hundred and forty-two pounds each: the rest were alloyed and weighed about a hundred and fourteen pounds. He also caused the image of a lion to be made of refined gold, in weight some five hundred and seventy pounds. This statue, when the temple at Delphi was burnt down, fell from the gold bricks which formed its base and lies today in the Corinthian treasury. It lost about two hundred pounds weight in the fire, and now weighs only three hundred and seventy pounds.

This was by no means all that Croesus sent to Delphi; there were also two huge mixing bowls, one of gold which was placed on the right-hand side of the entrance to the temple, the other of silver, on the left. In addition Croesus sent four silver casks, which are in the Corinthian treasury, and two sprinklers for lustral water, one of gold, the other of silver. There were many other gifts of no great importance, including round silver basins; but I must not forget to mention a figure of a woman, in gold, four and a half feet high, said by the Delphians to represent the woman who baked Croesus' bread. Lastly, he sent his own wife's necklaces and girdles. These, then, were the offerings which Croesus sent to Delphi.

His Questions

The Lydians who were to bring the presents to the temples were instructed by Croesus to ask the oracles if he should undertake the campaign against Persia, and if he should strengthen his army by some alliance. On their arrival, therefore, they offered the gifts with proper ceremony and put their question in the following words: "Croesus, king of Lydia and other nations, in the belief that these are the only true oracles in the world, has given you gifts such as your power of divination deserves, and now asks you if he should march against Persia and if it would be wise to seek an alliance." To this question both oracles returned a similar answer; they foretold that if Croesus attacked the Persians, he would destroy a great empire, and they advised him to find out which of the Greek states was the most powerful, and to come to an understanding with it.

Croesus was overjoyed when he learnt the answer which the oracles had given, and was fully confident of destroying the power of Cyrus. To express his satisfaction he sent a further present to Delphi of two gold staters for every man, having first inquired how many men there were. The Delphians in return granted in perpetuity to Croesus and the people of Lydia the right of citizenship for any who wished, together with exemption from dues, front seats at state functions and priority in consulting the oracle.

When Croesus had given the Delphians their presents, he consulted the oracle a third time, for one true answer had made him greedy for more. On this occasion he asked if his reign would be a long one. The Priestess answered:

When comes the day that a mule shall sit on the Median
throne,
Then, tender-footed Lydian, by pebbly Hermus
Run and abide not, nor think it shame to be a coward.

This reply gave Croesus more pleasure than anything he had yet heard; for he did not suppose that a mule was likely to become king of the Medes, and that meant that he and his line would remain in power for ever. He then turned his attention to finding out which of the Greek states was most powerful, with a view to forming an alliance. Now when Croesus had gathered information, he sent messengers to Sparta with presents, to ask for an alliance. They were instructed what words to use, so on their arrival they said that they came from Croesus, king of Lydia and other nations, with the following message: "Men of Lacedaemon, I the King have been advised by the oracle to make the Greek my friend, and because I am told that you are the most eminent of the Greeks, I am obeying the oracle in asking for your help. I wish to be your friend and ally, without deceit or underhand dealing."

Now the Lacedaemonians, who had themselves heard about the oracle, were very glad that the Lydians had come with the proposal from Croesus, and made a pact of friendship and alliance with him.

The Unheeded Warning

Croesus, who had failed to grasp the true meaning of the oracle, now prepared an expedition against Cappadocia, sure of success in bringing down the power of Cyrus and the Persians. But while the preparations were going on, he received a piece of advice from a Lydian named Sandanis, who was already known for his good sense, and by the opinion he then expressed greatly increased his reputation amongst the Lydians. "My lord," he said, "you are preparing to fight against men who dress in leather—both breeches and everything else. So rough is their country that they eat as much as they have, never as much as they want. They drink no wine but only water. They have no good things at all, not even figs for dessert. Now if you conquer this people, what will you get from them, seeing they have nothing for you to take? And if they conquer you, think how many good things you will lose; for once they taste the luxuries of Lydia they will hold on to them so tightly that nothing will make them let go. I am thankful myself that the gods have never put it into the Persians' heads to attack the Lydians."

Croesus did not take this advice—though Sandanis was right: the Persians before their conquest of Lydia had no luxuries of any kind.

The Campaign

Croesus sent to ask the oracles about his invasion of Persia, and, when the ambiguous answer arrived, interpreted it in his own favor and began the war. When he reached the Halys, he crossed it by the existing bridges. When the army was over the river and had reached the district called Pteria in Cappadocia, Croesus encamped and began to devastate the crops on the Syrians' land. He captured the town, enslaved the inhabitants, and took all the neighboring settlements, driving the Syrians from house and home without any provocation.

Cyrus meanwhile had collected his army and was on his way to meet him, increasing his forces as he went by levying troops from all the peoples that lay on his route. He marched to Pteria, and when he had pitched camp in the face of Croesus' army, there was a trial of strength between them. After a sharp struggle in which both sides lost a number of men, night fell and the battle was broken off without a decision.

Croesus laid the blame for his lack of success upon the size of his army, which in that engagement was much smaller than the army of Cyrus; so when on the next day Cyrus did not advance to the attack, he marched back to Sardis with the intention of [gathering reinforcements]. Thus, with reinforcements added to his own army, he proposed to wait until winter was over, and attack the Persians in the following spring.

With this purpose in mind, Croesus, as soon as he reached home, sent instructions to his allies to send troops to Sardis after an interval of four months. All the mercenary troops he disbanded and sent home, for he did not for a moment suppose that Cyrus after so close a fight would venture to advance to Sardis.

When Croesus started for home after the battle in Pteria, Cyrus was sure that he would disband his army as soon as he arrived; so after consideration he found that the best course was to press on to Sardis with all speed before the Lydian forces had time to muster again. Indeed he was his own messenger—for so swift was his advance into Lydia that Croesus had no news that he was on the way. This unexpected turn of events put Croesus into a very difficult position; however, he made an attempt to resist the invader. (In those days, by the way, there were no stouter or more courageous fighters in Asia than the Lydians.)

The armies met on the level ground in front of Sardis; it is a broad expanse, bare of trees. When Cyrus saw the Lydians take up battle positions on this plain, his fear of their cavalry led him to adopt a suggestion of Harpagus, one of the Medes; this was to get together all the camels (they were used as pack animals to carry equipment and stores), unload them and mount men armed as cavalrymen on their backs. He then ordered them to advance as the first line of attack against the cavalry of Croesus, with the infantry following and his own cavalry bringing up the rear. Having made his dispositions, he reminded his troops of their duty to kill without mercy every Lydian they met—except Croesus. Croesus was on no account to be killed, even if he tried to resist capture.

The reason for confronting the Lydian cavalry with camels was the instinctive fear which they inspire in horses. No horse can endure the sight or smell of a camel. This is the fact upon which the strategem was based, and its object was to render useless Croesus' cavalry, the arm in which the Lydians expected to distinguish themselves. The ruse succeeded, for when the battle began, the horses turned tail the moment they smelt and saw the camels—and Croesus' chief ground of confidence was cut from under him. The Lydians, however, did not play the coward; seeing what had happened they leapt from the saddle and engaged the Persians on foot. Both sides suffered heavy losses, but finally the Lydians, forced to retire, were driven within the city walls, where they were besieged by the Persians. This was how Sardis was taken. On the fourteenth day of the siege Cyrus sent officers to ride round his lines and tell the troops that he promised a reward for the first man to scale the wall. Following this an attempt was made in force, but it failed and was abandoned; then a Mardian called Hyroeades resolved to try at a point in the fortifications which was unguarded, because a successful attack there had never been supposed possible. It was a section of the central stronghold so precipitous as to be almost inaccessible. On the previous day Hyroeades the Mardian had seen one of the Lydians fetch a helmet, which had rolled down this precipitous slope, and the sight of the man climbing down had set him thinking. He had then made the ascent himself, and other Persians followed; after them a great many more climbed up, and Sardis was taken and sacked.

What happened to Croesus remains to be told. I have mentioned his son who was dumb, but in other ways a fine enough young man. In the time of his prosperity—now gone—Croesus had done everything he could for the boy, not even omitting to ask advice from the Delphic oracle. The Priestess had replied:

O Lydian lord of many nations, foolish Croesus,
Wish not to hear the longed-for voice within your palace,
Even your son's voice: better for you it were otherwise;
For his first word will he speak on a day of sorrow.

When the city was stormed, a Persian soldier was about to cut Croesus down, not knowing who he was. Croesus saw him coming; but because in his misery he did not care if he lived or died, he made no effort to defend himself. But this dumb son, seeing the danger, was so terrified by the fearful thing that was about to happen that he broke into speech, and cried: "Do not kill Croesus, fellow!" Those were the first words he ever uttered—and he retained the power of speech for the rest of his life.

In this way Sardis was captured by the Persians and Croesus taken prisoner, after a reign of fourteen years and a siege of fourteen days. The oracle was fulfilled; Croesus had destroyed a mighty empire—his own.

O, Solon!

The Persians brought their prisoner into the presence of the king, and Cyrus chained Croesus and placed him with fourteen Lydian boys on a great pyre that he had built; perhaps he intended them as a choice offering to some god of his, or perhaps he had made a vow and wished to fulfill it; or it may be that he had heard that Croesus was a godfearing man, and set him on the pyre to see if any divine power would save him from being burnt alive. But whatever the reason, that was what he did; and Croesus, for all his misery, as he stood on the pyre, remembered how Solon had declared that no man could be called happy until he was dead. It was as true as if God had spoken it. Till then Croesus had not uttered a sound; but when he remembered, he sighed bitterly and three times, in anguish of spirit, pronounced Solon's name.

Cyrus heard the name and told his interpreters to ask who Solon was; but for a while Croesus refused to answer the question and kept silent; at last, however, he was forced to speak. "He was a man," he said, "who ought to have talked with every king in the world. I would give a fortune to have had it so." Not understanding what he meant, they renewed their questions and pressed him so urgently to explain, that he could no longer refuse. He then related how Solon the Athenian once came to Sardis, and made light of the splendor which he saw there, and how everything he said—though it applied to all men and especially to those who imagine themselves fortunate—had in his own case proved all too true.

While Croesus was speaking, the fire had been lit and was already burning round the edges. The interpreters told Cyrus what Croesus had said, and the story touched him. He himself was a mortal man, and was burning alive another who had once been as prosperous as he. The thought of that, and the fear of retribution, and the realization of the instability of human things, made him change his mind and give orders that the flames should at once be put out, and Croesus and the boys brought down from the pyre. But the fire had got a hold, and the attempt to extinguish it failed. The Lydians say that when Croesus understood that Cyrus had changed his mind, and saw everyone vainly trying to master the fire, he called loudly upon Apollo with tears to come and save him from his misery, if any of his gifts had been pleasant to him. It was a clear and windless day; but suddenly in answer to Croesus' prayer clouds gathered and a storm broke with such violent rain that the flames were put out.

This was proof enough for Cyrus that Croesus was a good man whom the gods loved; so he brought him down from the pyre and said, "Tell me, Croesus; who was it who persuaded you to march against my country and be my enemy rather than my friend?"

"My lord," Croesus replied, "the luck was yours when I did it, and the loss was mine. The god of the Greeks encouraged me to fight you: the blame is his. No one is fool enough to choose war instead of peace—in peace sons bury fathers, but in war fathers bury sons. It must have been heaven's will that this should happen."

The Conversation

Cyrus had his chains taken off and invited him to sit by his side. He made much of him and looked at him with a sort of wonder, as did everyone else who was near enough to see.

For a while Croesus was deep in his thoughts and did not speak. Then he turned, and seeing that the Persians were sacking the town, said: "Should I tell you, my lord, what I have in mind, or must I now keep silent?" Cyrus replied that he might say what he pleased without fear, so Croesus put another question: "What is it," he asked, "that all those men of yours are so intent upon doing?"

"They are plundering your city and carrying off your treasures."

"Not my city or my treasures," Croesus answered. "Nothing there any longer belongs to me. It is you they are robbing."

Cyrus thought this carefully over; then he sent away all the company that was present, and asked Croesus what advice he saw fit to give him in the matter.

"Since the gods have made me your slave," Croesus said, "I think it my duty, if I have advice worth giving you, not to withhold it. The Persians are proud—too proud; and they are poor. They are ransacking the town, and if you let them get possession of all that wealth you may be sure that whichever of them gets the most will rebel against you. So do what I advise—if you like the advice: put men from your guard on watch at every gate, and when anyone brings out anything of value, let the sentries take it and say that a tenth part of the spoil must be given to Zeus. If you do that, they will not hate you, as they certainly would if you confiscated the things by mere authority. They will admit that it is an act of justice, and be willing to give up what they have got."

Cyrus was delighted with this advice, which he thought was excellent. With many compliments to Croesus, he gave orders to the guard to put the proposal into practice. Then turning to Croesus, "I see," he said, "that though you are a king you are ready to do me good service in word and deed. I should like to make you some return: ask, therefore, for whatever you wish, and it shall immediately be yours."

The Last Gift to Delphi

"Master," Croesus answered, "you will please me best if you let me send these chains to the god of the Greeks, whom I most honored, and ask him if he is accustomed to cheat his benefactors." Cyrus asked the reasons for this request, whereupon Croesus repeated the whole story of what he had hoped to accomplish and of the answers of the oracles, and dwelt at length upon the rich gifts he had sent and on how his belief in the prophecies had emboldened him to invade Persia. Then he ended by repeating his request for permission to reproach Apollo for his deceit. Cyrus laughed, and told Croesus he should have what he wanted, and anything else he might ask for, no matter when. Croesus, therefore, sent to Delphi, and instructed his messengers to lay the chains on the threshold of the temple; then, pointing to the chains, they were to ask the god if, when such things were the fruits of war, he was not ashamed to have encouraged Croesus by his oracles to invade Persia in the confident hope of destroying the power of Cyrus. And they were also to ask if it was the habit of Greek gods to be ungrateful.

It is said that when the Lydian messengers reached Delphi and asked the questions they had been told to ask, the Priestess replied that not God himself could escape destiny. As for Croesus, he had expiated in the fifth generation the crime of his ancestor, who was a soldier in the bodyguard of the Heraclids, and, tempted by a woman's treachery, had murdered his master and stolen his office, to which he had no claim. The God of Prophecy was eager that the fall of Sardis might occur in the time of Croesus' sons rather than in his own, but he had been unable to divert the course of destiny. Nevertheless what little the Fates allowed, he had obtained for Croesus' advantage: he had postponed the capture of Sardis for three years, so Croesus must realize that he had enjoyed three years of freedom more than was appointed for him. Secondly, the god had saved him when he was on the pyre. As to the oracle, Croesus had no right to find fault with it: the god had declared that if he attacked the Persians he would bring down a mighty empire. After an answer like that, the wise thing would have been to send again to inquire which empire was meant, Cyrus' or his own. But as he misinterpreted what was said and made no second inquiry, he must admit the fault to have been his own. Moreover, the last time he consulted the oracle he failed also to understand what Apollo said about the mule. The mule was Cyrus, who was the child of parents of different races—a nobler mother and a baser father. His mother was a Mede and daughter of Astyages, king of Media; but his father was a Persian, subject to the Medes, and had married his queen to whom he was in every way inferior.

When the Lydians returned to Sardis with the Priestess' answer and reported it to Croesus, he admitted that the god was innocent and he had only himself to blame.

Such are the facts about the reign of Croesus.

Such they are. . . . In Herodotus' telling, the saga of Croesus is not only political and military history but philosophical and moral drama in which the Delphic oracle makes only partial revelations, providing opportunities for insight without imposing a specific outcome. Let us pick up this tapestry at its far edge, the interview between a great teacher and a great ruler, and follow along. In the later art and literature of many nations, the dialogue of king and sage became a conventional but reliably fascinating theme. North Indian miniatures, for example, eloquently capture the moment: the secular power—king or emperor—has ridden forth from a lavish palace to the isolated cave where the hermit saint lives the life of the spirit reduced to fewest necessities. The richly dressed king sits before the half-naked sage to ask questions or seek a blessing, while the holy man offers the warm detached gaze in which all traditions read wisdom. The tension implicit in this encounter of opposites is understated but palpable. Herodotus offers us such an image in the visit of wise

Solon to the court of Croesus—and by doing so places the events to come in a philosophical theater.

Herodotus is careful to imply (in a passage abridged from our version) that Solon has not called on Croesus as a professional teacher in order to earn fees and gifts. No, Solon was wandering for a period of ten years because the Athenians to whom he had given a code of law had solemnly sworn not to repeal any part of the code without his participation in the first ten years. His deliberate absence held them to the task of living by law. While Herodotus is willing to attribute to Solon delight in "the pleasure of foreign travel," he arrives at Sardis without ulterior motive.

As Croesus courts his good will, the king is deftly shown to be a man divided within himself. On the one hand he wishes to dazzle the philosopher with his hospitality and unparalleled wealth. On the other hand he is drawn to Solon and willing to risk with him a question that is universal and egotistical at one and the same time. In their rather one-sided exchange concerning—"Who is the happiest man?"—Croesus comes off as a man driven by self-interest yet intelligent, for whom conversation with one of the lights of the Greek world is not a small occasion.

Solon takes him through three successive answers to his question, the second of which, recalling Cleobis and Biton, lays down a line between the Delphi of Herodotus' era and Delphi today: the statues of the brothers now offer their commanding physical presence and imperishable smiles at the Delphi Museum. The third of Solon's answers, unveiling the arithmetic of man's days with the intent to overwhelm Croesus in the dimension he best understands—quantity—is one of the gems of Greek literature. The flow of numerical calculation and busy adjustment for calendrical shifts ends in utter simplicity: "Mark this: until [a man] is dead, keep the word 'happy' in reserve. Till then, he is not happy, but only lucky." Solon goes his way, leaving behind him a thoroughly offended royal presence.

The ensuing trial of the oracles is another gem. A contest between narrow self-interest and the boundless oracles, it again dramatizes the divided nature of Croesus: on the one hand he impudently challenges the holy institutions, on the other hand his challenge is intelligently constructed and he acknowledges "with profound reverence"—why not believe it sincere?—his discovery of the genuineness of Delphi. The first lines of Apollo's reply, already recalled in chapter 3, are well worth reexamining.

> *I count the grains of sand on the beach and measure the sea;*
> *I understand the speech of the dumb and hear the voiceless.*

Apollo's first statement of credentials bears on measuring along the horizontal axis of life: counting the sand, measuring the sea. It is a statement of His mastery of the physical world. The second statement asserts, differently, that the Lord's knowledge and contact penetrate to the depths—specifically to the depths of human nature even where most hidden. It is a statement of His intimacy with human beings and, beyond that, conveys His compassion for those, dumb and voiceless, who cannot enforce their rights or speak their minds. Croesus does well to be impressed not only with the accuracy of Apollo's insight but also with His power and love.

And so Croesus sets about seducing God by gift and sacrifice: holocausts of livestock and precious objects, gold ingots, a weighty golden lion, gold and silver mixing bowls, gold and silver casks and basins, his wife's jewelry. . . . Coercively, he advises the good citizens of Sardis to sacrifice as richly as they can. And then he celebrates what he takes to be a positive reply from the oracle by sending a pair of gold coins to each citizen of Delphi. He had become the most munificent patron that Delphi would ever see, and the Delphians, not insensitive to his gestures, gave him everything possible in return. They could not give him Apollo.

You may have been struck by his odd gift of a golden figure of the woman who baked his bread. The story behind this is not in Herodotus, but Plutarch centuries later set it down at a time when the statue had disappeared but its legend survived. When Croesus was a young man, his stepmother plotted with the palace baker to poison his bread, but the baker secretly told Croesus and served the bread to the stepmother's children: a folk motif seemingly out of Grimms' fairy tales, but no less at home in the world of early Greek history and legend.[3]

We should pause a moment over Croesus' reception of the two key oracular messages: that a mighty empire would fall, that he had nothing to fear from the Persians until a mule reigned. His arrogance prevented any genuine attempt to interpret them, to doubt if even a little, to consider alternatives. Willing to test the veracity of the oracles through an elaborate hundred-day experiment, careful enough to check the census of the Delphic population before showering it with wealth, he was unable to direct his cunning, let alone his intelligence, toward his own situation. He took his arrogance with him onto the field of battle. His brutal treatment of the Cappodocian townspeople elicits what amounts to an outraged editorial from Herodotus. His assumption that he could set the pace of war left him vulnerable to the attack that Cyrus intuitively chose to press at once against Sardis itself. However rigid the destiny imposed on Croesus by the sin of Gyges, the distant founder of his line, destiny found its means within Croesus' own nature.

"Cyrus chained Croesus and placed him on a great pyre." At this point, when Croesus is confronted with the fruits of his arrogance and of the forgotten sin of his line, the philosophical drama resumes. We have left the field of battle, we are again in the field of ideas and of qualities of being. Croesus sighs bitterly and calls out three times the name of Solon. Showing himself to be a man not unlike Croesus, Cyrus insists on an explanation from the condemned man concerning this Solon. Croesus replies briefly as the flames begin rising around him. Touched, Cyrus orders his men to dowse the fire, but it is already out of control. Only the intervention of Lord Apollo saves the day—Apollo, to whom Croesus appeals for rescue with tears of anguish, "if any of his gifts had been pleasant to him." The scene is perfectly spectacular. Our great king has been reduced to utter need, to hopeless tears, literally passed through the fire. When he is invited to sit beside Cyrus in the intimacy that has unexpectedly appeared between them, he is a new man. His very first words to Cyrus radiate compassion and thoughtfulness.

From within the ruler on the world stage, cunning, self-interested Croesus, has emerged another man whom Herodotus allowed us to glimpse but never fully encounter, perhaps for the best of reasons: he had never encountered himself. Stripped of worldly position but heir now to his inner wealth, Croesus is free to counsel Cyrus in the same grave and persuasive tone with which Solon once counseled him. There is no finer narrative in any literature of the capture of spirit by worldly power and the release of spirit when power departs.

Cyrus offers Croesus a boon, the gift of anything at all he pleases. Croesus asks only for the opportunity to confront the Delphic oracle. In explanation, Croesus tells his story to Cyrus; he himself is the first bard to convert this flow of events into a tale. Cyrus laughs, for he finds this obsession with the oracle to be retrospective and pointless. He acts on his view by offering Croesus yet another boon, presumably expecting him to request something more substantial. But Croesus is authorized to enact the little theater he has conceived: his men are to go to Delphi with his chains, to cast them on the temple threshhold, and to ask taunting questions. Is it the habit of the Greek gods to be ungrateful?

In response, Apollo explains all through the Pythia, and explains well. He places the blame for Croesus' loss of empire on his own shoulders and those of his treacherous ancestor. He reveals the occult dynamics of the event, whereby He postponed an implacable destiny but could not avert it. And He coolly critiques Croesus' approach to the oracle: Croesus had failed to ask the appropriate follow-up question and had failed to cudgel his brain about the metaphor of the mule, which Apollo apparently believed to be transparent enough and, on the whole, quite a good oracular message. Faced with Apollo's explanations and strong in his new perspective, Croesus can only admit that "the god was innocent and he had only himself to blame." With this recognition his story ends. We do not hear of him again.

The ancients never forgot this tale. Croesus, too, by his dialogue with Delphi was impoverished and enriched.

7

A Chapter of Tales

Pausanias repeats a parable heard on his travels that serves well to convene us for a chapter of tales. Not a Delphic tale, it has a comparable atmosphere and cast of characters—a blind seer, a confused populace, people selfish and giving.

God Anchored in the Middle

> Once the people of the coastal city of Erythrai looked out to sea and saw a strange raft drifting toward them. Upon it stood a tall and ancient statue of a god. Stranger still, no crew tended the raft. As if by a higher will, it advanced on its own. At the same moment, the townspeople on the nearby island of Chios also looked out to sea and sighted the mysterious raft. There was tremendous excitement in both towns. And then groans of dismay—for instead of easing onto shore the raft ran aground on a shoal midway between Erythrai and Chios.
>
> Both towns at once sent boats with strong men and tow ropes. As they approached, they recognized the image of Herakles, half-god, half-mortal, who by his exploits earned full membership among the gods. Each team of oarsmen lashed onto the raft, churned their oars. . . . To no avail: it was hard aground. Turning their energies on one another, the men of Erythrai and Chios threatened each other with dire fates. The holy image was theirs and theirs alone. Whose? The god paid no attention.
>
> Days of confused stalemate passed until one morning a blind fisherman of Erythrai reported a dream that had come to him in the

> night. "I dreamed," said Phormion, "that if our women cut off their hair and the men plait it into a long cable, we can draw the statue into port."
>
> The Erythraian women would have none of it—cut off their hair? But there were other women in the city, slaves and freedwomen of Thrace, valued for their labor and charm but little else. And these women said yes. "Yes, we shall cut off our hair to make the great cable, we shall help you." So they did, without a whimper. It wasn't long before the Erythraians towed the raft home.
>
> A shrine sacred to Herakles was built in the city to house the image. By public ordinance only the women of Thrace were allowed access to it. People still preserve the rope of hair. And they say that the fisherman's eyes were opened. For the rest of his life, he could see.[1]

This is a richly encoded tale, folklore of course, and fantasy of great appeal, but endowed with another dimension through its suggestions about relationship—between humanity and the divine, between men and women. The divine freely and inexplicably makes itself known, but it remains at a distance and does not enter our lives without persevering effort on our part and the sacrifice of things dear to us, however unimportant in reality, however easily replaced. In face of the sacrifice required, people caught up in the pleasant routines of life refuse to participate in the drama of earning intimacy with the divine, but others with fewer attachments step forward in their stead. The last shall be first.

There is more encoded in the tale. The solution to the riddle of the grounded god is reached not by logical means but by the magical "seeing" of a blind man, visited from above in a dream. The merely human solution—roping up, churning oars—was ineffectual. While the townspeople of Chios remained within the realm of the narrowly human, those of Erythrai, however reluctantly, were responsive to the inspired message reaching them through their impromptu seer. And then, something is encoded here about the relations between men and women. Ancient Greek men, thoroughly patriarchal, limited the scope of their wives' and daughters' lives, but the tale relates a challenge in symbolic form which could only be met by cooperation between the sexes and by stepping over social boundaries. The men were hopeless without the women, the women hopeless without the men, the center of society hopeless without those on the margin. The mysterious cultural act of bringing the god home from a wild place was a joint venture.

Intensity of religious and moral content beneath a folkloric surface, the central role of an inspired message, and a permeable border between things divine and human are outstanding features of this tale and of many Delphic tales that follow in this chapter. Because the border is permeable but real, communication by signs and the interpretation of signs are the rule: the oracle may "give signs," as Heraclitus tells us, or inquirers may call upon it to unveil the meaning of signs encountered in the course of life. This is the gist of the next tale, so brief that it is more like an image impressed on the mind than a story unfolding through time. It refers to an unnamed oracle, not necessarily Delphi. During the long sojourn of this tale in my research file, Herodotus' casual prose anecdote became verse.[2]

The Honey Head

General Onesilos besieged the Amathusians—
An event long since past
Among a vanished people.
Why remember?

Why not remember?
The Amathusians overcame his troops,
Captured him
Lopped off his head
Hung it from the gates
Bloody.

Over time
The head hollowed out
And bees settled inside.
They filled it with rich honeycombs
Overflowing.
They buzzed
Through the hot day.

The Amathusians could not ignore
The change
From blood to honey
From bitter to sweet
From decay to a sign.
They consulted an oracle.
"Retrieve the head.
Offer it the funeral
Owed the man.
Make annual sacrifices
To honor the hero Onesilos.
If you do these things,
Your lives will be better."

The image of the honey head, grotesque and holy, repellent and saturated with beauty, conveys the magical atmosphere of much Delphic storytelling. I am drawn to place this head over the gateway to the tales, implying as it does that events, even those that are harshest, are not unattended in our lives, and that utter transformation from death into life may await us. But because the honey head is a harsh image, why not place another nearby that is full of harmony? There was a sculpture at Delphi—and at Lokri, as well—to commemorate the following tale:

The Missing Note

The Halex River marking the boundary between Rhegion and Lokri passes through a deep ravine. An odd thing happens there: while the cicadas on the Lokrian bank sing, those on the other bank are silent. Local people think that the Rhegian side is so densely shaded that the cicadas are too wet with dew to sing, while those on the sunny side are dry and musical.

Eunomos of Lokri and Ariston of Rhegion—both acclaimed for their singing to the lyre—were once competing against each other at the Pythian games. Eunomos claimed, extravagantly, that contestants from Rhegion had no right to participate in the contest, since in their country even the cicadas were mute. Ariston was in fact the favorite and hoped for victory. In the event, Eunomos won and in the oddest way. During the contest one of his strings broke. It seemed that he would have to withdraw from competition. Then out of nowhere a cicada hopped onto his lyre. When Eunomos resumed his song, the creature faithfully supplied the missing note. How could he not have won?[3]

It is difficult to imagine a sweeter story. We naturally take it to be modest, unworthy of special notice in later times. But strangely enough this harmless tale became the object of a strident Christian revision by Clement of Alexandria, a third-century Father of the Eastern Church. In his obsessive critique, Clement puts his finger on some interesting features. He begins with a swipe at the Delphic legend of Pytho, the demonic serpent whom Apollo slew in combat, and goes on from there.

The Missing Note, Corrected Version

A solemn assembly in honor of a dead serpent gathered at Delphi, and Eunomos sang a funeral ode for the reptile. Whether his song was a hymn in praise of the snake or a lamentation over it I cannot say, but there was a competition, and Eunomos was playing the lyre in the heat

> of day at the time when cicadas, warmed by the sun, sing under the leaves along the hills. The cicadas were singing, you see, not to the dead serpent of Delphi but to All-Wise God—a spontaneous, natural song, better than Eunomos' song.
>
> A string broke in his hand. Then a cicada settled on the neck of the lyre and began to twitter as if upon a branch. At once the minstrel adapted his song to the cicada's song so that it *seemed* as if the cicada was supplying the missing note. It was not Eunomos who drew the cicada by his song, although this is suggested by the bronze figure at Delphi showing Eunomos with his lyre and the cicada perched on the instrument. No, the cicada flew of its own accord, and sang of its own accord, although the Greeks thought it was responding to the music.[4]

What seems most to bother Clement is the possibility that a pagan artist, Orpheus-like, deserved Nature's cooperation. While literally accepting the legend, he goes to great length to abolish the miraculous kinship between Eunomos and the cicada, and to drive home the point that even a cicada's dry song is more holy than a pagan hymn. In Clement's corrected version the pagan must cooperate with Nature, rather than the other way around. The cicada remains the hero of the tale, but it is now a pious Christian cicada.

Now we have begun to furnish a suitable gateway to tales of Delphi: above us, the honey head; to our right, a splendid bronze of Eunomos, his diminutive ally perched on the neck of his lyre. The view through the gateway? To a distant shoreline, where a boat labors into port with a raft in tow. Perhaps we'll come in time to a tale that asks to be placed on the left flank of the gateway, to complete this ensemble.

THE SEVEN SAGES AND OTHER FAVORITES

The Delphi of the mind—the Delphi of which people even in remote regions of the ancient world could hear and dream—was associated with a circle of semi-legendary founders known as the Seven Sages. They were founders not of the Delphic institution itself but of aspects of its style of communication and its wisdom that all people took to be quintessentially Delphic. Philosophers and enlightened rulers of the seventh and sixth centuries B.C.E., they were given by many authors as Bias of Priene, Chilon of Sparta, Kleobolos of Lindos, Periander of Corinth, Pittakos of Mitylene, Solon of Athens, and Thales of Miletus (Plato recorded Myson of Chenai as the seventh in place of Periander, according to Pausanias;[5]

we shall meet Myson). A number of utterly satisfying tales about them have survived.

The Revelation of the Seven Sages

After a long day at sea, some fishermen of the island of Cos returned with a plentiful catch, which strangers from nearby Miletus bought wholesale without examining each and every fish. As the fishermen transferred the catch to the strangers' cart, an object flashed by, more brilliant than the fishes' iridescent scales. There was a sudden hush. One of the fishermen reached into the mass of fish and groped for the mysterious object. He drew out a small tripod of pure gold. Now there was a legend that, on the voyage home from Troy, Helen had thrown overboard just such an object. This must be it, precious beyond all imagining!

A sharp dispute broke out between the fishermen and the strangers. Who owned the tripod? The fishermen maintained that they had sold fish, and fish only. The strangers contended that they had bought the entire day's catch—seaweed, fish, and all, and if the lot happened to include a golden tripod, so be it. The issue could not be resolved. Within days their cities had taken up the quarrel. It seemed as if war would break out when a few wiser heads in Cos and Miletus agreed to refer the dispute to the Delphic oracle.

A mixed and irritable embassy made the journey to Delphi. They put their question.

The tripod belongs neither to the party of Cos
Nor to the party of Miletus,
But to the wisest man of Greece.

The disputants calmed down. The oracle had posed an intriguing problem. Who, after all, was the wisest man of Greece? They gave it serious thought. In time they agreed that no one was wiser than Thales of Miletus, the first scientist, the great geometer and metaphysician. The delegation returned to Miletus and with due ceremony offered him the tripod. But Thales declared that Bias of Priene was a wiser man than he. "He is the man who must have the tripod!" The delegates had no choice but to obey good Thales.

Bias, in turn, sent it to another whom he regarded as much wiser than himself. And that man sent it to another. And so it went the round of seven great men, refused by each in turn and sent on to another . . . until at last it came to Thales for the second time.

These were the Seven Sages. They are said to have met together at Delphi, and again in Corinth. The passing round of the tripod, and their modesty and good will, contributed much to their fame.[6]

There could hardly be a vehicle more entertaining than this story to invite our acknowledgment that true leadership appears almost magically, of itself, rather than by manipulation, and, further, that true leadership does not exclude modesty. While the Seven Sages were said to be individually responsible in their time for complex intellectual and political achievements—the development of codes of law, the first steps toward empirical science—Plato makes clear that their *joint* wisdom was held to be of another order. The Seven Sages were "admirers and disciples of Spartan culture," he wrote, "and their wisdom may be recognized as belonging to the same category, consisting of pithy and memorable dicta. . . . Moreover they met together and dedicated the first fruits of their wisdom to Apollo in his temple at Delphi, inscribing those words which are on everyone's lips, 'Know thyself' and 'Nothing too much.' "[7]

And so the ancients (at least some—unanimity was rare) believed that the key Delphic commandments were given by this early board of overseers rather than by Apollo through His priestess. While "Know thyself" was universally considered the prime commandment, "Nothing too much" was often recalled in the same breath. The virtue of *sophrosyne*, moderation or evenness of mind, was central to the regulation of a fiercely competitive society in which individuals and city-states pitted themselves against one another for whatever prizes they currently coveted.

The Seven Sages were not remembered as icons of piety. On the contrary, they were tough-minded, resourceful, practical. A tale of Bias reflects something of this:

Bias to the Rescue

The story is told that Alyattes, father of Croesus, once besieged Bias's native city, Priene. There was hunger in the city. Events were taking a poor turn. Bias reflected. Some days later, he was to be seen moving past the city gates, driving a pair of fattened mules before him. Like a peasant innocently seeking forage for his beasts, he drove them into the enemy camp. When Alyattes saw the plump mules, he was stunned. If even this peasant's mules were so well fed, Priene must have all but limitless resources to withstand the siege! Taking the measure of his own difficulties in prolonging the siege, he decided to send a messenger to the city on a pretext—his real mission was to see how people were faring.

Bias was ready. He had the townspeople pile up heaps of sand with a layer of corn on top, and he made certain that the diplomatic talks took place within easy sight of them. The messenger left the city with the only message that made sense: Priene was in no difficulty whatever.

> Informed of the abundance behind the walls, Alyattes made peace with the people of Priene.[8]

The same practical wisdom is reflected in a tale of Myson. Not included by all ancient commentators as one of the Seven Sages, Myson recalls later traditions such as the Jewish legend of "the just man" who safeguards the world and the Shi'ite Muslim tradition of the "hidden imam," incomparably wise, living in obscurity. Here is the tale:

Who is Wiser?

> The Scythian prince Anacharsis gained a reputation for wisdom even among Greeks of the sixth century. Once he came to Delphi, where it occurred to him to ask the oracle who among the Greeks was wiser than he. The Pythia replied:
>
> *A man of Oeta, Myson, they say,*
> *Is more gifted with intelligence.*
>
> Myson was a peasant from the village of Chenai, who never strayed far from it. He enjoyed no renown whatever. Hearing of this answer, Solon of Athens was curious to meet this hidden sage. He made the overland trip to Chenai and found Myson beside his barn, fitting a handle to a plow. To put the man to test, Solon offered the thought, "This is not the season for the plow." "Not to use it," replied Myson, "but to get it ready."[9]

In another version, Anacharsis himself goes to meet and test Myson. He finds the hidden sage, again fitting a handle to a plow, and offers the same probing observation: "This is not the season for the plow." "No," replied the other, "but this is the season to repair it."[10] The tale can leave one feeling sadly reduced in stature. Myson's simple insistence on timing and preparation carries such weight.

The Seven Sages and Anacharsis were sixth-century figures. Deeper in the well of legend, perhaps the eighth century, the Delphic oracle had adopted another sage, Lycurgus of Sparta, as a favorite. More legendary than historical—yet, like Pythagoras, insistently present and convincing—Lycurgus was the founding lawgiver in Sparta during years when he served as regent to a young king. Lycurgus involved the Delphic oracle in his process of detailing the code of law and of infusing it with divine prestige so that Spartans would be more ready to respect it. The oracle, in turn, treated Lycurgus from the very first encounter with a respect that struck the ancients as unique:

Lycurgus' First Inquiry

> At first the Spartans were among the worst of men, violent with others, scarcely less violent with one another. Then Lycurgus appeared among them. He saw the promise of this people. Some say that he decided to seek a code of law from the Delphic oracle, others say that he adapted the constitution of Crete. Those who favor Delphic origins tell that when he entered the temple, the Pythia immediately addressed him as follows:
>
> *Is it you, Lycurgus, come to my rich temple?*
> *Lycurgus, dear to Zeus and to all that dwell*
> *In the halls of Olympus?*
> *I ask myself whether I must address you*
> *As a god or as a man.*
> *I see a god in you, Lycurgus.*
> *You have come in search of laws:*
> *I shall give them to you.*[11]

Plutarch gives us reason to imagine Lycurgus shuttling back and forth between Sparta and Delphi to collect the elements of his code. When it was complete in his own mind, he returned to Delphi with a striking entourage:

The Endorsement of Law

> Before delivering his laws to the people of Sparta, Lycurgus journeyed to Delphi, accompanied by the most important citizens. There he asked whether, according to the established formula, it was "better and more good" for Sparta to obey the laws he had prepared under divine guidance. When Apollo answered that it was better in every way, Lycurgus enacted a further law: refusal to obey a code given by Apollo at Delphi was not just unlawful but evil. Then he gathered the people to explain everything in detail.[12]

Plutarch evokes the long process of adjustment and addition through which Lycurgus embedded the new code into the life of Sparta. Finally satisfied that everything was in place, the sage enigmatically recognized a need about which he could tell no one. Plutarch's language has qualities of stateliness and force worth retaining for this episode:

Lycurgus' Last Ruse

When Lycurgus' principal institutions were at last firmly fixed in the customs of the people of Sparta, and the state had the strength to support and preserve itself, Lycurgus was filled with joyful satisfaction. But so far as human forethought could manage, he ardently desired to make this order of life immortal and go down unchanged to future ages.

Accordingly, he assembled the people and told them that the provisions already made were sufficient to secure the prosperity and virtue of the state, but that something of the greatest weight and importance remained, which he could not lay before them until he had consulted the god at Delphi. They must therefore agree to abide by the established laws without any change until he returned from Delphi. Then he would do whatever the god thought best.

When they had agreed and urged him to set out on his journey, he exacted an oath from the kings and senators and the whole people that they would abide by the established order until his return; he set out.

On reaching the oracle, he sacrificed to the god and asked whether the laws he had established were good, and sufficient to promote a city's prosperity and virtue. Apollo answered that the laws were good and that the city would be held in highest honor for as long as it retained them. This Lycurgus wrote down and sent to Sparta.

But for his own part, he sacrificed again to the god and, resolving never to release his fellow-citizens from their oath, decided to put an end to his life where he was. Abstaining from food until he died, he made his death guardian of the blessings he had secured for Sparta.[13]

Not all great leaders came to Delphi with the prestige and assurance of Lycurgus. Consider, for example, Lucius Junius Brutus, known to tradition as the founder of the Roman Republic, about whom the following tale is told. Its setting is the sixth century, when the Tarquin kings reigned in Rome.

The Fool Who Was No Fool

Lucius Junius, nicknamed Brutus (simpleton or fool), was the prime mover in the expulsion of the tyrants. Brutus's father was Marcus Junius, a man of merit who ranked among the most illustrious Romans of that period. His mother was Tarquinius, a daughter of the first King Tarquin. Brutus enjoyed the best education that his country could provide, and his nature was drawn to noble accomplishment. But the king had his father murdered secretly—together with many other good men—not for any crime but simply out of greed for Marcus's wealth.

Still a boy and now orphaned, Brutus decided to pretend to be a simpleton, although he was in fact most intelligent. From then on, he acted the fool—hence his nickname—until perhaps the moment would come to reveal himself. Contemptuous of the young fool, the king took Brutus's inheritance away and left him only a small allowance for daily needs. But he kept him in the royal household as a companion for his sons, not to show him the kindness due a kinsman, as he falsely explained to his friends, but to provide his sons with amusement.

Some years later, a plague descended on Rome that preyed on children and, even more fiercely, on pregnant women. The king decided to dispatch two of his sons, Arruns and Titus, to consult the Delphic oracle. At their request he sent along Brutus to keep them amused during the journey.

When the boys reached the oracle and received answers concerning the plague, they made rich offerings to Apollo—and burst into laughter when Brutus offered nothing more than a wooden staff. In reality, Brutus had secretly hollowed it out and inserted a rod of gold.

The king's sons asked Apollo to reveal which of them was destined to be the next king of Rome. The god answered,

The one who shall first kiss his mother.

Missing the meaning of the oracle, the brothers secretly agreed to kiss their mother at the same time. They wanted to be kings together.

But Brutus understood. As soon as he landed in Italy, he stooped and kissed the ground, for the Earth is our common mother.

Such were the early events in the life of the man destined to free Rome.[14]

This version of the tale is based on a text from the first century B.C.E. Another version, some two centuries later, offers a lucid interpretation of Brutus's offering: "It was a kind of staff, apparently possessing no point of excellence and making him all the more a laughingstock, and it furnished a sort of image of the affliction he feigned. For he had hollowed it out and secretly poured in gold to indicate that concealed behind the contempt he suffered for his stupidity was a sound and estimable intelligence."[15] The interpreter also recorded a related tale. Like many tyrants, Tarquin was nervous about his longevity in office. He brought his question to the Delphic oracle. He would be driven from office, the Pythia told him, "*only when a dog uses human speech.*" He was, of course, confident that such a thing would never come to pass, just as Croesus had been confident that a mule would never rule in Persia. The dog was our friend Brutus, a secret favorite of the oracle.

The trait of cunning intelligence so evident in Brutus appears in other tales of Delphi concerning not only inquirers but also benefactors. Herodotus tells about another striking sixth-century figure, the Egyptian pharaoh Amasis. When the temple at Delphi accidentally burned in the course of the century, the Delphians launched a national and international fundraising effort to rebuild. Herodotus describes them as wandering from city to city begging for gifts. Among the greatest donors they encountered was Amasis.

A Truly Clever Pharaoh

Amasis became king. Now at first the Egyptians made little of Amasis and held him in no esteem, because he was formerly a man of the people and of no very distinguished house. But afterwards Amasis conciliated them by his cleverness and his want of stiff-neckedness. He had countless treasures, among them a golden footbath, in which Amasis himself and his fellow guests washed their feet on each occasion of need. Amasis cut this up and made out of it an image of a god and set it up at the most suitable part of the city. The Egyptians, as they came constantly to the image, showed it great reverence. Amasis noticed what was done by the citizens, and he summoned them together and made them clear about the matter; he said that the image had been made out of a footbath in which formerly the Egyptians used to vomit and piss and wash their feet, and now they reverenced it mightily. So now, he said to them, he himself was just like that footbath. For if he had been formerly a man of the people, he was now and in the present their king, and so he bade them honor and respect him.

That is how Amasis conciliated the Egyptians to the justice of their slavery to himself, and the following is how he ordered his way of life: in the early morning, until when the market was full, he would zealously do all matters that were brought to him; but from then on he drank and joked with those who drank with him and was indeed an easygoing and sportive companion. Certain of his friends were aggrieved at this and chid him, saying, "My lord, you do not take due care for yourself in bringing yourself so low. You ought rather to sit solemnly all day on a solemn throne and conduct business, and so the Egyptians would know they were governed by a great man and you would have a fairer fame. What you are doing now is not the least royal." He answered them: "Those who have bows string them when there is need. If they were strung all the time, they would break, and

> so their owners would not have them to use when they needed them. A man is just like that. If he will be serious always and never let any part of him trifle, he will, without knowing it, become crazy or idiotic. I know that, and so I give each part its due." That was how he answered those friends of his.
>
> It is said that Amasis, even when he was a private person, was one who loved drink and jokes and was altogether not a serious man; and whenever, in his drinking and enjoying himself, the supplies ran out, he would go around stealing. The people who said, in spite of his denials, that he had taken their goods would hale him to the oracle, wherever there was one among them. Many times he was convicted by the oracles, and many times he got off. Now, as soon as he became king, he took no care at all of those shrines that had acquitted him of thievery, nor would he make any contribution to their decoration, nor would he go there and sacrifice; for he saw them as nothing worth but possessed of lying oracles. But those of them that had strictly convicted him of being a thief, those he took good care of, as being truly gods and possessed of oracles that knew not lying.[16]

Amasis, too, with his versatile intelligence and penetrating humor, must have been a favorite of the oracle.

PYTHAGORAS ET AL.

The legendary lives of three sages, Pythagoras, Zeno, and Diogenes, were guided at key moments by the oracle. Zeno's story is the most concise, and perhaps the one, despite chronology, to remember first. A philosopher of the first half of the fifth century, about whom little is known apart from a few ingenious philosophical paradoxes, Zeno once came to Delphi with a question. The encounter, briefly told, has weight:

The Complexion of the Dead

> As a young man, the philosopher Zeno asked the oracle how he should go about attaining the best life. The god replied:
>
> *Take on the complexion of the dead.*
>
> Perceiving what this meant, Zeno studied ancient authors.[17]

This is one of few examples in which the inquirer is not floored by Delphic ambiguity—in which he at once sees the meaning, however densely disguised, and knows how to act on it. Zeno showed his promise at this moment. When the Delphic transaction involves such an intelligent inquirer, it is anything but clumsy or unfair: like speaks to like, Apollo to His own, and the shared language is transparent. The metaphor endowed with multiple meaning, as always, left Zeno free to choose his course. Arguably, he could have adopted the ascetic practice of meditating in graveyards, or he might have interpreted that the oracle was urging him to cultivate extreme detachment from day-to-day life. His actual choice conformed with his nature and destiny. As always, it matters not at all whether Zeno factually received this answer at Delphi; it matters only that tradition held him to have done so, and that readers in ancient times welcomed the wisdom of the tale.

A somewhat comparable tale, set in the legendary aftermath of the Trojan War, involves the form of government adopted by the city of Megara.

The Majority Vote

> When the last king of Megara was killed, the people decided to elect governors from among themselves and form a council of advisors. Aisymnos, one of the leading men of the city, took the precaution of making the journey to Delphi to ask how the city could best prosper.
>
> *You will prosper*
> *By making your decisions*
> *With the majority.*
>
> Unclear words, yet promising. What could they mean? After exhaustive debate, the people of Megara made the intuitive leap that by His word "majority" Apollo must mean the dead. And so they built their council house directly over the site where their heroes and most notable ancestors were buried.
>
> There the ancient tale ends.[18]

Among philosophers, none was more closely linked to the oracle than Socrates, but we can piece together from fragments of the legend of Pythagoras a comparable intimacy, in this instance not merely from birth but, according to the poets, from his conception as a child of Apollo. Like many other figures of the sixth century, Pythagoras is known to us through a later literary tradition that assembled fact and legend indiscriminately, so much so that all facts are questionable and many legends may have a germ of fact. The tale in Iamblichus is worth hearing in a close equivalent to its original, rather stately wording.

The Birth of Pythagoras

> That Pythagoras was the son of Apollo is a legend due to a certain Samian poet, who thus described the popular recognition of his noble birth. Sang he,
>
> Pythais, the fairest of the Samian race,
> From the embraces of the God Apollo
> Bore Pythagoras, the friend of Zeus.
>
> Mnesarchos had gone to Delphi on a business trip, leaving his wife without any signs of pregnancy. He enquired of the oracle about his return voyage to Syria, and he was informed that his trip would be lucrative, and most conformable to his wishes, but that his wife was new with child and would present him with a son who would surpass all others who had ever lived in beauty and wisdom, and that he would be of the greatest benefit to the human race in everything pertaining to human achievements. When Mnesarchos realized that the God, without waiting for any question about a son, had by an oracle informed him that he would possess an illustrious prerogative, and a truly divine gift, he immediately changed his wife's former name Parthenis to one reminiscent of the Delphic prophet and her son—naming her Pythais, and the infant, who was soon after born at Sidon in Phoenicia, Pythagoras, by this name commemorating that such an offspring had been promised him by the Pythian Apollo. The assertions of Epimenides, Eudoxus, and Xenocrates that Apollo, having at that time already had actual connection with Parthenis, causing her pregnancy, had regularized that fact by predicting the birth of Pythagoras, are by no means to be admitted. However, no one will deny that the soul of Pythagoras was sent to mankind from Apollo's domain, having either been one of his attendants, or more intimate associates, which may be inferred both from his birth and his versatile wisdom.[19]

The name Pythagoras was variously explained by preservers of his legend; for example, Aristippus of Cyrene suggested that "Pythagoras derived his name from the fact of his speaking (*agoreuein*) truth no less than the God at Delphi (*tou Pythiou*)."[20] The implied association between Delphic truth and Pythagorean truth is, as we shall see, not accidental.

When he came of age, Pythagoras set off on a voyage of study, lasting decades, that took him to all of the great centers of learning in the ancient world. His first master was Thales of Miletus, whom we have encountered as one of the Seven Sages. After many years, Thales sent him on to Egypt to study with the priests and learn the mysteries. Pythagoras' voyage to Egypt was broken by an interlude in Phoenicia, where he not only learned much, but also learned, as Thales had insisted, that Egypt was the fountainhead of knowledge. He spent the next twenty-two years in Egypt, according to legend, after which he was captured by Persian troops and transported to Babylon. There he "was overjoyed to be associated with the Magi, who instructed him in their venerable knowledge and in the most perfect worship of the Gods."[21] Captivity fell within the divine plan for this exceptional man, who returned to Greece at the age of fifty-six, fully prepared to teach.

Somewhere in this pattern—our authors are not clear—Pythagoras is also said to have sojourned in Delphi, where he studied with the Pythia of his time, variously named Aristokleia and Themistoklea by the sources:[22] "He had learned from the Magi, who call God Horomazda, that God's body is like light, and his soul is like truth. He taught much else, which he claimed to have learned from Aristokleia at Delphi." Another ancient source is no less definite: "Aristoxenus asserts that Pythagoras derived the greater part of his ethical doctrines from Themistoklea, the priestess at Delphi." And so we encounter the claim that Pythagoras, master of all teachings of the ancient world, was a living embodiment of Delphic wisdom in its metaphysical and ethical dimensions. As we have seen in an earlier chapter, Pythagoras' mode of speech was also viewed as Delphic: condensed, symbolic, full of implication, challenging the listener to grasp meanings that were hidden, not out of haughty disregard for the ordinary person but because fundamental truth is best expressed in economical language stripped of personal graces.

The tone and focus of these abbreviated Pythagorean teachings recall the wisdom of the Seven Sages:

> The beginning is the half of the whole.
> Poke not the fire with a sword.
> On starting a journey, do not turn back.
> Help a man to take up a burden, but not to lay it down.
> Sacrifice unshod.
> Do not speak of Pythagorean matters without light.[23]

Each is a teaching in itself. It is worth remembering that Pythagoras—averse to bloody sacrifice, a vegetarian, and teacher of a moderately ascetic way of life—sacrificed only at a bloodless altar in Delos, the legendary birthplace of Apollo. The sacrifice he recommended is likely to have been the characteristic sacrifice of his path: of everything unnecessary.

The ancients had astonishingly long memories. Events and persons from many centuries past could be conjured in an instant to shed light on some matter of current interest. Among these long-remembered figures was one Phalaris, the exceptionally evil tyrant of Akragas in early sixth-century Sicily, who periodically reappears in literature, even many centuries later, as the epitome of cruelty and bad rule. He is curiously woven at several places into the fabric of Delphic tales, in the present instance as an embodiment of pure evil against whom our hero Pythagoras, embodying all that is good and wise, brings to bear his message of cosmic and human order. The legend of Pythagoras holds that he was anything but shy of the political arena: "He dissolved tyrannies, ordered confused commonwealths, and emancipated cities, he ended illegalities, and impeded the activities of insolent and tyrannical men."[24] In glorious illustration of this capacity, Iamblichus tells the tale of Pythagoras taken captive by Phalaris.

Pythagoras in Captivity

> Detained by the cruel tyrant Phalaris in Akragas, Pythagoras spent his days in serious conversation with a visiting philosopher, Abaris. Phalaris would listen. Pythagoras would say, for example, that from the heavens above to creatures of the air and land there is a certain descending communication, and so on. It was the grandest of philosophical exchanges. Phalaris sometimes lost his temper with these self-possessed men. He would interrupt their talks with curses and blasphemies—yet, for reasons of his own, he liked to listen.
>
> Pythagoras intuited that Phalaris intended to put him to death. Yet he knew that he was not destined to die at this man's hands. With this secret knowledge encouraging him, he gradually turned the focus of conversation to Phalaris himself. Pythagoras evoked for the tyrant's edification the power and vastness of heaven, and the source of law and ethics in the divine. His teaching ranged over the whole of reality. And ultimately Pythagoras gained some small influence over Phalaris. As he did so, the moment approached for the fulfillment of an oracular message from Apollo. For years the message had circulated secretly in Akragas.
>
> The oracle had foreseen that the cruel tyranny of Phalaris would end when his subjects became better men and learned to cooperate with one another. As the teaching and influence of Pythagoras reached out to the unhappy people of Akragas, this is just what occurred: a light dawned among them. What proof do we have that Pythagoras led Phalaris to his fate? On the very day the tyrant condemned Pythagoras and Abaris to death, he fell victim to a coup in which he lost his life.[25]

This was Pythagoras, perceived by the ancients as a true son of the Delphic oracle and as one whose words had that authority. One would think that such an ancient figure could be safely forgotten, but it's not quite so. Pythagoras was the first Western guru, first teacher in our part of the world of an intensive way dedicated to educating and refining the whole person rather than mind alone. "He danced certain dances which he thought conferred on the body agility and health."[26] Incomparable.

We can conclude this chapter by remembering Diogenes the Cynic, yet another ancient figure who grips hard. According to tradition, his life too involved a key encounter with the Delphic oracle. Student of a student of Socrates, and a contemporary of Plato's, Diogenes was a thoroughly complex figure whose views, way of life, and sharp humor cannot be captured in brief. His home for some years was a large clay pot. When some pranksters broke it, the Athenians voted to replace it at public expense. He lived among his fellow men and women as a rude, truthful witness. He shocked and railed. He created deliberate public scandal. He respected few. By these means, he pressed society toward honesty, detachment, and breadth of thought to a degree that most citizens found inconvenient. He has been compared to a Beatnik, a drifter at the fringe, and compared with equal justice to a Zen master. His memory is limited for most of us to a few vignettes: Diogenes walking about in daylight with a lantern, muttering, "I am looking for a real man"; Diogenes encountering Alexander the Great.

Alexander had come to see him in Corinth. At the time, Diogenes was taking a sunbath. Alexander approached with his entourage and, by way of recognizing Diogenes' fame, asked, "What can I do for you?" Diogenes: "You can stand out of my light." Alexander withdrew with his followers. They were laughing: "What a foolish man!" To which Alexander said only, "If I weren't Alexander, I would wish to be Diogenes."

There is much more; Diogenes awaits rediscovery. He is the patron saint of more than a few people living today. One has to go looking for one's patron saint. The best hide. The Delphic tale about Diogenes is curiously muddled, as if tradition couldn't quite decide whether this man of acknowledged greatness had committed a crime in his youth or merely suffered the consequences of another's crime.

Change the Currency

> Diogenes was a native of Sinope on the Black Sea, and the son of Hikesios, a banker. Some say that he went into exile because his father, entrusted with the state mint, debased the coinage to his own advantage and was found out. Others say that Diogenes himself committed the crime and was forced into exile with his father. According to the

> second account, Diogenes was appointed supervisor of the mint, and the artisans there tempted him to reduce the precious metal in the coins and sell what was left for private profit. Diogenes was torn. Here the account that attributes crime to Diogenes goes astray, because it claims that he went to Delphi—or to the Apollo oracle in his own city—to ask whether he should do what these men urged. But no one in his right mind would ask the oracle to condone crime. Be that as it may, the oracle's reply is the same in all accounts: the god urged him to change the city's currency *(politikon nomisma).*
>
> *Nomisma* means not only coinage and currency but also custom and usage. What then did the god mean? According to some, Diogenes failed to grasp the subtle meaning. Instead, he literally changed the currency for his personal profit and, when his crime came to light, either fled or was banished.
>
> But consider the other version. According to it, after his father was imprisoned for the crime, Diogenes fled to Delphi and, in despair over his uncertain future, asked what he should do to gain the greatest reputation. "*Change the nomisma of the city*!" the Pythia charged him, using the imagery that was so much in his mind, but transforming it. If his father had changed the coins, he must now change the way of life.[27]

A complex tale, difficult to tell smoothly. . . . But you understand?

8

Tales Mostly of War

The fourth-century Athenian leader Phokion, ultimately martyred by the people he served, was elected general no fewer than forty-five times. A faithful defender of the Athenian way of life, he was not one to suffer fools gladly and often defied popular opinion. Once a message from Delphi was received in the Assembly: *When all Athenians agree*, it stated solemnly, *there will be one who differs*—and that man, the Athenians understood, would be worth hearing. Phokion came forward. "Seek no further," he said, "I am that man." No one doubted him.

Some time later, he was giving his opinion on a weighty matter before the Assembly when he found, to his surprise, that everyone agreed with him. Turning to nearby friends, he asked in a stage whisper: "Am I making a poor argument without knowing it?"[1]

The Delphic oracle was not always taken solemnly; humor plays at the edges of the Center of the World, laughter mixes with the chant.

A Cure for Giddiness

> The people of Tiryns decided to confront a longstanding problem: the other city-states considered them a fun-loving community, good drinking companions, but when the time came to do business, the most desirable trading partners turned elsewhere. No one fully trusted them. They were giddy, irresponsible. Such was their reputation—and they

thought it time to live it down. They turned to Delphi with their question. "How," asked their delegates, "can we free ourselves from this weakness?"

> *You will free yourselves if you sacrifice a bull to Poseidon*
> *by casting it into the sea without a smile.*

The way was clear. The great sacrifice was arranged, a bull of extraordinary strength and beauty was selected from the herds, and as an extra precaution the people forbade their children to attend the ceremony for fear that they would take it lightly and cause a disturbance—perhaps even smile.

Bright and promising, the great day arrived. In their finest gowns the people assembled at the shore. The foremost citizens led the garlanded bull to the water's edge. An atmosphere of intense seriousness enveloped every gesture.

As it happens, a boy had managed to mingle with the crowd. His diminutive gowned figure darted here and there. Finally someone in authority noticed him and ordered his immediate removal. The people nearest him tried at once to drive him away.

"What's the matter?" the boy shouted. "Are you afraid I'll upset the bull?"

And at this everyone burst into laughter.[2]

The transmitter of this tale adds from his wisdom that Apollo had really meant to show the people of Tiryns that it is not easy to rid oneself of a habit.

Delphic humor—or what can only seem it, from this distance—even crept into rather solemn tales of war and peace. In the early fourth century, for example,

Do you agree with your Father?

Sparta was poised to launch a campaign against nearby Argos when their adversaries abruptly declared a holy truce, due to a lengthy holiday falling just at that time. This was not an unfamiliar ruse of war: the festival calendars of city-states differed from one another, and holy truces could be called at a moment's notice when the going got rough.

Agesilaos, king and commander of the Spartan troops, thought that he detected in this sudden burst of religious observance just such a strategy. But he had his doubts. Not wishing to offend the gods, he traveled to the oracle of Zeus at Olympia in search of an indisputable view. There he explained that the Argives had raised the issue of sacred months only *after* the Spartans had made their warlike intentions clear.

Zeus replied through his oracle that there can be no violation of divine law when a holy truce is declared out of season.

Agesilaos was satisfied. On the other hand the ephors—the ruling council of Spartans—felt that further verification was needed. Upon his return from Olympia, they sent Agesilaos straight on to Delphi.

There he asked Apollo whether He held the same opinion as his Father. Apollo replied that He agreed unreservedly.

Agesilaos led the troops into battle.[3]

Another set of wartime oracular messages is endowed with something of the same dynamic. While the tale is humorous only to the degree that it illustrates cunning Greek intelligence at grip with circumstance, it again constructs consultation with the gods as a family situation in which the divine generations freely pass judgment on each other's messages. We are in the year 479 B.C.E., and in feverish preparation for the battle at Plataea in which the Greek allies won their decisive victory over the Persian invader.

Zeus Clarifies Apollo: The Oracle in War

Aristides, commander of the Athenian army at Plataea, sent a delegation of fellow-citizens to Delphi in search of advice on which gods to invoke for help in the coming conflict. The oracle was prodigious in instruction: they would win the battle if they made vows to Zeus, Hera, Pan, and certain nymphs, if they sacrificed to no fewer than seven specific heroes, and if they engaged the enemy on their own soil in the plain of Eleusinian Demeter and Kora. The delegation returned with these instructions.

Aristides found them, in part, puzzling. There could be no doubt about oaths and sacrifices to the gods, and the heroes designated by the oracle had a long history of worship in Plataea, as did the specified nymphs (they were said to live in a nearby cave). But the command to take the field in the plain of Eleusinian Demeter, and the promise of victory only if the battle was fought there, made no sense: the only field of Eleusinian Demeter he knew lay at a good distance from Plataea, between Athens and the sacred city where the Eleusinian mysteries were celebrated. If they were to make their stand near Eleusis, a major shift in strategy would be needed.

One night soon after the oracular message had been received, the Plataean general Arimnestos dreamed that he was approached by Zeus himself. The father of the gods asked him what strategy had been adopted for the impending battle. "Tomorrow, my Lord," replied Arimnestos in his dream, "we shall march to Eleusis and make our

> stand against the enemy there, in obedience to the Delphic oracle." "What?" roared the father of the gods. "You are making a terrible mistake! If you search, you will find the theater of battle foretold by the oracle much closer at hand, in your own Plataea."
>
> As soon as Arimnestos awoke from this vivid dream, he called together the elders of Plataea and conveyed the god's words to them. They mentally searched the geography of their beloved region, which they knew as well as their own hands, until one of them suddenly recalled an ancient, half-ruined temple dedicated to Eleusinian Demeter and Kora. It stood at the foot of Mount Kithaeron.
>
> Summoning Aristides, they set out together to scout the site. They soon realized that it naturally favored their infantry against a Persian force of cavalry. The plain spreading in front of the temple was bordered by rocky terrain and cliffs that would limit the free movement of horses. And in further confirmation that this was the chosen theater of action, they found nearby a shrine dedicated to one of the heroes mentioned by the Delphic oracle.
>
> Now all but one of the oracle's conditions had been met, namely, that the army was to meet the enemy "on their own soil"—Athenian soil, since the delegation to Delphi was Athenian. What to do? The Plataean elders voted on the spot to grant certain lands to Athens—including the chosen field of battle. The ground on which they stood was now Athenian. Here the Greek allies would defend home and country, in accordance with the oracle.[4]

The tale is not "esoteric"; it contains no secret wisdom. It does, however, invitingly reflect a time and place when human beings dealt more familiarly with the gods, when oracles and dreams were lines of connection with the divine, and rapidly struck bargains of a very human kind were as central to the fulfillment of divine command as solemn sacrifices and other acts of ritual.

Another tale of the oracle's influence at Plataea has been passed down, and here is no doubt the place to remember it. A tale of curious power, it is capable of stirring archaic memory, of reminding us that the "feel" of a circumstance may call for action even when, materially, the action changes nothing. It is a tale of the replacement of fire with fire.

Renewing the Fires

> After the great victory at Plataea, the Greek allies sent a delegation to Delphi to ask what grateful sacrifices should be made. The Pythia responded that the Greeks were to raise an altar to Zeus the Deliverer

in Plataea itself, but they were not to sacrifice upon it until they had extinguished all fires across the land and renewed them. The fire at every hearth had been polluted by the passage of the barbarian army. In this respect all Greece was one. And the only solution was to rekindle the fires from a single source: the temple hearth at Delphi.

The oracle's command was extreme. It imposed massive effort. But the symbolic is real, the command was obeyed. The process of death and rebirth began at Plataea itself, as the field generals spread the word to smother all fires throughout the camp. Soon a thick blanket of smoke hung over the camp. A volunteer was needed, someone willing to make the journey to Delphi at top speed to obtain the sacred fire and return. Euchidas stepped forward.

We know nothing of him beyond this tale. Perhaps he was a runner hardened by training for the Pythian or Olympic Games. We know that he was a pious soul yet proud of his stupendous effort, because when he arrived in scarcely more than a half-day at distant Delphi he purified himself by sprinkling his body with holy water and crowned himself with laurel, as if a victor in the Games. Then, taking live embers from the hearth and sheltering them in his soldier's carrying case, he turned back toward Plataea.

He arrived before sunset. With unutterable emotion he greeted his countrymen, passed on the sacred fire—and collapsed. He died soon after.

The Plataeans gave him burial in their sanctuary of Artemis, tireless runner of the forests.[5]

Like a mirror reflecting light toward us from a very distant place, the tale reveals some timeless sensitivity to the power of symbol. Materially, fire is fire; there can be no difference between the pure fire of Delphi and the fires that saw the Persians' angry passage across the land. But the oracle required of all Greeks everywhere to mark the moment when their lives and homes were again secure, and to mark it unmistakably through concerted action. The inconvenience, even the price of a hero's death, mattered less than enacting the purification without compromise. The tale presses against our current unease with ritual: the language of symbolic action is for many of us alien, not our own, and we are uncertain how or whether to reclaim it. The tale suggests that symbolic action is necessary, that what seems merely a symbol to the mind—fuss with no measurable result—is the natural language of the feelings.

The ancient way of healing psychic wounds through symbolic action is evident in the tale of Aristinos. It is the tale of an individual, not of an entire people, but the role of symbol is the same.

A Man of Later Fate

We do not know the exact circumstances—perhaps a distant military campaign, a long commercial voyage—but when Aristinos failed to return to his city after many, many months, his grieving family gave up hope of seeing him again and had his funerary rites pronounced.

One fine day he returned. Instead of greeting him with open arms, his fellow-citizens shunned him, acted as if he was not there. By the ancient code, he was *polluted*: this was the unyielding judgment against those for whom last rites are performed and who have the indiscretion to return among the living.

Aristinos was unwilling to live out his life as No One. Again circumstances are unclear, but it seems that he went to the outskirts of Delphi and sent a surrogate questioner to the oracle to ask what he must do to erase the pollution.

You must be born again.
Then offer a sacrifice
To the blessed gods.

Aristinos somehow grasped that the Pythia should be taken literally. He sought out the midwives of Delphi and struck a bargain with them. Soon after, he went to their quarters, stripped off his clothes, and gave himself into their care as naked as the day he was born. They washed him as if he had just emerged from the womb, wrapped him in swaddling clothes, offered him their breasts. He was reborn.

He let it be known by messenger that all had been done as the oracle commanded. He would soon be home, with the legitimate hope of a better welcome.

Those like Arimnestos who must be born again are called "men of later fate."[6]

MY LORD, DO YOU CARE FOR THESE SUPPLIANTS?

Surviving tales of Delphi address all levels of human experience, from the archaic simplicity of these tales of ritual healing to matters of human conniving. A fine tale of the lame poet Tyrtaios in wartime falls into the second category, although the gods ably contrive to lift events from the realm of calculation to their preferred realm of destiny.

A Lame Gift

Some 40 years after the fall of their principal city to the Spartans, the people of Messenia rebelled against the conquerors' yoke. Sparta roused itself to defend what it took to be its own. But before launching a campaign of pacification, the ephors consulted the Delphic oracle with the hope of obtaining assurance or strategic hints from the highest source.

"*Consult the Athenian!*" they were told. They immediately sent a delegation to Athens to announce these holy words and to ask for the man—whoever he might be—who was destined to guide them.

The news threw the Athenians into a predicament. If they were to obey the oracle by sending a seasoned strategist to the Spartans' aid, this would only strengthen the Spartans' position, and who could guarantee that in time they would not come knocking at the gates of Athens? On the other hand, were the Athenians to deny help, they would disobey the god at Delphi. How to respond?

At last they found a solution. There lived among them a teacher of writing and a poet, Tyrtaios, who was generally regarded as obnoxious. He was also lame in one foot. After due reflection, this is the man they sent to the aid of Sparta.

But as later generations would say, God is not mocked. Just as the Athenians expected, Tyrtaios exploited his new setting to cultivate the great men of the city. He recited his verses at tedious length wherever he found captive listeners. And yet. . . . The war took a bad turn at a place called Boar's Grave. Standing with priests on high ground behind the field of battle, Tyrtaios witnessed the rout and something changed in him. The Spartans returned in despair from the field, ready to abandon the campaign. But Tyrtaios sang new songs that were inspiring and deeply encouraging. The men under arms were moved.

Tyrtaios did more than sing. As an outsider unfamiliar with the strict Spartan code, he felt free to recruit replacements for the army among poor serfs whom the Spartans had never respected enough to invite to fight by their side. Suddenly there was a new leader in Sparta. His name was Tyrtaios.

Despite themselves, the Athenians had sent the right man. It is said that, even long after, the Spartans sang his songs as they marched to war.[7]

Delphic tales of war almost always have an unexpected twist. One of the most compact and patterned concerns the little island people of Lipari, between Sicily and the mainland, who once faced the overwhelming threat of the piratical Etruscan navy.

The Value of Small Increments

> I discovered a most extraordinary thing that the people of Lipari pulled off against the Etruscans. The Delphic oracle ordered them to fight against the Etruscan fleet with as few ships as possible. What does that mean? they asked themselves. How can we mount a defense without the full navy? With heavy hearts they submitted. Against the line of colorful Etruscan warships bobbing on the swell out to the horizon, they brought into forward positions just five ships of their own.
>
> The Etruscans could not believe their eyes: five ships? Was this how the little island folk planned to do battle? Counseling among themselves, they decided as a matter of honor—and with a touch of malice—to engage just five ships of their own.
>
> But things did not turn out quite as the Etruscans had foreseen: with the courage of desperation, the Liparians devastated the five Etruscan ships. The enemy again took counsel; they sent a second strike force of five ships into battle. Again the result was the same, and again and again. The Liparians prevailed in each miniature battle until the Etruscans, in profound humiliation, withdrew over the horizon and went home.
>
> The people of Lipari dedicated at Delphi a statue of Apollo for every ship they took.[8]

This is a magical tale, embodying fundamental good sense in an attractive form. The Etruscan navy may never have borne down on the Liparians, the Liparians may never have turned in anguish to Delphi, but the tale remains to convey the value of small incremental gains. The islanders received a clear message from the oracle; the difficulty was to obey it.

The situation was very different for the legendary king, Kodros of Athens, when the Spartan army besieged his city. The oracle gave him no instructions whatever. He had to invent a future in harmony with a message from the oracle that had been delivered to someone else. His tale is told by Lycurgus of Athens, a mid-fourth century statesman.

Kodros: A King's Tale

> Remember the reign of Kodros. Remember the year when the Spartans' crops failed, and they decided to march against our city to steal our land. They were cautious enough, as you recall, to send a delegation to

> Delphi with the usual question: Are we going to capture Athens? The god told them that they would prevail—as long as they didn't kill Kodros. And so they issued the secret order to preserve the king's life, no matter what the circumstance, and took the field against us.
>
> We were not without friends at the time. A Delphian sympathizer caught wind of the oracle's message and sent word to us here in Athens.
>
> The siege was bitter. Shut inside the walls, short of food and of everything that makes life bearable, our ancestors held out bravely. Kodros pondered. What could he do? What *should* he do?
>
> Informing no one, seeking advice from no one, one morning he disguised himself as a beggar and slipped out of the city. He made his way to a brushy hillside near the main Spartan camp. There he began cutting firewood with a peasant's sickle. Sentries noticed him. They approached. "How fare things in the city?" they asked. "Are the people weakening?" Stooped over his task, Kodros remained silent. The sentries came closer. When they were very close, Kodros abruptly rose and killed one with a single pass of his sickle. The other drew his sword. Thinking Kodros a miserable slave, he returned blow for blow, and the brave king died.
>
> It did not take the Athenians long to piece together an account of their king's lonely accomplishment. With mixed sorrow and pride, they dispatched a herald to the Spartan camp to explain the unexpected event and request return of the body for burial.
>
> The Spartans complied. And in light of the oracle's words, they abandoned hope of victory. They retreated to their own parched lands.[9]

Lycurgus used this tale to illustrate a point in a lawyerly address before an Athenian jury. We probably owe its preservation to its aptness as an example of heroic, independent action—of willingness to do that which no one justly can ask of another. The Delphic oracle left the field of events open to individual choice but planted, so to speak, a single marker; this Kodros noticed.

Pausanias adds an arresting footnote to the tale of Kodros. The Spartans in retreat inadvertently left behind a band of warriors who had sneaked into Athens under cover of night and now were marooned. Some of their number managed to rejoin the withdrawing troops, but the majority, fearing for their lives, fled to the Hill of Ares, god of war, and to its altars sacred to the Furies. There they took refuge as suppliants, seekers of sanctuary. The right of sanctuary was all but unquestioned in the ancient world; it assured enemy soldiers, fugitives, strangers, all who were tracked and defenseless, their safety at a temple or altar. Sanctuary imposed a pause for negotiation in events otherwise likely to end in violence. In his narrative concerning the Spartan suppliants, Pausanias records a message from the oracle of Zeus at Dodona, delivered in very distant times, which alerted the Athenians to the special status of the band now before them:

> *Think of the Hill of Ares;*
> *Think of the smoking altars of the Furies;*
> *Here Spartans, captives of the spear,*
> *Shall make supplication. Do not cut them down:*
> *Supplication is pure and consecrated.*

To this bold but helpless band of Spartans the Athenians gave safe passage.[10]

Herodotus tells a tale from the era of Croesus in which the right of supplication was questioned. The divine agent in the tale is Apollo, but not our familiar Delphic Apollo. The scene is coastal Asia Minor, near Apollo's oracle at Branchidae.

The Wrong Question

> Paktyes, a general in the army of Croesus who had been defeated in the field, fled to the Greek city of Kyme, where he invoked the sacred right of sanctuary. Not far behind, a pursuing Persian force had orders to take him alive and bring him before the Persian king. Mazares, leader of that force, stopped before the walls of Kyme and sent a message within, demanding the surrender of Paktyes.
>
> The people of Kyme were anguished. The Persian force was almost certainly more than they could withstand; therefore they could hardly deny Mazares' demand. Yet they had never refused sanctuary to a suppliant. What to do? In their misery, they dispatched their cleverest spokesmen to temporize with Mazares while a small delegation, led by noble Aristodikos, made its way to Branchidae to consult the god.
>
> "Lord," asked Aristodikos, "Paktyes the Lydian has come to us as a suppliant, pursued by Persians who will sooner or later kill him, of that we can be sure. They demand his surrender. We are afraid of the Persians, but never until this day have we given over a suppliant. Guide us, Lord: which path must we follow? To save our city by surrendering the suppliant or to defend him even at the cost of many lives?"
>
> This was the question, and Apollo declared unhesitatingly that Paktyes should be released to the Persians.
>
> While some of his fellow-citizens were secretly relieved at this answer, Aristodikos withdrew into deep silence. Suddenly, spear in hand, he rose and began circling the temple, jabbing angrily at the birds' nests

> sheltered here and there in niches. The nests plunged chaotically to the ground, birds wheeled in the air. Then a voice boomed from within the temple:
>
> *"Wicked man, how dare you disturb the suppliants to my temple!"*
>
> Aristodikos had his answer ready:
>
> "My Lord," he said, "do you care for these suppliants of yours but care nothing for ours?"
>
> The god answered:
>
> *"I commanded you to surrender your suppliant—so that you commit more quickly the crime you have in mind, so that you are more quickly destroyed, so that you never come to my temple again to question the surrender of a suppliant!"*
>
> The men of Kyme, few of them made of the same stuff as Aristodikos, nonetheless found a way to live another day. Dreading the consequences of offending the Persians, dreading the consequences of offending God, they decided to send Paktyes secretly to the neighboring city of Mytilene. Ah, the Greeks . . .[11]

Among all tales of ancient oracles, this is one of the most attractive. Aristodikos' inspired mime makes it a drama, and the booming voice from within the temple provides the satisfaction of a moment of outright magic, temporarily exempting us from the ritual of inquiry and the mediation of the priestess.

But there is something more: the tale probes the real basis of acts of conscience and suggests that certain decisions or gestures are matters of first principle, axioms of community. One does not even *think* of doing certain things. If the thought nonetheless strays through one's mind, it is quickly rejected because one *feels* that the actions would ignore axioms of community. In the ceaselessly violent ancient world, the inviolability of sanctuary was one such axiom: it protected each from all, and people had little difficulty acknowledging that events could reduce even the most secure person to the status of an undefended fugitive.

Kyme needed the help of the three-eyed man. He appears in a tale recorded by Pausanias, which harks back to the aftermath of the Trojan War. Not specifically a Delphic tale, hardly a tale at all but more like a single haunting image, it is infused with the love of riddling language and the imperative to solve the riddle through personal astuteness. The three-eyed man represents an early occurrence in folklore of the helper figure who is in some way "other"—a well-spoken fox, a wise but testy gremlin—whom the hero must obey because the helper knows the way.

The Three-Eyed Man

When Eleios was king of Elis, his expeditionary force gathered to make its victorious return from Troy to their west Peloponnesian homeland. An oracle had commanded them to take "the three-eyed man" as their guide on the homeward journey. The three-eyed man? The words defied understanding. The army delayed its departure. Its leaders, Kresphontes among them, feared what the price might be for starting off without "the three-eyed man." But was there such a person?

In time a man passed through camp, driving a one-eyed mule before him. Kresphontes looked up casually; and then found himself suddenly staring. Was this the man? Hope dawned. It made sense. He approached the weary-looking mule driver and offered the hospitality of camp. As Kresphontes conversed with him over food and drink, he brought the talk around to the journey that lay ahead. The mule-driver, Oxylos, persuasively advised against the overland route and mapped out a sea route. As it happens, he had spent decades piloting a merchant fleet.

Under his guidance, the Elians made their way home.[12]

The three-eyed man is both "lower" and "higher" than the soldiers to whom he offers practical wisdom: seemingly a peasant who cannot afford better than a disabled mule, he is in reality endowed with greater vision. In the language of story, he possesses a third eye. In later folklore, the wise helper is often cloaked in such a modest or off-putting appearance, and it is among the tasks of the hero to recognize reality behind appearance.

Kadmos, too, stooped to conquer—humbled himself, at the invitation of the Delphic oracle, to accomplish a very great mission. The events occurred in the era of myth, when the gods still mingled with human beings.

Follow the Cow

Zeus in the form of a bull kidnapped Europa, and her brothers, including young Kadmos, were sent by their father to find her. It was a task with no clue to shape it, no dream or hint to guide it. In despair, Kadmos came to Delphi to ask the oracle to unlock the secret of his aimless search.

Kadmos, you travel the world in vain.
You seek a bull never born of a cow,
A bull no mortal can track.
Give up that task, assume another:

Take an earthly cow as your guide
And follow its footsteps patiently
Where it may lead, until it stops to rest.
At that place you will found a great city.
This is your true task.

Kadmos could not but accept the Pythia's charge. He purchased a magnificent cow with the image of the moon on its flanks and, with his companions at arms, set out full of faith behind it. Sometimes seeming only to wander, sometimes following a definite path, the cow moved tirelessly toward the northeast, beyond Delphi, into the far reaches of Boeotia. Finally, in a well-watered, pleasant place it sank to the ground to rest.

Here, after many trials, Kadmos founded Thebes, one of the great cities of the Greeks, home of Oedipus.[13]

The tale can be viewed from many vantage points, but surely its keynote and the source of its quiet fascination is the image of the founder of a great city humbly following a cow. As in the tale of the three-eyed man, there is a play of "lower" and "higher": the cow has nothing like the prestige of the Founding Father yet it is moved by a higher power and shares in that power. Modest willingness to accept guidance from whatever source it may come, glamorous or not, is Kadmos' great virtue.

Tales of war and tales of the founding of cities occasionally coincide. Herodotus tells one:

His Shout of Welcome

Peoples often march out of total obscurity into the ring of light around the Delphic oracle where we meet them, and then return to the obscurity from which they came. So it is with the Dolonki, a tribe from Thrace in the north, which was locked in war with the neighboring Apsinthians. Despairing of victory, the Dolonki sent their kings to implore a strategy session with Apollo the Far-Shooter at Delphi. The Pythia spoke surprising words to them, words that seemed to ignore their immediate need:

Whoever first offers you hospitality
When you leave my temple,
Take this man to your hearts,
He is the founder of your future.

We do not know how the kings received this command, but it must have been with good cheer because they turned toward home along the

> Sacred Road through Phokis and Boeotia, alert to every farm and village as they passed. Perhaps someone would hail them in.
>
> No one paid the least attention. Eventually they joined the road to Athens. Athens was ruled at the time by the benevolent tyrant Pisistratos. Among those excluded from power was a nobleman, Miltiades, who lived in a suburb of the city. Miltiades happened to be sitting on his porch when the column of Dolonki passed by. He studied their dress and weapons with curiosity: clearly strangers, somehow intriguing, not the least threatening.
>
> "Well, men," he shouted, "why don't you share my food and roof for the night?" The column halted. The kings of the Dolonki looked across the hot fields toward the first to offer hospitality.
>
> That evening, after the customary meal and politely evasive conversation, the kings revealed to Miltiades the message they had received from the Delphic oracle. They asked him to obey the god. Within himself, Miltiades had little hesitation: perhaps these good people truly needed him, as the Athenians under Pisistratos did not. But he took the precaution of making the journey to Delphi, to ask the oracle whether he should yield to their demand.
>
> The Pythia said yes.[14]

The oracle sets in motion what amounts to a folktale. The anxious Dolonki warriors from the northern wilds make their way to the Center of the World to receive a message that challenges their narrow agenda, bids them face a broader, more promising unknown. They are given a task of openness: it is not theirs to choose who will first offer them hospitality. The unemployed nobleman follows his warm impulses into what quickly emerges as the destined opportunity to remake his own life. The tale assures us, behind its words, that those who need each other will find each other and that we ourselves, whether we are forced to the margin of life, like Miltiades, or facing heavy opposition, like the Dolonki tribesmen, can find our way.

In its meander among tales mostly of war, this chapter is moving toward, and can only be moving toward, the encounter between Athens and the oracle at the height of the Persian Wars. The pair of oracular messages from that moment and the resulting turmoil of the Athenians are narrated by Herodotus not only as solid fact but as an historic turning point. Although scholarship casts doubt on the historical reality of the Delphic pronouncements and the Athenian debate they touched off,[15] from the perspective of the Delphi of the mind, this passage in Herodotus is especially revealing of the language, function, and limitations of the

Delphic oracle. On the way toward that charged narrative, however, we might do well to meander a little more. There remain a few tales from other wars, earlier and later, that should not be missed. Here is one, a dour little tale showing our honored oracle in an unpleasant light.

Respect the Limit

> Knidos is remembered today for the exquisite Aphrodite, carved by Praxiteles in the mid-fourth century, which made Knidos a port of call in the ancient world. But two centuries earlier Knidos was a city living in fear. Harpagos, a ruthlessly competent general in the Persian armies of Cyrus, was scooping up the free Greek cities of Asia Minor one after another. Knidos was next. Since it was situated on a narrow peninsula jutting from coastal Asia Minor into the sea, the city's leaders fixed on a last, desperate strategy to preserve their independence: to dig a wide canal between the peninsula and the mainland and artificially create an island fortress. The project was not unreasonable; a narrow isthmus of land invited the attempt.
>
> The able-bodied citizens of Knidos set furiously to work, excavating, transporting debris. But something strange began to occur: there were many injuries, especially to the workers' eyes, more than made sense. The Knidians felt confronted by a force greater than themselves. In dismay, they sent a delegation to Delphi to ask what stood in their way.
>
> *Do not make a barrier. Do not dig.*
> *Had He wished, Zeus would have made Knidos an island.*
>
> The Knidians lay down their tools and surrendered to Harpagos.[16]

This, too, is the Delphic oracle as its memory is preserved: on occasion clumsy—or is it unpatriotic?—in its wartime counsel; uningenious; advising flight or surrender when the human impulse was to make a stand. In its advice to Knidos there is no ambiguity, no invitation to *complete the oracle* through the community's own initiative. The record of Delphic advice in wartime is patchy: in an imperfect world, an imperfect oracle. At the end of the fifth century, Thucydides must have spoken for many when he noted that oracles had predicted the length of the Peloponnesian War, and he went on to comment that "for those who put their faith in oracles, here is one solitary instance of their having been proved accurate."[17] Yet not everyone reads the tale of Knidos in the same way. Some feel, and why not, that the will of Zeus represents objective law, to which human beings can only acquiesce. In this perspective, the surrender of the Knidians is neither sad nor happy but required, and the tale puts us on notice that some incidents in life are neither sad nor happy but required.

The Knidians were defending themselves. Curiously, there is another tale in which the aggressors adopted a strategy of literally engineering reality to conform with a prediction from Delphi. The tale takes us to the early fourth century B.C.E., when Rome had begun its relentless expansion at the expense of its neighbors—in this instance the Etruscan city of Veii, just nine miles' distance from early Rome. Here is rough handling of Delphic truth.

An Engineering Solution

The Romans had the storied Etruscan city of Veii under siege when a strange natural event occurred. The season was high summer and dry, but a lake in the nearby Alban mountains inexplicably rose. Overflowing its banks, it forced a channel through a mountain valley and poured into the plain below. It was as if a new river had appeared. The event filled the Romans with anxiety: had they offended a god? They turned to the soothsayers, but the soothsayers preferred to refer the problem to the Delphic oracle.

An embassy was dispatched. Meanwhile, the siege continued. It happened one day that a citizen of Veii who had inherited the ancient prophetic science of the Etruscans was standing his tour of duty on the city wall. Down below, he caught sight of an acquaintance from better days, a Roman centurion. They struck up a conversation.

"I pity you," said the centurion. "I pity all of you when we take your city."

The seer laughed. "You know that I have a certain sense for the future—and you Romans have none. Here you are, besieging us month after month as if you were going to prevail. If your leaders only knew what our ancient oracles have told us—that our city can be taken only "*when the waters of the Alban lake no longer mingle with the waters of the sea*"—perhaps you would stop wasting your time and energy, and stop making our lives miserable!"

The centurion moved off thoughtfully from the conversation. This man was a respected seer from an ancient line. He could be right about the destiny before them all. The centurion made a plan, shared it with the tribunes to whom he reported, and returned the next day, unarmed, to the base of the wall.

"Ho!" he hailed the seer, who was again on duty. "I need to ask you about signs and premonitions we've had on the Roman side. I'm unarmed, as you see. Join me down here as a friend."

The seer's clairvoyance must have been limited to great events but not those right under his nose, for he decided to trust the centurion and made his way down. The two walked off together in discussion—unobtrusively guided by the centurion toward the Roman camp. When they were well away from Veii, the Roman suddenly picked up the seer by the waist and took him, kicking and protesting, into camp.

The tribunes interrogated him. What did he know of ancient Etruscan prophecies concerning the course of the Alban lake and the fall of Veii? Lofty assurances that divine predictions cannot be thwarted by the will of man and threats of torture if he failed to reveal everything he knew gradually convinced the seer to divulge his knowledge. Satisfied that he had an important tradition to report, the tribunes sent him in chains to the Senate at Rome, where he repeated what he had told the tribunes. Some senators thought him deceptive, perhaps an agent of the Veiians sent to mislead them. Others thought he spoke sincerely.

While they were debating the issue, the embassy returned from Delphi with a message from the oracle that matched in detail the seer's prophecy.

The gods and daimons who protect Veii
Guarantee the city's welfare
For so long as the Alban lake
Overflows and runs down to the sea.
Were it to turn from its course
So that its waters no longer reach the sea,
Veii would fall. This the Romans can achieve.

The Romans felt invited to try. They called in their most astute engineers, who devised a plan to dig channels that would divert the water from the sea to the plain.

The corps of engineers was about to begin work when a solemn delegation of Veiian elders, under diplomatic protection, entered Rome to address the Senate. They had heard from a Roman prisoner how their enemy intended to proceed, and they sensed that all was lost unless they could persuade the Senate to accept a peaceful surrender of the city. The exchange in the Senate was sharp and fruitless. The Senate voted to continue the war.

All of the Veiian envoys, save one, filed out of the hall. He was the most prominent member of the delegation, a seer himself. He stopped at the portal and turned to the assembled Senate. His fiery eyes scanned them.

"You Romans claim to lead because you are better men, more courageous and principled than others. But you refuse to accept the

> surrender of an ancient city, you wish instead to cause its utter disappearance from the Earth. You fear neither the anger of Heaven nor the opinion of mankind. You may accomplish the evil in your hearts. But I tell you: Veii will be avenged by the gods who love it. You will suffer, as you intend to make us suffer. By destroying Veii, you destroy Rome!"[18]

THE ATHENIANS COULD NOT AGREE

At the time of the Athenians' greatest folly in their conduct of the Peloponnesian War, tradition records that the Delphic oracle provided more than enough magical signs and coded counsel to bring them to their senses. It was the year 415: Athens was about to launch a great armada to conquer Sicily, in a vast and foolish diversion from the war at home. Among other signs fruitlessly offered by the god at Delphi, there was this: the oracle instructed the Athenians to bring from Klazomenai, a member city of their alliance, a certain priestess of Athena. They did so and, as Plutarch writes, "lo! her name was Peace. And this, as it seemed, was the advice which the divinity would give the city at that time, namely, to keep the peace."[19]

Sound advice—but the oracle was not always able to preserve its reputation for "counsel that cannot fail," in the ancient words of the Homeric Hymn, where the fortunes of war were concerned. The clash between human need and the oracle's tendency to assess the size of armies in pragmatic terms and advise accordingly is nowhere clearer than in the Athenians' most urgent hour, when the Persians were poised to invade Attica and ravage their city.

The Wooden Wall Shall Not Fall

> It was the Athenians who—after God—drove back the Persian king. Not even the terrifying warnings of the oracle at Delphi could persuade them to abandon Greece; they stood firm and had the courage to meet the invader.
>
> Prepared as they were to listen to the oracle's advice, the Athenians had sent their envoys to Delphi, and as soon as the customary rites were performed and they had entered the shrine and taken their seats, the Pythia Aristonice uttered the following prophecy:
>
> *Why sit you, doomed ones? Fly to the world's end, leaving*
> *Home and the heights your city circles like a wheel.*
> *The head shall not remain in its place, nor the body,*

Nor the feet beneath, nor the hands, nor the parts
between;
But all is ruined, for fire and the headlong God of War
Speeding in a Syrian chariot shall bring you low.
Many a tower shall he destroy, not yours alone,
And give to pitiless fire many shrines of gods,
Which even now stand sweating, with fear quivering,
While over the rooftops black blood runs streaming
In prophecy of woe that needs must come. But rise,
Haste from the sanctuary and bow your hearts to grief.

The Athenian envoys were greatly perturbed by this prophetic utterance; indeed they were about to abandon themselves to despair at the dreadful fate which the oracle declared was coming upon them, when Timon, one of the most distinguished men in Delphi, suggested that they should reenter the shrine with branches of olive in their hands and, in the guise of suppliants begging for a better fate, put their question a second time. The Athenians acted upon this suggestion and returned to the temple. "Lord Apollo," they said, "can you not, in consideration of these olive-boughs which we have brought you, give us some kindlier prophecy about our country? We will never go away until you do; indeed no: we'll stay here till we die."

Thereupon the Pythia uttered her second prophecy, which ran as follows:

Not wholly can Pallas [i.e., Athena] *win the heart of*
Olympian Zeus,
Though she prays him with many prayers and all her
subtlety;
Yet will I speak to you this other word, as firm as
adamant:
Though all else shall be taken within the bound of
Kekrops
And the gold of the holy mountain of Kithaeron
[i.e., from the region of Athens to a mountain
far to the northwest],
Yet Zeus the all-seeing grants to Athene's prayer
That the wooden wall only shall not fall, but help
you and your children.
But await not the host of horse and foot coming from
Asia,
Nor be still, but turn your back and withdraw from
the foe.
Truly a day will come when you will meet him face
to face.

Divine Salamis, you will bring death to women's sons
When the corn is scattered, or the harvest gathered in.

This second answer seemed to be, as indeed it was, less menacing than the first; so the envoys wrote it down and returned to Athens. When it was first made public upon their arrival in the city, and the attempt to explain it began, amongst the various opinions which were expressed there were two mutually exclusive interpretations. Some of the older men supposed that the prophecy meant that the Acropolis would escape destruction, on the grounds that the Acropolis was fenced in the old days with a thorn-hedge—the "wooden wall" of the oracle; but others thought that by this expression the oracle meant ships, and they urged in consequence that everything should be abandoned in favor of the immediate preparation of a fleet. There was, however, for those who believed "wooden wall" to mean ships, one disturbing thing—namely, the last two lines of the Pythia's prophecy:

Divine Salamis, you will bring death to women's sons
When the corn is scattered, or the harvest gathered in.

This was a very awkward statement and caused profound disturbance amongst all who took the wooden wall to signify ships; for the professional interpreters understood the lines to mean that if they prepared to fight at sea, they would be beaten at Salamis. There was, however, a man in Athens who had recently made a name for himself—Themistocles; and he it was who now came forward and declared that there was an important point in which the professional interpreters were mistaken. If, he maintained, the disputed passage really referred to the Athenians, it would not have been expressed in such mild language. "Hateful Salamis" would surely have been a more likely phrase than "divine Salamis," if the inhabitants of the island were really doomed to destruction. On the contrary, the true interpretation was that the oracle referred not to the Athenians but to their enemies. The "wooden wall" did, indeed, mean ships; so he advised his countrymen to prepare at once to meet the invader at sea.

The Athenians found Themistocles' explanation of the oracle preferable to that of the professional interpreters, who had not only tried to dissuade them from preparing to fight at sea but had been against offering opposition of any sort. The only thing to do was, according to them, to abandon Attica altogether and seek a home elsewhere.

The Athenians determined at a council, which was held after the discussion on the oracle, to take the god's advice and meet the invader at sea with all the force they possessed, and with any other Greeks who were willing to join them.[20]

Such, according to tradition, was the Delphic oracle in the life of the Greeks at war: a source of advice both clear and unclear, the stimulant of citywide debates, sometimes a cunning strategist, sometimes cowardly, sometimes disregarded, sometimes taken as the absolute voice of God. Consultations with the oracle were deeply woven into the fabric of the ancients' process for making decisions in time of war, so much so that even the Persians checked with their Greek allies for intelligence reports out of Delphi.[21] According to Thucydides, the very first point in a late-fifth-century declaration of armistice between Athens and Sparta reflected the primacy of Delphi in the minds of men at war:

> With regard to the temple and oracle of the Pythian Apollo we agree that all who wish should have the right to consult the oracle without fraud and without fear, according to the established laws of each man's country.[22]

Without fraud—meaning that the adversaries renounced any effort to subvert the objectivity of the oracle, on which all relied. Without fear—meaning that no one would bar the way to or from Delphi.

Let the Oracle-Bearer Go!

> In the era of war between Messenia and Sparta, the Messenians decided to send a sacred ambassador to Delphi. They chose Tisis, who was thought to understand more than most about prophecy. On his way home from Delphi, Tisis was suddenly surrounded by a Spartan squadron. He refused to be taken prisoner. He defended himself, took some wounds. Suddenly a voice from nowhere cried out: *"Let the oracle-bearer go!"* The Spartans stepped back to let Tisis pass.[23]

BLESSED BE THE COLONISTS

The most entrepreneurial acts of the ancient Greek world were warring and colonizing. They were also the most dangerous. Those who engaged in them were not slow to seek the counsel of Delphi in war or its blessing upon a small fleet preparing for a migratory voyage. The destination might be to the west, somewhere on the Italian peninsula or its neighboring islands, which came to be known as Greater Greece. It might be to the northern wilderness of Thrace or to the coast of Asia Minor where Greek civilization eventually flourished with as much sophistication as in the original homeland. It could be to the south, the African littoral. Warring and colonizing were closely related because not every region that drew the adventurers was an empty paradise: often the colonists displaced an indigenous people by force of arms, always they had to be prepared to defend their holding as it prospered. And then, these were voyages into little explored regions in light craft that guaranteed more adventure than safety.

The Greeks were driven to colonize not just by a venturesome spirit but by the agricultural limits of the homeland. Between 750 and 550 B.C.E.—years during which the Delphic oracle appeared and earned its prestige—more Greek cities than in any later period dispatched colonists who, if and when they prospered, became valued trading partners and allies. The activity was heroic, it spawned legends "of the frontier" not so different in character from American frontier legends, and it was pressed forward not only by the lofty metaphysical approval of Apollo at Delphi but by His active intervention as counselor, *provocateur*, and cartographer. The Center of the World was committed to creating a well-populated and prosperous circumference. Delphic tales associated with migrations range from examples of divine Realpolitik and the perennial taste for riddles to the breathtakingly romantic.

Rain from a Clear Sky

Before setting out to found a colony somewhere on the Italian peninsula with his family and comrades at arms, Phalanthos took the customary precaution of appearing at Delphi to ask the oracle's blessing on the enterprise. Apollo graciously offered His blessing and added a puzzling clue:

You will know that you have reached your new home
When rain falls from a clear sky.

An expedition leader is a busy man. Although the clue meant nothing to him, Phalanthos did not resort to the professional interpreters serving in and around the temple. The oracle had offered its blessing, and this is what mattered.

The adventurers set sail. In time they approached the coast of southern Italy. The rich landscape drew them into one verdant natural harbor after another as they sought a suitable place for settlement, but everywhere they encountered fierce tribesmen who forced them offshore. Patience began to run short. Disease was taking its toll. The expedition seemed destined for failure.

Landing unobserved at a particularly inviting spot, Phalanthos could no longer find the courage that had sustained him for so long. He flung himself on the ground in despair. His wife, Aithra, came to his aid. Sitting beside him, she took his head into her lap to comfort him. Distractedly combing her fingers through his hair, she plucked the lice from it. As if making a dying man's review, he spoke to her of his hopes and disappointment, of all the trials they had faced to no purpose. As she listened to him sorrow, she was moved to tears. Her tears rained down upon him. Opening his eyes, he looked past her face toward the clear blue sky.

And he grasped the meaning of the oracle.[24]

Few tales in the Delphic repertory record such a poignant moment of recognition. Similarly, there are few signs of easy intimacy between men and women. The tale is rare.

Phalanthos founded Tarentum. The Tarentines of a later generation faced, in turn, a challenge from colonists emigrating, like their forebears, from the regions dominated by Sparta.

A Day and a Night

A clever-minded leader, Leukippos, asked the god at Delphi where it was that he and his colonizing party were destined to settle. Apollo commanded them to sail to Italy and settle that region where they would spend "*a day and a night.*"

As fate would have it, the party made their landfall near Kallipolis, a small port belonging to the people of Tarentum. Leukippos liked everything about the site. As a Greek addressing fellow-Greeks, he found it easy enough to secure permission from the Tarentines to camp there for "a day and a night." And so they did—in fact several days and nights.

Their hosts gradually lost patience. They approached the camp: "You were welcome to camp here for a day and a night. Several days and nights have passed." Offering an opportunistic grammar lesson, Leukippos corrected their memory of the agreement: "You gave your word that we could stay here 'day and night.' For as long as either of these exists—day *or* night—we shall not give up this land."

We do not know what influenced the people of Tarentum to stand back. Perhaps the memory of their own arrival, generations ago, as colonists? Perhaps a sense of kinship despite themselves. The Tarentines accepted them as neighbors.[25]

Explorers setting off with no sure destination valued the oracle's hints about landmarks on the unfamiliar coastlines they surveyed. Artimedes of Chalkis, another intrepid leader, was given a Delphic riddle that served him well.

Where Apsia, Most Sacred River, Falls into the Sea

Like so many other enterprising Greek colonizers, Artimedes of Chalkis asked the Delphic oracle to reveal a sign by which he could recognize the place destined for a new city. And as so often, the god in reply was generous—and enigmatic:

Where Apsia, that most sacred river,
Falls into the sea, and where upon its shore
The female covers the male, found your city.
That land is your gift.

A small indication, and obscure, but Artimedes set sail with confidence that he would recognize the sign. Perhaps a part of what made the oracle's message memorable was its reversal of standard sexual code: men of the era were *not* interested in being covered by their sexual partners—that was passive, an insult to virility.

In due course Artimedes reached the mouth of the Apsia river, but he saw no peasants coupling along the shoreline, no animals or birds coupling, no males covering females, let alone females covering males.

He was puzzled. . . . After a time his distracted gaze fell on a vine entwining a sturdy wild fig tree. The sight was somehow prepossessing. He found his thoughts wandering from the reality at hand to philological matters: "vine" is feminine in Greek, while "fig tree" is masculine. . . . This embrace of vine and fig tree has an almost erotic flavor. . . .

It burst upon him that the oracle was fulfilled.

There were barbarian settlements. War was inevitable. Rising from the place of discovery, he moved energetically among his followers: "Who is ready," he cried, "to win immortal glory in exchange for a mortal life? Who will be first to say, 'I give my life for this generation and generations to come?'"

Throwing the natives back, Artimedes and his followers founded the city of Rhegium.[26]

"Recognition of the place" is a recurrent theme. The oracle characteristically provided a riddling description, and it was up to the expedition leader to solve the riddle through an offbeat perception of landscape features. There is a quality of serious play in the pattern. The ancients did not expect the gods to make matters easy, but they did expect a hint. Without a hint, possibility was too vast. Podaleirios received such a hint. He was not an expedition leader, but he too needed to find his home.

If the Sky Falls

Podaleirios, son of the half-divine founder of medicine, Asklepios, was one of two physicians who served in the Greek camp during the seige of Troy. After the war, Podaleirios made his way from Troy to Delphi to ask where he should settle for the remainder of his life.

Make your home where, if the sky should fall,
You will suffer no harm.

Had you received this message, what would *you* look for? The legendary physician chose to live in a city ringed around by high mountains.[27]

Two heroes of the age of colonization were physically impaired, and both needed special urging from Apollo to accept their missions—a curious configuration, on the whole encouraging.

The Stuttering King

Battus means "stutterer" in Greek, and "king" in the language of Libya. Between these two meanings lies a tale. A young man who came to be known as Battus because he stuttered was born to an aristocratic family on the island of Thera. When he was old enough to set his own course, Battus made the pilgrimage to Delphi to ask the oracle for a cure to his stuttering, which burdened him as he sought his place among the leaders of his community. The Pythia had a surprise in store:

Battus, you come for a voice, but our king, Phoebus Apollo,
Sends you to Libya, sheep country, to found a colony.

Battus could not help but break the tranquillity of the temple with his protest: "My Lord, I have come to consult you about my voice. But you speak of something else, you speak of the impossible. What power do I have to lead a colony into Libya? What strength of hand do I have?" But he could not dissuade the oracle. As if to smother the young man's protests, the Pythia began insistently chanting the god's instructions. Battus attempted to break through, but she offered no further recognition. In utter confusion, he left the temple while the Pythia chanted on.

The confusion continued. Battus returned home, fully prepared to ignore the oracle, but both his own affairs and those of the island deteriorated. Another delegation went to Delphi. Obstinately, the oracle told them that if Battus would do as he was told, things would go better for all concerned. The delegation reported the new message and

> Battus was summarily outfitted with the minimum requirements of a colonist and sent on his way.
>
> He and his comrades managed to find North Africa, but they quickly discovered that they lacked the skill to make a respectable settlement. Rather than insist overmuch, they reembarked and set sail for Thera.
>
> The Thereans were less than warmly receptive, since their return would throw the island back into the cycle of difficulty that their departure had been intended to solve. The islanders launched an attack on the would-be colonists, who decided that the better part of valor was to ship out again.
>
> These lost souls made for North Africa, where they settled on an offshore island that seemed to offer the simplest solution to their dilemma. Not surprisingly, after two years of fitful effort, they left a member of their band on the island while the rest set sail for Delphi, the author of all their woes.
>
> Before the Pythia, they were all explanation. "We have done what you said we must do, and we have nothing to show for it. We have been to Libya, we have founded a colony, and we are miserable." She responded:
>
> *You say that you know Libya better than I do!*
> *You have not been there. I have.*
> *Your knowledge is indeed surprising.*
>
> Our band of settlers returned to their island outpost and picked up their lonely comrade. Then they sailed on to the mainland where, this time, they obeyed the oracle. The city that rose, in time a very great one, was Kyrene.[28]

Like much of the Delphic record in Herodotus, the attitudes and circumstances in this tale were vividly etched in the memories of ancient readers. Plutarch offered this retrospective comment: "Battus had a lisp and a shrill thin voice, but [he] also had the qualities of a king and a statesman and was a man of sense."[29]

Curiously, there is another disabled expedition leader, the hunchback Myskellos. Like Battus, Myskellos came to Delphi for what amounted to medical assistance: he did not expect a cure for his physical deformity, but he was concerned about the difficulty he and his wife were having in conceiving children. The Pythia's exchange with him, over several visits, went far beyond his immediate concerns. It rings out even now.

Receive the Gift

It is said that the hunchback Myskellos came to Delphi to inquire not about a colonizing venture but to seek the oracle's help on a matter close to home: the birth of an heir. The Pythia spoke:

Hunchback Myskellos, you are beloved of Apollo
Who works afar, and He shall give you children.
But this first is His command:
Found great Croton.

Myskellos did not understand. He had presented himself as a desperate and humbled husband. He was being addressed as an *oikistes*, proud leader of a migration. The Pythia was moved to offer a visionary lesson in geography:

To you Apollo Himself now speaks: pay heed.
Here lies the Taphian region
Untouched by plow, and Chalkis there,
And there the home of the Kuretes, sacred soil,
And there the Echinades' islands,
And past them a mighty sea.
Guided by these landmarks,
you cannot miss the Lakinian Headland
Nor sacred Krimise, nor the Aesaros River
By which Croton is destined to rise.

Myskellos organized an expedition and set out for the destined place with good will, but when he put in at the immensely rich city of Sybaris, his will weakened considerably. It seemed only reasonable to him to found his own city a good deal closer to Sybaris than Apollo had planned, since the region of Sybaris offered every advantage. Sybaris itself was proof that events might unfold very favorably.

He returned to the Delphic oracle. "*Hunchback Myskellos,*" said the Pythia,

In seeking things apart from those
That God commands, you seek only tears.
Receive the gift He offers.[30]

We are not quite done with Myskellos, nor he with us. In the following tale, Myskellos is presented not as a reluctant hero but as a very willing one:

Wealth or Health?

The story is told that Archias, future founder of Syracuse, happened to be in Delphi at the same time as Myskellos. They were approaching the oracle for the same purpose: to receive a blessing and guidance before setting out to found new cities. They came together into the presence of the Pythia.

Do you choose wealth or health?

The men grasped at once that they were confronting a great question. The answer would surely determine many things in the future. After long hesitation, Archias spoke: "I choose wealth." And Myskellos: "I prefer health." Thus Apollo granted Syracuse to Archias and Croton to Myskellos.

Croton was a marvelously healthful city in southern Italy. It was spared much of the plague and drought that periodically assailed Greeks elsewhere. Syracuse was one of the most sumptuous cities of the ancient world.[31]

We should not imagine that all necessarily went well with established colonies. They entered into the play of forces that swept the Greek world—a world of endless rivalry between cities. Under these conditions, the competition for rule of the little town of Leuke seems perfectly understandable:

A Ruse

Leuke was founded on a rocky height between the older cities of Kymae and Klazomenae. After the death of its founder, who had deftly managed to preserve Leuke's independence, each of the neighboring cities discovered good reasons why it, and it alone, should be recognized as the paramount power in Leuke.

The first instinct was to make war; the second, to consult the god at Delphi. After some indecisive but sobering skermishes in the field, a truce was declared and a joint embassy dispatched to Delphi to ask which of the two cities was fated to be master of Leuke.

Recognizing that the warring cities would accept some form of competition to settle the matter, the Pythia decreed that each city, on an agreed day, precisely at sunrise, was to send its champions to Leuke. Whichever team arrived first and completed a sacrifice would win the prize.

The people of Kymae calculated that they had a decisive advantage: their city was closer to Leuke. The people of Klazomenae were keen enough to make the same calculation—and another. Choosing by lot a group of colonists from among their own citizens, they secretly founded a daughter-city quite close to Leuke. By the time of the contest, the new "city" was nothing worthy of notice, but even a village served the purpose.

The great day arrived, the sun rose, the champions raced through the streets of Kymae and burst out the gates on the road to Leuke. Meanwhile from the new village a few less hasty champions made their way to Leuke. There, with all proper ceremony, they conducted a sacrifice and won the prize. To commemorate their victory, Klazomenae instituted an annual festival called "Anticipation."

It is unclear to this day whether they won fairly.[32]

There is another tale of conflict, in this instance between a colony and its rivals for sovereignty at sea. The Delphic oracle was consulted only when the play of events released consequences that dwarfed human understanding and demanded the insight of a god.

Justice

The Phokaean colonists on the island of Corsica had become ruthless pirates, preying on the sea lanes of greater powers. The Etruscans and Carthaginians, each a strong maritime power, decided to make common cause against them. They assembled a fleet of 60 ships and sailed to the Sardinian Sea, where the Phokaeans massed 60 ships of their own to engage them. The battle was joined.

By nightfall it was clear that the Phokaeans had carried the day, but no fewer than 40 of their ships had been sunk or drifted helplessly, and the remaining 20, no longer battleworthy, were forced to retreat, leaving many Phokaean sailors to the mercy of the enemy.

Defeated in the battle at large, the allies were only too happy to look for satisfaction elsewhere. They cast lots for possession of the crews of the drifting Phokaean ships. The Etruscans of Agylla won the greatest number. The laws of war condemned these unfortunate Phokaeans to be sold into slavery, but the Agyllaeans were so angry over their defeat that they brought the men ashore and stoned them to death. At last appeased, they flung the corpses into a common grave and thought no more about them.

In the months that followed, every living thing—man or beast—that passed near the makeshift grave became twisted, crippled, paralyzed. The normal way of life in Agylla sputtered to a halt. Nearly every family was touched by an invisible miasma. The city was dying.

The people recognized the angry hand of Justice. They sent a delegation to the Delphic oracle. "What must we do to overcome this calamity?" they asked. "How can we make amends?"

The Pythia replied starkly:

You must institute a religious festival
To honor the Phokaean dead.
You must hold great athletic contests
And stirring horseraces.
Only in this way can they find peace.
Only in this way can you find peace.

So it is even today. The people of Agylla celebrate a splendid yearly festival to honor the Phokaeans, against whom they fought a just war to an unjust conclusion.[33]

9

The Sybarites' Question: Tales of Wisdom and Wrongdoing

In his essays on everything, Ananda Coomaraswamy once paused to savour a first principle of the American Shaker community: we must work, they said, as though we had a thousand years to live, and as though we were to die tomorrow.[1] Framed as a work ethic among these craftsmen and religious seekers, the aphorism encourages endlessly patient craftsmanship and the will to leave nothing undone today. Yet it resonates beyond its workshop context, touches on our relations with time and eternity, suggests a way of life that infuses a brisk daily agenda with a sense of ultimate safety.

The Shakers' saying has echoed in my mind for years. It captures in few words an uncommon view of the human condition, which seems the height of good sense. I had never heard or read anything of the kind elsewhere: like an herb restricted to a certain region and elevation, it appeared to have grown out of the experience of the Shaker workshops, where spirituality and craftsmanship enriched each other. Therefore the surprise of encountering the following words attributed to "the Lord of the Oracle" by the poet Bacchylides, who was old when Socrates was young:

> As a mortal you must have two convictions: that you shall see but one more day's sunlight, and that you shall have fifty years of a life of ample wealth.[2]

The essential identity of this passage from Delphic wisdom and the saying of a rural fellowship, connected only by Bible to the ancient world, is an arresting shred of evidence, reminding us that wisdom is not of one place and time to the exclusion of others, nor is it likely to be much different in one place and another, one time and another. Symbol systems differ, as do source revelations and their subsequent histories—Christian, Buddhist, or Delphic—but they point in much the same direction.

This is a chapter of Delphic tales of wisdom and wrongdoing. Naturally, they have their own genius, but they also focus and animate the common wisdom of the world. One of the most impressive concerns the Sybarites' question.

The Sybarites' Question

Few of us recall that Sybaris was a Greek city on the south Italian coast, which reached its height in the sixth century before our era. But even today we all know that "sybaritic" is a mordant word for those who love luxury. We retain this token of the overwhelming pleasure of life in Sybaris.

The people of Sybaris were worried. How long would their lives remain so pleasant? Perhaps this question disguised just another kind of greed, but they sent one of their best men, Amyris, to ask the Delphic oracle.

Happy, O Sybarite, happy will you be forever
In the abundance you enjoy
For as long as the deathless gods
Are honored in your city.
But were you ever to honor a man
More than a god,
War and destruction shall find you.

Amyris made the return journey to Sybaris with a glad heart. When he solemnly restated the oracle's message, the ensuing debate about its meaning uncovered no danger. It was inconceivable that Sybarites of this or any future generation would honor a man more than a god. Their wealth would endure to the end of time.

One day a householder of the city flew into a rage against one of his slaves. He whipped the man mercilessly. Seizing his opportunity, the slave leapt up and ran for his life to the nearest temple. His incensed master pursued him into the sanctuary, threw him to the ground, continued whipping him. The slave again struggled free and fled, this

> time to the tomb of his master's father. He clung trembling to the monument. His master rushed to the entrance, raised his whip—and lowered it in reverence for his father.
>
> In the year 510, the rival city of Croton leveled Sybaris in a savage attack. After emptying the city of its wealth, they redirected a nearby river to flow over the site.[3]

The people of Sybaris were doomed by their failure, so understandable, to remember the underlying order of things and put first things first. The oracle's command in this tale is conservative. Many clues in ancient writings attest to its conservatism on most matters of behavior. "Follow the norms of the state,"[4] it would advise. Questioned by an embassy of Spartans wavering between courses of action, the Pythia counseled them to remember the oaths they had *already* sworn and assured them that "it would be better and much more desirable to keep them."[5] Similarly, as in the tale of the sanctuary seeker left to the uncertain mercy of Kyme, the oracle would often point out the obvious truth, however difficult that truth might prove to be for the questioner. Yet its calculus of right and wrong, wisdom and folly, was not wholly predictable. Witness the following tale, which tweaks the noses of the Delphians themselves.

The Price of Love

> The wealthy Etruscan city of Spina maintained a Treasury at Delphi in the centuries before the rise of Rome, and in that fabulous Treasury there were exquisite statues of two boys. It happened that a pilgrim to Delphi forgot his pious business there and conceived a passion for one of the boys. He was beside himself. He could think of nothing but the bronze boy. Finally, driven by his passion, he concealed himself in the Treasury at dusk and spent the night of love for which he longed.
>
> Before leaving the next morning, he placed a wreath of finely braided leaves and flowers at the boy's feet as the price of his favors. Unlucky man, as he darted off he was seen by the Treasury's caretakers. When they found the wreath and pieced together the outrage he had committed, they searched for the fellow and arrested him. They had no idea what to do next. There was nothing on the subject in the regulations.
>
> The Delphians were not shy about consulting their oracle. Others might come from great distances to inquire of the god; the Delphians crossed the street. Easy to imagine the watchmen with bunched keys jangling from well-rounded waists as they climb the wide steps to the temple and wait their turn. At last they put their question. The word of God arose from behind the curtain:

Let him go. Let him go,
For he has paid the price.[6]

The transmitter of this tale is a sophisticated Greek scholar of Roman imperial Egypt, and it is quite in character for him to enjoy a risqué tale of the oracle, but his tale is no less a part of the Delphi of the mind than solemn ones. Between the poles of the grave injunction, "Follow the norms of the state," and the laissez-faire advice to "let him go," there are many Delphic tales of wisdom and wrongdoing.

For example, the following tale of strict advice, which takes us back to the legendary early years of Athens.

The Tale of Strict Advice

Some years after the death of their father, King Pandion of Athens, who had been driven into exile by rivals, his four sons marched against the city and recovered the kingship. They wished to share power among themselves, but as time went on Aigios prevailed over his brothers in day-to-day affairs. On the other hand, his brothers had numerous children while his own marriage was barren. He remarried, but destiny continued to deny him offspring. This promised nothing very inviting for the future. In dismay, Aigios made the questioner's journey to Delphi. He asked the god what, if anything, he could do to give birth to an heir.

The bulging mouth of the wineskin, O best of men,
Loose not until you have reached the height of Athens.

Obscure words. . . . They said nothing of children, nothing of wives. With a heavy heart, Aigios began the return journey to Athens. At dusk, it occurred to him to stop for the night with Pittheos, king of Troezen, a man widely acknowledged for learning and subtlety of mind. Perhaps he would understand the oracle's words?

Pittheos and his lovely daughter Aethra received Aigios with pleasure. As the night of congenial drinking and conversation wore on, Aigios felt that the time had come to seek the benefit of his host's wisdom. "Pittheos, my friend," he began, "you know that I have just received counsel from Pythian Apollo—but I have not confessed to you how little I understand the god's meaning. 'The bulging mouth of the wineskin, O best of men, Loose not until you have reached the height of Athens.' I am grateful for the god's compliment—this much I understand. But I do not grasp his larger meaning. You and I have been drinking together, but I do not think the god means anything so plain-spoken as 'refrain from wine'—that is not his way of addressing us."

> Pittheos' eyes brightened. For a moment he seemed to understand the oracle's words, but then he passed his hand over his forehead in puzzlement. He confessed that it made no sense to him, either. "Let us continue drinking," he said warmly, "perhaps the wine will teach us what our own dry thoughts cannot!"
>
> Pittheos had understood at once. He continued to ply Aigios with drink and companionship until his willing victim was thoroughly drunk, and then he did everything necessary to have Aigios sleep with his daughter. His motives? Unknown—perhaps he had long wished for blood kinship with the ruling house of Athens. The result? Well known: from that night of love, in which the "bulging mouth of the wineskin" loosened in more than one sense, was born Theseus, great hero of Athenian legend.
>
> But the god's words were not empty. Many years later, when Theseus was returning in triumph from Crete after slaying the Minotaur, the young adventurer forgot to hoist white sails as he approached Athens by sea, as an agreed signal to his father that all was well. Carelessly, he left aloft the black sails of sorrow with which he had started his voyage. In anguish at what he took to be a sure sign of his son's death, Aigios threw himself from a cliff into the sea.[7]

Aigios's error in interpreting the oracle's words was excess of subtlety. Had he been willing to take the oracle literally, even without understanding the fine points, he would have fared better.

THE MAGNESIANS ARE NOT MY CONCERN

The Sybarites' question and the tale of strict advice have moved us into the realm of Delphic morality. For the most part, the code of conduct proposed by the oracle makes permanent sense, based as it is primarily on concepts of fair dealing and due penance. Great wrongs can often be set right by great acknowledgments. On the other hand, not every sin can be redeemed. Among those to whom the oracle could offer no redemptive path was the Spartan Glaukos, thrust into the role of a banker. The "moral" of his story is obvious, but the highly detailed narrative suggests that Herodotus, who tells the tale, and his ancient audiences were interested not only in the *process* of agreement and its corruption, but also in the vast scale of the oracle's pronouncement, which goes well beyond issuing a judgment on financial fraud.

The Banker's Tale

There lived in Sparta a man named Glaukos who was widely known for integrity and a keen sense of justice. Drawn by his reputation, a Milesian once traveled to Sparta to speak with him about a matter of some importance.

"I am from Miletus," began the stranger, "and I have sought you out, Glaukos, because I too hope to benefit from your good character. Throughout Greece and as far as my native Ionia, people know of your spotless reputation for integrity. I have thought about this—I have thought that Ionia rattles along in a nearly constant state of upheaval, that among us peaceful ownership and undisturbed inheritance cannot be relied upon, while your country is just the opposite, steady and undisturbed. For this reason, I decided that the best course of action—I hope you are willing—is to convert half of my assets into silver and bank the sum with you, knowing that it will be safe with you and a legacy, in time, for my heirs. And so I ask you: are you willing to take these funds into safekeeping? Here is a written record detailing everything I wish to entrust to you. In the future—I really can't say when—members of my family or our representatives will come to you with a duplicate record, and you will know that the sum is to be returned to them. We will reward you very generously for your service at that time."

So spoke the stranger from Miletus. Glaukos accepted the deposit on the terms proposed.

Many years later, the Milesian's sons made the journey to Sparta. They easily found Glaukos, although now he was quite an old man. They showed him the duplicate record, faded but legible, and asked for the return of their father's deposit. Unexpectedly, Glaukos answered:

"You know, I'm an old man. . . . I just can't remember this affair. Your record doesn't jog my memory. I'll go over my accounts, and I'll do the right thing. If I have this money, I'll return it at once. But if I have no records and can't manage to remember what this is all about, I will have to call the matter to the attention of the court, as is our custom. Please be good enough to return to Sparta for my answer, let's say in four months."

Outraged, speechless, the brothers withdrew. They were certain in their hearts that they had lost the family fortune forever. And what of Glaukos? Curious fellow, he went to Delphi to consult the oracle, for the virtuous man that he had been and the grasping one he had become were at war in him. He remembered, remembered very well. No one knows what he was thinking—perhaps that the value of the deposit, held for so long, now equaled the safekeeping payment he should receive.

> At Delphi he asked the god whether he could keep the money by pronouncing a solemn public oath stating that he had never received the Milesian deposit. Perhaps he even explained in the quiet of the temple how he rationalized the whole affair.
>
> *Glaukos, you are free to take an oath*
> *And a profit.*
> *Swear! Do not hesitate! For death also comes*
> *To those who keep their word.*
> *But Oath has a nameless child*
> *Without hands or feet*
> *Who is nonetheless swift in pursuit*
> *Until he seizes all of a man's heirs*
> *and destroys them,*
> *Together with all that is theirs,*
> *While the seed of a man who keeps his word*
> *Grows stronger in each generation.*
>
> When Glaukos heard these relentless words, he begged the god's forgiveness for his error in bringing such a question to Delphi. The Pythia responded with great simplicity:
>
> *To tempt the god and to commit the sin are the same.*
>
> Upon his return to Sparta, Glaukos sent for the Milesians and returned their money. Yet the child without hands or feet found him: his descendants suffered the fate predicted by the oracle.[8]

The clarity of motive, judgment, and consequence in this tale prompted later authors to return to it; it seems to have been one of the best remembered Delphic tales. In his discussion of Philip of Macedon, father of Alexander the Great, Pausanias produces it as a lesson in conduct:

> If Philip had paid attention to Glaukos of Sparta and remembered that verse at each of his actions,
>
> *and the seed of a man who keeps his oath*
> *grows stronger after him,*
>
> I do not believe that a god would so unreasonably have extinguished at a single stroke Alexander's life and with it the power of Macedonia.[9]

Glaukos sought the oracle's ratification of his intended crime. This was rare. More often, individuals and communities sought Delphic counsel *after* events had taken a disastrous turn and they had reached their wits' end. Herodotus tells such a tale:

A Heavy Price

Euenius' story was an odd one, and I will here relate it. In Apollonia there is a flock of sheep sacred to the sun; during the daytime these sheep graze along the banks of the river which rises on Mt. Lacmon and, after running through Apollonian territory, joins the sea by the harbor of Oricus. At night, however, they are looked after by men specially chosen from the wealthiest and most distinguished families—each man having one year's spell of duty. The people of Apollonia value these sheep very highly because of an oracle they once received concerning them. The place where they are penned for the night is a cave, a long way from the town, and here it was that Euenius, who had been chosen for the task, was keeping watch. One night he fell asleep on duty, and some wolves got in and killed about sixty of the sheep. When, on waking, he saw what had happened, Euenius kept silent and told nobody about it, intending to buy some more sheep to make good the losses. But the people of the town got to know of the disaster, and at once brought the culprit to trial and condemned him to have his eyes put out for sleeping at his post. The sentence was carried out, and immediately afterwards the sacred ewes had no more lambs, and the land ceased to produce the normal harvests.

The oracles both at Dodona and Delphi were consulted upon the reason for this calamity, and the answer in each case was that it was due to the fact that Euenius, the guardian of the sacred sheep, had been unjustly deprived of his sight: it was the gods themselves who had set the wolves on the sheep, and they would continue to punish the people of Apollonia for the wrong they had done Euenius, until they made him such amends as he himself might choose. And when this was done, they, too, would give him something, for the possession of which many men would call him blessed.

The people of the town did not make this oracle generally known, but instructed certain men to carry out the arrangements with Euenius, which they did in the following way. They went up to him as he was sitting on a bench, and, taking their seats beside him, entered into conversation on various topics, leading up to an expression of sympathy for his misfortune. Having thus drawn him on, they asked him what he would choose by way of reparation, should the townspeople undertake to offer it. Euenius, who knew nothing of the oracle, replied that if he were given So-and-so's land (naming the men whom he knew to possess the two best estates in the community), and a certain house, which he also knew was the finest in the town, he would consider that adequate reparation had been made, and would bear no further resentment. "Euenius," came the answer, "the citizens of Apollonia will grant what

> you ask, in compensation for the loss of your eyes, according to the advice of the oracle."
>
> On learning the whole story, Euenius was angry at what he considered to be the deception which had been practiced on him. The townspeople, however, bought the house and the two estates from their owners, and gave them to him; and immediately afterwards he found that he had the power of divination—just as if it had always been there—so that he became a famous man.[10]

This tale may be viewed as the account of a seer's initiation, thrown off course by the Apollonians' vindictive judgment and retrieved by the gods through messages from Delphi and Dodona. On the other hand, it was not out of character for the gods to blind the human vessel predestined to become a seer. Locally, the tradition goes back to blind Homer, the bard of the Greeks, and in worldwide myth and folklore the condition of physical blindness underscores the special character of a seer's second sight by giving material form to the spiritual reality of a seer's detachment: he or she tells truth, without regard to appearances or personal advantage. Teiresias, seer of ancient Thebes in the legendary era of Oedipus, was blinded by the gods for an unintended transgression. By sending wolves to attack the sacred herd, the gods were evidently putting Euenius's fate "in play"; they had great plans for him, he would suffer accordingly. After events seemingly went awry, they resorted to the primitive but persuasive means of inducing general agricultural failure. When the suffering city inquired at the oracles, the gods could resume control, the enactment of due penance could unfold through a colorful process of bargaining, and Euenius could go on to become the man they had foreseen.

But the ambiguity of this sequence of events is hardly lost on us. Since the gods sometimes blinded their chosen seers, were they, after all, behind the pattern of events? Was it the Apollonians' judgment in court, or theirs? How many lessons from divine tutors are being taught here? As Herodotus observed, the tale is an odd one.

There is a comparable sense of entangled wills, human and divine, in the tale of Lame Labda's son, which again we have through Herodotus.

Lame Labda's Son: A Tale of Corinth

> The city of Corinth was dominated by a ruling class whose grown children were guided by the elders to marry exclusively among one another. One of this fortunate few, Amphion, had a lame daughter

named Labda who was overlooked in the calculation of marriage partners. Sadly, no one wanted her. Finally a husband was found in Eetion, son of Echekrates, of the outlying township of Petra. He was something of a country bumpkin, but under the circumstances he would do.

As time went on, Eetion had no children either by Lame Labda or by any other woman. He was concerned, so much so that he made the journey to Delphi to ask what might be done. As he entered the temple, the Pythia addressed him at once without waiting for the customary question:

> *Eetion, you are rich in honor, yet no one honors you.*
> *Labda will conceive, and she shall bear a rolling rock*
> *That will fall upon the princes and mete out justice in Corinth.*

There is no record of how Eetion received these ominous words, but it is easy to imagine that he had grievances against the grandees of Corinth. He could not have been displeased. On the other hand, thanks to what must have been a well-developed spy network at Delphi, the oracle's words found their way back to Corinth. The leading men were reminded of an earlier oracular message about their city, which had puzzled the best minds at the time but now seemed all too clear:

> *An eagle shall breed in the rocks*
> *And give birth to a lion,*
> *A savage eater of raw flesh.*
> *He shall loosen the knees of many.*
> *Men of Corinth, be warned.*

Perhaps the child foreseen by the oracle was this "savage eater of raw flesh." It was possible.

The top men secretly decided to do away with the child as soon as possible after its birth. When they heard that the child was born, they sent ten of their number on the heartless errand. Entering the courtyard of Eetion's home in Petra, they asked pleasantly to see the baby. Labda had no reason to fear them. She thought they might have come out of good will toward her husband. She brought the baby out of the house and placed it gently in the arms of one of the visitors.

Now was the time to act. They had agreed that whichever of them had his hands on the child first would smash it to the ground. But just as the one holding it was about to do the deed, providence intervened: the child smiled at him. The would-be murderer melted. He couldn't harm it. He handed the child to a second man, and the second to a third. The child passed from hand to hand around the circle. No one could bring himself to harm it. With the compliments you might expect, they returned her baby safely to Labda and withdrew.

Just outside the courtyard gate, moods suddenly changed for the worse. The men berated each other for hesitating, especially the one who had first held the child. After calming down, they decided to go in again. This time, all of them would share in the murder.

But fate had determined that evil would flourish in Corinth through this child. Standing unseen on the other side of the gate, Lame Labda had heard everything. She was sure now that they would shame each other into doing what they had come to do, and so she took her baby and hid him in the most unlikely place, a chest. The men returned. Not bothering to conceal their intentions, they searched everywhere. But the child was nowhere to be found. They counseled with one another and decided to abandon—but to tell their peers in Corinth that the raid was a success. And so they did.

Eetion's son grew up peacefully. Because he had found safety in a chest, he was given the nickname Kypselos. When he grew to manhood, he consulted the Delphic oracle about his future and received a message that encouraged his greatest ambition: to raise an army against Corinth and make the city his own. The Pythia spoke as follows to him:

Happy is this man who enters my palace,
Kypselos Eetides, king of renowned Corinth.
Happy you and your sons.
But not your sons' sons.

This was the oracle's message, and it was enough for Kypselos, who lived for the moment, not the future. He soon held absolute power in Corinth—and drove his adversaries into exile, murdered them, stripped them of their wealth. Kypselos reigned thirty years and died a happy man, with a son to succeed him.[11]

Kypselos represents something like a fever, and the gods are not prepared to spare the body politic its experience of fever. They seem to be of two minds about him: he will "mete out justice," but he is a "savage eater" whose line is not destined to continue beyond the third generation. The tale comes to life through its awkward encounter between the men of Corinth and Lame Labda: the transformation of their stark political mission into a courtesy call is deeply comical, while Labda's maternal protection of the child has the taste of tragedy averted. Perhaps there was another solution to this puzzle, which the gods created through their oracular messages, but no one was astute enough to find it. The rolling rock broke free.

The gods' wishes are ambiguous in the tale of Lame Labda. But in many Delphic tales of wrongdoing and the setting right of wrongs, the oracle is as clear as can be.

Crow's Tale

"Crow" (this was his *nom de guerre*) was a seventh-century warrior who met in battle an adversary named Archilochos (perhaps also a *nom de guerre*—it means First Sergeant). Like Crow, Archilochos was a veteran of many campaigns. He was also a poet famous in his own day, known to us even now through wonderfully arch and fragrant verse fragments.

I weep that the people of Thasos
Are in trouble;
The Magnesians
Are not my concern.[12]

So he spoke as a warrior, with acute recognition of his irony. As a lover, he spoke no less well:

I said no more, but took her hand,
Laid her down in a thousand flowers,
And put my soft wool cloak around her.
I slid my arm under her neck
To still the fear in her eyes,
For she was trembling like a fawn.[13]

It was this man whom Crow fought and killed on a campaign day like any other. He did not know whom he had killed. There was no reason to know the name and quality of an enemy soldier. But later, when people mourned the warrior-poet's death, he realized what he had done. In the spirit of Archilochos himself, Crow must have felt in response that "the Magnesians are not my concern"—the fortunes of war are what they are.

But not even in death do the gods forget the good. Apollo could not overlook his death. The day arrived when Crow made his way to Delphi to ask certain questions. As soon as he entered the temple, the Pythia called out to him:

You have killed the Muses' servant!
You must leave at once!

Crow was unwilling to be driven off so easily. He made his case before the Pythia and the assembled priests. "You must respect the fortunes of war, as I do. Had I not killed Archilochos, he would have killed me—of that there is no doubt. I am not an evil-doer. On the day of battle,

> your 'servant of the Muses' was a faceless adversary with blood on his sword. I did not wish to add my blood." Yet Crow cursed the day he met Archilochos. In the presence of the sacred company, he solemnly swore that, had he known, he would have preferred his own death to the poet's.
>
> Apollo was moved to compassion. The Pythia spoke:
>
> *Go to Taenaros where Archilochos is buried,*
> *And give peace to his soul with libations.*
> *Then you shall be received in this temple.*
>
> The good soldier obeyed—and earned his release from the wrath of Apollo, Leader of the Muses.[14]

Few Delphic tales reflect the life of the temple or the inevitable improvisation that attends any human activity. In Crow's tale, the steady ritual of inquiry at the temple is broken, the priests and the Pythia abandon station to gather in debate around Crow. The heavenly court becomes a human one. And the problem is solved as so many problems must be, by groping, until the god intervenes. Apollo's decision casts Him as a participant in the drama, willing to reverse Himself in response to obvious and painful sincerity. Crow is not devious like Glaukos. Penance and the renewal of his purity remain within reach.

The Delphic oracle did not look kindly upon deviousness. The most pungent tale on this theme is a short but memorable one from Aesop, the sixth-century spinner of fables.

The Fall of a Sparrow

> A malicious but cunning man made a bet with one of his cronies: he could prove beyond doubt that the Delphic oracle is all guesswork, that it sees nothing of the truth of things. On the agreed day he captured a sparrow, hid it under his cloak, and made his way to the temple. In time he came before the oracle and asked: "Is the object in my hand living or dead?" Were the Pythia to say that it is dead, he had decided to produce the living sparrow. Were she to say that it is alive, he would crush the bird instantly and produce it dead for all to see.
>
> But Apollo saw through him. The Pythia spoke:
>
> *Enough! For it depends on you alone*
> *Whether what you have in hand lives or dies.*
>
> The Divine cannot be taken by surprise.[15]

The legendary life of Aesop is strangely bound up with Delphi.[16] The storyteller became the subject of a late classical novella comparable in its deliciously sly humor, plainspoken wisdom, and raciness to that ultimate masterpiece of storytelling, the *Arabian Nights*. The novella depicts Aesop at the height of his fame, wandering from court to court like a minstrel, bringing tales and inspired common sense. He was curious to visit Delphi, and finally did so. He came not as an inquirer but as the Mark Twain of the ancient world, a public speaker comfortable on any platform. In return, he expected and was typically offered handsome fees. The Delphians enjoyed him—who didn't?—but when the time came to pay for their pleasure, they suddenly displayed the miserliness for which the ancients sometimes mocked them. Never slow to speak his mind, Aesop offered the following instructive comparison:

> "Men of Delphi, you are like a piece of driftwood floating on the sea; when we see it at a great distance, tossing on the waves, we think it is something worthwhile, but then when we approach and come to it, we find that it is a very insignificant thing of no value. So it has been with me; when I was far away from your city, I was impressed with you as men of wealth and generosity, but now that I see you are inferior to other men in your breeding and in your city, I recognize that I was mistaken. I shall carry away a bad impression of you."[17]

He added other insults. The Delphians, counseling privately, decided that the man had to be stopped for fear that he would damage their reputation in the world at large. They decided to frame Aesop by hiding a temple treasure among his belongings and then arresting him for theft. As he struggled to escape the circle closing in on him, there ensued a remarkable sequence in which, like Scheherazade, he told tale after tale in an effort—ultimately vain—to change the Delphians' minds. When all was lost and he stood at the edge of the cliff from which they meant to throw him, he continued telling tales, now to mock them and warn them of the punishment sure to overtake them. Then he leaped over. The Delphians were indeed soon punished by a divinely ordained famine and by human avengers from many places in the ancient world, who knew the value of Aesop. In the spiritual economy of the ancient world, the Delphians themselves did not escape censure for wrongdoing.

The Delphic oracle and its peers conveyed in their answers an authority well beyond that of human institutions. A hint of this authority, transcending even that of kings, is preserved in a haunting detail from Plutarch.

Message of the Shooting Star

> Every year the elected leaders of Sparta, who serve the two hereditary kings, select a clear and moonless night, and sit out in silence to watch the face of the heavens. If a star shoots across the sky, they take it as a sign that their kings have erred in their dealings with the gods and suspend them from office until an oracle from Delphi or Olympia comes to the aid of kings thus found guilty.[18]

Overseen with dedication by the ephors, the dual kingship of Sparta was, according to Spartan legend, the joint creation of a solicitous queen mother and the Delphic oracle. Its origin tale is a classic example of the imperious need to *complete the oracle* through one's own ingenuity.

Adding Cleverness to Wisdom

> The Spartans held their first king, Aristodemos, in highest honor: he had led them to the region where they were to flourish for many centuries. Soon after they settled, Aristodemos' wife gave birth to twins, but the king lived scarcely long enough to see them born before he fell sick and died. The Spartans decided to make the elder of the twins their king, but soon realized that they had no idea which was which: the boys were identical in all respects. Naturally, they turned to the mother. Which is older? Which is our king? She replied that she had no idea herself. In fact, she knew very well but nursed the hope that the boys could share the kingship.
>
> The Spartans were at a loss. In their anxiety, they sent an embassy to Delphi. The Pythia instructed:
>
> *Make both children king—*
> *But honor more the elder.*
>
> Her words still left them in confusion because they had no idea which child was the elder whom they should honor more. The Pythia had set a goal but provided no means of attaining it.
>
> At this moment of crisis, a man from Messenia made a clever suggestion: they should watch the queen mother secretly to discover which of the twins she washed and fed first. Were she found to be caring for the children always in the same order, then the Spartans

> would know beyond reasonable doubt their order of birth. On the other hand, if she made no distinction, then it would be obvious that she really did have no idea which was firstborn. In that case, the Spartans would just have to think of something else.
>
> In keeping with this proposal, the Spartans secretly observed the queen mother—and discovered that she invariably looked after the needs of one of the boys first. Now they knew which young king was to be more honored.
>
> From that time forward, dual kingship was the rule in Sparta.[19]

The outcome of this tale is happy in all respects: the Spartans found their foremost king, the oracle's message was respected, the queen mother's wish was fulfilled. There is another tale—an anecdote, really, but powerful—in which multiple rule takes shape under the darkest of clouds. It is a tale in which the partnership between Pythian Apollo and those who come to question Him is made dramatically clear.

To Their Sorrow, Then

> When Deinomenes of Sicily asked about his sons' futures, the answer was that all three should rule as tyrants. Deinomenes replied, "To their sorrow, then, O Lord Apollo." The god said that he granted this also, and added it to the response.[20]

I know of no sadder Delphic tale; it has the taste of ashes.

CHARLATANS AND SEERS

Plutarch was not especially given to protest, but he drew the line at Onomakritos and his like. Such men were "oraclemongers," specialists in retailing oracular messages to a paying public that ranged from kings to peasants. "I forbear to mention," writes Plutarch without much forbearance,

> how much blame men like Onomakritos, Prodikos, and Kinaethon have brought upon themselves from the oracles by foisting upon them a tragic diction and a grandiloquence of which they had no need, nor have I any kindly feeling toward their changes.
>
> However, the thing that most filled the poetic art with disrepute was the tribe of wandering soothsayers and rogues that practiced their charlatanry about the shrines of the Great Mother and of Serapis, making up oracles, some using their own ingenuity, others taking by

> lot from certain treatises oracles for the benefit of servants and women, who are most enticed by verse and a poetic vocabulary.[21]

So there was riffraff: versifiers, already encountered at Delphi, who dressed up oracular messages in finer words; counterfeiters; most notoriously, collectors who "recycled" oracular messages by one method or another—Plutarch mentions drawing lots—to satisfy the needs of clients. The concept was that oracular messages retained value over time. By insight or method, an expert could identify the applicable message and reinterpret it.

Some oraclemongers had collections "from Bakis," a name that scholars now take to indicate not a specific early seer but rather an ancient status: certain women were designated "Sibyl," certain men were designated "Bakis." Others had scrolls inscribed with the oracular messages of Mousaios—a pupil, they say, of the ancient poet and wonder-working musician Orpheus. Onomakritos was the possessor of such a collection and drew considerable attention in later sixth-century Athens when he "edited" Mousaios for contemporary use. To his misfortune, he was discovered interpolating material into the collection that did not belong, and was summarily banished from Athens. We pick up his trail in Persia some years later in the service of the Great King Xerxes, who was contemplating war against the Greek cities. Onomakritos attended Xerxes in the company of traitorous Athenian exiles who hoped to ride with the king's army to power:

> Whenever he came into the King's presence, [the exiles] would make very solemn reports of him, and he would give readings of some of his oracles. If there was among these one that bore on some defeat of the barbarian, nothing was said of that; he picked out the most fortunate, spoke of the bridging of the Hellespont (to be done by a Persian), and sketched the course of the invasion. This man, with his oraclemongering, made great assaults on Xerxes.[22]

Curiously, in this world of freelance talent lying well past the sacred precincts of the institutional oracles, there were not only opportunists, down-at-heel scholars, and rascals. There were also true seers and sages who acted strictly for the welfare of their fellowmen. Some, of unknown affiliation and background, left traces in ancient literature that even today ring with authenticity. We cannot quite decipher what they were or sort fact from fiction, but there are enough reports to persuade us that wandering sage and compassionate seer were archetypes well filled, and well served, in ancient Greece.[23] The legendary blind seer of Thebes, Teiresias, comes at once to mind, as do Mopsos and Kalchas, both of the era of the Trojan War.

> . . . what the Lord Teiresias
> sees, is most often what the Lord Apollo
> sees.[24]

These are words of the Chorus in Sophocles' *Oedipus Tyrannos*, endorsing reliance on Teiresias to uncover the cause of the plague afflicting Thebes under Oedipus' rule—interesting words because they nearly equate the insight of a saintly and gifted human being with that of an oracular god. Teiresias is a figure of legend, but the type persisted in historical times, for example the wandering sage and healer, Apollonius of Tyana, whom we have already encountered. He is said to have gone to Delphi and other oracular temples and "corrected the rites" in each place. The priests willingly drew around him for instruction.[25]

Some few stood close to Apollo. And many, although they pretended, did not. In this respect Hipparchos was far from the worst offender. He is said to have pitted his own wisdom against that of Delphi. Coruler in Athens during the lifetime of the oraclemonger Onomakritos, he is remembered for his patronage of the arts and crafts but also for the following odd venture.

Delphi's Competitor

> It mattered to Hipparchos, coruler of Athens in the late sixth century, to be admired for his wisdom. Athenians living in the city were won over. But that left a sizable suburban and rural population who knew not Hipparchos, at least not in the way he wished. He decided to remedy this difficulty. It had long been the custom to commemorate events and preserve important inscriptions on so-called herms—partially sculpted images, sometimes of the god Hermes, sometimes of honored persons, which had flat surfaces suitable for inscription. Hipparchos contracted with stonecarvers to set up herms at the halfway point on every road from Athens to outlying communities, each inscribed with a maxim that generously shared his wisdom with passersby. His name was included to leave no doubt of authorship. Hipparchos went so far as to hope that Athenians reading these words would think them superior to the wisdom of Delphi—to "Know thyself," "Nothing too much," and other familiar sayings. One side of the

> herm reported travelers' information: you are halfway from Athens to the town of. . . . The other side was tutorial:
>
> This is a reminder of Hipparchos: As you walk, think righteous things.
>
> On the road to Steiria, there was another:
>
> This is a reminder of Hipparchos: Deceive not a friend.
>
> Was this the birth of propaganda?[26]

Hipparchos was more high-minded than the professional oraclemongers. Aristophanes, the comic playwright, is a wonderful source of insight into the hustling demimonde that lived in the long shadow of Delphi and its sister institutions. Two of his vividly characterized oraclemongers—Hierocles in *Peace*, and an unnamed role in *The Birds*—have unusually sensitive nostrils: they show up just as a sacrifice gets under way, with its promise of a banquet. In the first of these plays, a worthy Athenian farmer, Trygaeus, is supervising a sacrifice to Peace at a time when a treaty with Sparta is imminent:

Trygaeus: I see someone coming. He's got a laurel wreath on his head.
Slave: Who is he? Some kind of puffed-up quack, I can see that. Is he an omen expert?
Trygaeus: Not quite. It's Hierocles the oraclemonger. Let's pretend not to see him.
Hierocles: What is this sacrifice and to whom is it being made? [They ignore him.]
Hierocles: Begin carving, and let me have the priest's dues.
Trygaeus: Do you know what you can do?
Hierocles: If you'll be so kind as to tell me.
Trygaeus: Keep your mouth shut. We are in the middle of a sacrifice to Peace.
Hierocles: [ignoring him]: *Who in their folly, not knowing th'inscrutable purpose of heaven,*
Rashly, though human, made peace with the golden-eyed monkeys of Sparta—
Trygaeus: Ha! ha! ha!
Hierocles: What, may I ask, is amusing you?
Trygaeus: Golden-eyed monkeys! Ha! ha! ha!
Hierocles: *You like storm-fearing petrels are trusting the word of the foxes,*
Treacherous of heart and treacherous of mind—
Trygaeus: This meat is roasting beautifully. I hope the same happens to your windbag lungs!

Hierocles: *For if the Nymphs tell the truth unto Bakis and Bakis to mortals,*
And if the Nymphs tell the truth unto Bakis—
Trygaeus: One more Bakis and I'll murder you!
[They discuss the wisdom of making peace with Sparta. Hierocles challenges Trygaeus to think of an oracular message that justifies the peace treaty. Trygaeus recites a passage from Homer but concludes:]
And to the oraclemonger a cup was given by *no one*!
Hierocles: That's a fake! That's not in the Sybilline collection.
[The encounter reduces to a brawl.]
Hierocles: Help! Assault! Is there a witness? Help!
Trygaeus: Yes, I'm a witness! I witness that you're a greedy swine who talks a lot of rot![27]

Much the same good-humored mockery occurs in *The Birds*, where the scene is another interrupted sacrifice.[28] The third sortie by Aristophanes, in *The Knights*, is a marvelously droll contest between two opportunists seeking the favor of a character named "Demos" or People—the people of Athens. Each of them "throws Sibylline dust in master's eyes." Asked what his oracles are about, the first character assures Demos that they cover "all sorts of things: Athens, Pylos, you, me, everything." Not to be outdone, the second character replies to the same question as follows: "All sorts of things: Athens, lentil soup, Sparta, fresh mackerel, dealers wots give short measure of barley, you, me—."[29] The second list is clearly superior.

Aristophanes shows how some of the good people of Athens kept oraclemongers at bay, but there was, quite apart from comedy, a perennial audience for them. In the late sixth century we met Onomakritos in Persia, where business was obviously good. Some one hundred years later, Thucydides wrote that when a Spartan army was marching on Athens, "professional prophets came forward with prophecies of all kinds, which were eagerly listened to by the various parties."[30] And many centuries after Thucydides, at the height of the Roman Empire, the comic poet Juvenal could write of

fortune-tellers, Armenians, Syrians,
Who'll pry out the steaming lungs of a pigeon, predict
A young lover for the lady, or a good fat inheritance
From some childless millionaire. They'll probe a chicken's
Bosom, unravel the guts of a puppy. . . .
Chaldean astrologers
Will inspire more confidence: their every pronouncement
Is a straight tip, clients believe, from the oracular fountain

> Of Ammon. (Now that Delphi has fallen silent
> The human race is condemned to murky unknowing.)[31]

It is all tongue in cheek—but taken from life, the life that fascinated the Italian filmmaker Federico Fellini, who created unforgettable images of the thickly sensual, cynical world of Juvenal and other Roman satirists. If Delphi was the temple on the mount, there was much else besides.

Juvenal's younger contemporary, Lucian, dedicated a work of what amounts to investigative journalism to an especially celebrated rogue whom he had personally met: Alexander, dubbed "the false prophet." While Lucian's richly detailed account is too long to include at length, some of his observations will help us understand the demimonde surrounding the great oracles. Alexander could not have been more striking:

> He was tall and handsome in appearance, and really godlike; his skin was fair, his beard not very thick; his long hair was in part natural, in part false, but very similar, so that most people did not detect that it was not his own. His eyes shone with a great glow of fervor and enthusiasm; his voice was at once very sweet and very clear. In understanding, quick-wittedness, and penetration he was far beyond everyone else; and activity of mind, readiness to learn, retentiveness, natural aptitude for studies—all these qualities were his. But he made the worst possible use of them. In sum, imagine a highly diversified soul-blend, made up of lying, trickery, perjury and malice; facile, audacious, adventuresome, diligent in the execution of its schemes, plausible, convincing, masking as good, and wearing an appearance absolutely opposite to its purpose.[32]

Alexander formed a partnership with another fellow, and together they reasoned with nasty but impressive realism about the hidden forces that actually animated their fellowmen:

> They readily discerned that human life is swayed by two great tyrants, hope and fear, and that a man who could use both of these to advantage would speedily enrich himself. For they perceived that both to one who fears and to one who hopes, foreknowledge is very essential and keenly coveted, and that long ago not only Delphi but Delos and Klaros and Branchidae had become rich and famous because, thanks to the tyrants just mentioned, hope and fear, men continually visited their sanctuaries and sought to learn the future in advance, and to that end sacrificed and dedicated ingots of gold. By turning all this round and round and keeping it astir, they concocted the project of founding a prophetic shrine and oracle, hoping that if they should succeed in it, they would be rich.[33]

Their scheme succeeded beyond expectation; it was not long before they were established in a temple of their own—built at municipal expense by the city of Chalcedon—and pilgrims were flowing in from far and wide to consult what they took to be a grandson of Asclepius, the god of healing. The oracle became a thriving institution, with a full staff of "assistants, servants, collectors of information, writers of oracles, custodians of oracles, clerks, sealers, and expounders."[34] The expounders were charged a fee for the privilege of occupying their lucrative positions at the temple. And there were additional employees, for example publicists sent to distant places to talk up the oracle and a corps of spies who gathered intelligence that could be recast as divine messages. Among other fine calculations, to win the friendship of the established oracles Alexander would occasionally recommend that a pilgrim go to one of the Apollo oracles to inquire further. The carnival lasted for decades. Many doubted and mocked Alexander, but others flocked to him from as far away as Rome. Lucian presents all this as the greatest scam of antiquity. Alexander's oracle at Chalcedon was the diabolical mirror image of Delphi.

Wherever there are sages there will be charlatans, wherever there are authentic oracles there will be shams. A tradition of this type throws a shadow of that type. To this point, there was a tale that concludes with a proverb surprisingly familiar in form.

"Many cast lots . . ."

> They say that divination by casting lots—sorting beads or some other set of indicators—was invented by Athena. It wasn't long before the method became so popular under Her divine guidance that it overshadowed the Delphic oracle.
>
> This was not to Apollo's liking. He complained to His father. After deliberating, Zeus decided to undermine the practice of casting lots. His influence went out over the world—and ever after, the results yielded by lot were flawed, untrustworthy, outright lies.
>
> Some time after this divine intervention, a band of inquirers came to Delphi to ask what had happened. The Pythia replied:
>
> *Many cast lots, few are seers.*[35]

10

One Golden Celery Plant: A Delphic Audit

Delphi was, overwhelmingly, a city of art. "When we arrived in Apollo's famous territory," recalled a messenger in one of the plays of Euripides,

> We spent three entire days, from dawn to dark,
> Filling our eyes with all there was to see.[1]

Delphi was the attic of the ancient Greeks, not their sole attic but arguably the richest and most mysterious. Donors' offerings from long ago—once transparent statements of piety or victory, of a holy symbol or of events in which Apollo had a hand—could lose their transparency over time. A later generation of Greeks would be left to guess their meaning in a serious game that engaged, for example, Plutarch and his friends in the first century C.E. And while such weighty inquirers probed the more enigmatic monuments, a fraternity of paid guides swarmed the temple grounds with their pilgrim clientele, explaining everything in the absent patter that has not changed to this day. Herewith a selective audit of art at Delphi, which none of us can see except through story, for apart from a few fragmentary survivals, all of these works are long since lost.

One Golden Celery Plant (*selinos*). Gift of the people of Selinos. An admirably straightforward, modest self-representation, as if the people of New York City had sent a Big Apple.[2]

One Statue of Alexander the Great. Before which Kassander trembled. In the embattled years following the death of Alexander, one of his generals, Kassander, consolidated his hold on Macedonia and much of Greece by ruthless measures, including the murder of Alexander's family. Long after these events, Kassander was one day walking about Delphi surveying its statues when he came upon this image of Alexander. At the sight of it, he began to shudder, his head swam, he could scarcely recover.[3]

One Golden Statue of the Sophist Gorgias. Erected by the gentleman himself, a contemporary of Socrates and Plato. Mocked by Plato, according to ancient anecdote. Admired grudgingly by others. The facts of this ancient controversy concerning personal vanity and the uses of a sacred place can still be pieced together. Gorgias was a rich, famous, and long-lived teacher of "the art of persuasion," as he defined his calling in a Platonic dialogue named for him. From their first moment of encounter in that dialogue, Socrates cunningly casts doubt on Gorgias's integrity.

"Chaerophon," Socrates urges his pupil when they come upon Gorgias in the marketplace, "ask him."

"Ask him what?" "Who he is."[4]

At some point in Gorgias's illustrious career, he dedicated a statue at Delphi, depicting not a god or a moment of civic triumph for his native city, Leontini, but rather himself. Pausanias at Delphi does not miss the point when he observes with admirable economy that "the gilded portrait dedicated by Gorgias of Leontini is Gorgias himself."[5] Pliny the Elder reports that this statue was regarded, at least by some, as the first "solid gold statue of a human being," and he immediately editorializes, "So great were the profits to be made by the art of oratory!"[6] According to anecdote, Plato sneered at raising a statue to oneself: "The good and golden Gorgias has come to us," he is reputed to have let slip when they met.[7]

For his part, Dio the Golden-Mouthed once referred sympathetically to the problem of Gorgias's statue in a model courtroom summation. "One might urge many reasons," he argued, "in support of the claim that Gorgias the sophist should not have a statue at Delphi, and what's more, a statue on a lofty base and made of gold. However, while it is possibly legitimate to object at the outset, to try later to cancel the resolution authorizing the erection of a statue is a grievous wrong. Once statues have been erected they hold their position rightfully. What an absolutely crazy government it is whose statues are annuals, like crops!"[8]

A Golden Image of Phryne. Famous fourth-century courtesan who modeled for the sculptor Praxiteles. Created by Praxiteles and dedicated by herself, according to Pausanias[9]—but according to other sources, dedicated by her admirers. Dio pointed out the kinship between the golden statue of Gorgias and that of Phryne: how can you fret over Gorgias's dedication, he asked in his courtroom appeal, "when you may see [at Delphi] even Phryne of Thespiae, perched on a pillar like Gorgias?"[10]

Great is her glory, said Pericles, "of whom there is least talk among men whether in praise or in blame"[11]—his sentiment reflecting the Athenian and broadly Greek view of his era. In a society that with few exceptions restricted women to the home, if you wanted a conversation with a woman of wide experience and original opinions, you were more likely to find her among the sophisticated *hetaerai*, or courtesans, than in the women's quarters of the homes of the well-born. You might also have found her among educated priestesses who were exposed to a richer sample of the world—for example, Plutarch's friend Klea, whom we have already met. She was a woman who "had kept company with books,"[12] as he put it. Priestess or prostitute, marginalized upward or downward, women such as Klea and Phryne made their marks on the imagination of the Greeks.

The golden statue of Phryne at Delphi has long since vanished. We can recapture something of its svelte beauty through surviving copies of another Praxitelean masterpiece for which Phryne is said to have modeled, the nude Aphrodite "that many people sailed to Knidos to see,"[13] in which sensual warmth and cool distance must have been unforgettably blended by Praxiteles under the inspiration of his sacred subject and his nearby friend. However beautiful the golden Phryne at Delphi surely was, it fell victim to a fundamentalist graffiti attack from an unexpected quarter, the Cynic philosopher Diogenes. He is said to have scrawled across its base a new dedication: "From the boundless passion of the Greeks."[14]

Phryne once asked Praxiteles which of his works he considered most beautiful of all. He wouldn't answer—but promised that if she could guess, he would give it to her. She was stumped. A few days later, when Praxiteles was chatting amiably with her, one of her servants came rushing in with terrible news: Praxiteles' studio had caught fire, everything was going up in flames. "No!" cried the master sculptor as he rushed out the door, "if I lose the Satyr and the little Eros, I'll have worked all these years for nothing!" Phryne called him back, calmed him down. It had just been a ruse to trap him into revealing his masterpiece.[15]

The golden statue of Phryne at Delphi: first monument to the independent identity and freely disposed power of women.[16]

Bronze Portrait of a Very Old Man. His flesh sunken, mere skin and bones. A dedication by the people of Delphi, perhaps to Hippocrates.[17] Admirable counterpoint to the overwhelming physical beauty of the image of Phryne and to the intellectual pride of Gorgias. Without calculation or coherent instructional intent, Delphic art mirrored the whole that Greece was.

An Uncarved Natural Stone. Not quite a boulder, anointed daily with oil and piously offered unspun wool at every festival. A relic of most ancient times, testament to the reality of myth.

Rhea, beloved of Kronos, second ruler of the gods in the era preceding Zeus, bore him beautiful children. But Kronos had learned that one of his offspring would overthrow him. As each child came forth from Rhea's womb, he ruthlessly swallowed it to prevent the loss of his kingly office.

Unceasing grief seized Rhea. When she was about to give birth to Zeus, she begged her parents, Earth and Heaven, to help her conceal the birth and punish Kronos. They sent her to a hidden place on the island of Crete, where Earth secretly received the infant from Rhea. Ancient imagination adds with a flourish that when the newborn cried in his cave hideaway, a bodyguard of warriors danced around him and beat their shields to disguise the sound of his tears. Earth had another strategy to protect the child. Wrapping a stone in swaddling clothes, she gave it to mighty Kronos, who promptly swallowed it without a glance.

The years rolled on. In time, Kronos was persuaded by Earth to release his offspring, who were destined to become the earliest Olympian gods. Kronos vomited up first the stone, and then all of the children, magically intact. Soon war broke out in heaven between the newborn gods and their dreadful father and his allies. Victor in the great battle, Zeus took his place as king of the gods and set the stone "in the wide-pathed earth" at Delphi to be "a sign and a marvel to men."[18]

The tale has an abiding, grim fascination. The shadowy parental fear of usurpation by one's children, checked but not necessarily erased by love, is starkly written in its events. Kronos and Earth still vie within us. The great stone in the path at Delphi was one of few unworked monuments in a sacred place where all else was refined to the highest level of beauty.

A curious smallish boulder remains to this day at Delphi, uphill from the temple.

The Monument to the Victory at Plataea, where the Greek allies overwhelmed the invading Persians in 479 B.C. A great rope-like vertical shaft, rising to three snake heads, it supported a golden tripod and cauldron. Inscribed along its coils were the names of all the allies, perhaps the only dedication reflecting the unity of the Greeks rather than their restless rivalry. While Pausanias felt free to pass over without further comment the crowd of dedications to "athletes and obscure musicians,"[19] he dwelt on the vast number of war dedications at Delphi which provided an episodic but vivid history of Greece as a battlefield.

Herodotus captures the desolation of the Persian camp when the victorious Greeks swarmed over it to gather the spoils that were later converted into the Victory Monument at Delphi and comparable memorials at other sacred places. "Scattering all about the camp," he writes, "[the soldiers] found tents adorned with gold and silver, and couches gilded and silver-plated, and golden bowls and cups, and other drinking vessels; and sacks [containing] cauldrons of gold and silver; and they stripped from the dead that lay there their armlets and torques, and daggers of gold."[20] From a tithe of this vast wealth—the tenth that belonged to Apollo at Delphi from the fruits of any exploit—artisans fashioned the serpents and cauldron.

The history of the monument does not quite end there. Thucydides relates that Pausanias, the Spartan general and commander-in-chief at Plataea, had verses peremptorily inscribed on the monument when it was first erected:

> Leader of the Greeks in war, victorious over the Persians,
> Pausanias to the god Phoibos erected the trophy.[21]

Outrage. It was *not* his victory alone. The Spartans in time had the offending verses burnished out and replaced with the names of the entire roster of allies.

A Solemn Procession, Lifesize, with Sacrificial Animals. Bronze, gift of the people of Orneai.[22] At war with Sikyon and nearly defeated, the people of Orneai vowed to Apollo that if He helped them sweep the enemy from their country, they would offer a daily procession at Delphi with lavish sacrifices. In the event they prevailed and, mindful of their vow, they organized processions and sacrifices at Delphi. But the expense began to mount, the little nation could hardly keep up. . . . A solution was desperately needed. They hit upon the idea of commissioning an elegant bronze procession to fulfill their vow eternally.

This little tale has some of the force of an Aesop fable. It is tempting to affix the moral. But a moral abstracted from the foolishness and astuteness of the people of Orneai would miss the point by focusing on principle in a setting where improvisation ruled.

A Complex Military Dedication. Said by Pausanias to have been offered by the people of Tegea from the spoils of war with Sparta. Apparently lifesize, bronze. Pausanias' simplistic strategy as the author of a guidebook is to name the figures and their makers: Apollo and a Victory; the divine heroes of Arkadia where Tegea was to be found, and so forth.[23] A typical war dedication, in which the wealth of the vanquished enemy was invested to thank Apollo and glorify the victor.

But the fortunes of war kept shifting. Delphi was filled with conflicting monuments.

A Massive Spartan Dedication. Directly across from the Tegean memorial of its victory over Sparta, a massive Spartan dedication of bronze gods and thirty-seven bronze war leaders, memorializing the victory of Sparta over Athens at the naval battle of Aigospotamai in 405 B.C. Prominently including Lysander, a Spartan military leader of genius, and Agias, the soothsayer who helped him.[24] The base of this enormous dedication has been uncovered by archaeologists and its inscriptions recorded, among them this curious blend of unvarnished triumphalism and delicacy:

> Lysander dedicated this statue
> after his victory in the swift ships.
> He has destroyed the power of Athens
> And crowned Sparta the undefeatable:
> the akropolis of Greece:
> and the country of beautiful dances.
> Ion of Samos wrote this poem.[25]

While discussing this massive dedication, Plutarch provides a clue to the keen appreciation with which some visitors to Delphi approached its monuments. He speaks of a foreigner, a connoisseur not drawn like ordinary people to the realistic imagery and technique of the sculpture.

This learned visitor admired "the patina of the bronze, smooth and shining with a deep blue tinge, so that it gave an added touch to the sea captains, as they stood there with the true complexion of the sea and its deepest depths."[26] It is a subtle observation, of freely conceived poetry.

All of which yields few hints as to how visitors to Delphi from the separate city-states perceived their own victory monuments and those of rival states that at some point in the centuries of mêlée had defeated them. Pausanias implies that the battles may have been refought in the visitors' minds and their outcomes corrected or justified. Plutarch makes explicit that the beauty of the sculpture, quite apart from the triumphalism of its themes, provided connoisseurs with a rich experience. Yet, if we multiply the few victory monuments we have now passed in review by a factor of one hundred or more—the temple grounds were something of a war museum—we have to ask ourselves whether Delphi was a place of peace or war, of insight or propaganda. It was both. This sharp ambiguity was not lost on Plutarch and presumably many others.

The issue, surprisingly, returns us to the irrepressible matter of Phryne's golden statue. In one of Plutarch's dialogues, a participant is brooding over the immorality of this image when one of his companions interrupts him:

> You exclude from this shrine a poor weak woman who put the beauty of her person to a base use. But when you see the god completely surrounded by choice offerings and tithes from murders, wars, and plunder, and his temple crowded with spoils and booty from the Greeks, you show no indignation. Nor do you feel any pity for the Greeks when, on beautiful dedications, you read the most disgraceful inscriptions: "Brasidas and the Akanthians from the Athenians," and "The Athenians from the Corinthians," and "The Phokians from the Thessalians," and "The Orneatans from the Sikyonians," and "The Amphiktyons from the Phokians." Praxiteles should be commended, not criticized, for placing a golden courtesan beside these.[27]

A Statue of Apollo, Spear in Hand. Dedication of the Megarians to commemorate the battle in which they drove out the Athenians who occupied their city at the end of the Persian War. One of many images of Apollo, overshadowed by a figure of the god some seventy feet tall near the entrance to the temple. Peace-loving Theon, a participant in one of Plutarch's dialogues, retrospectively takes the Megarians to task for their monument, which in his view crudely co-opts the divine person of Apollo to their cause.[28]

A Golden Palladium or Statue of Pallas Athena. The image of Athena, divine guardian of Athens, modeled on an ancient, venerated carving and set beside a bronze date-palm with golden fruit and perhaps owls, sacred to the goddess. Dedication of the city of Athens from the spoils of the Persian War. Pecked and dismantled by crows a century later, as an unheeded sign to the Athenians of approaching catastrophe. Pausanias writes: "Kleitodomos, most ancient of the local historians of Athens, says that when the Athenians were readying the expedition to Sicily, an enormous flock of crows descended on Delphi and chipped at this statue and tore off the gold with their beaks. He says the crows broke off the spear and the owls and the fruit that was on the tree like a harvest."[29]

It was believed by some, not universally, that dedications at Delphi, like the portrait of Dorian Gray, reflected the fates of those whom they celebrated. When the Spartan general Lysander met his death in battle, his stone portrait at Delphi "put forth a growth of wild shrubs and grass in such abundance as to cover up the face"[30]—so they recalled at Delphi. Moved to explore this correspondence between event and symbol, Plutarch provides both sides of an argument that must have brewed for centuries between believers and rationalists. A traditionally minded participant in Plutarch's dialogue relies on time-honored references:

> Aristotle used to say that Homer is the only poet who wrote words of such vigor that they possess movement. But I would say that among offerings also, those dedicated here move in sympathy with the god's foreknowledge; no part of them is void or insensible, all are filled with divine spirit.[31]

To which another speaker replies cynically:

> Yes indeed, it is not enough to incarnate the god once every month in a mortal body, but we are bent on incorporating him into every bit of stone and bronze, as if we did not have in chance or accident an agent responsible for such coincidences.[32]

Plutarch, a born moderate and listener, would probably have come down toward the middle in this debate.

A Water Jar of Gold and Silver. Dedicated by the Opontians under unusual circumstances. In what came to be called the Second Sacred War, the Phokians occupied Delphi in defiance of the other city-states. To raise funds for their army, they converted masses of gold and silver offerings into coins. Collecting as many of these coins as they could recover, the Opontians had a magnificent water jar made from them and, when the Phokians were eventually sent packing, poignantly offered it to Delphi.[33]

The Fruits of the Harvest Fashioned from Gold. Dedications by the peoples of Myrina and Apollonia.[34] A timely reminder that the temple grounds at Delphi were not only a showcase for military sentiment.

A Bronze Wolf. Dedicated by the people of Delphi, who say that a thief made off with gold from Apollo's temple and hid in the uplands of Mount Parnassos where the forest was impenetrable. A wolf attacked him in his sleep and killed him. Every day the wolf would come to the city and howl. The Delphians gradually realized that the wolf must have something to do with the god. They followed it and recovered the gold.[35]

Theft was always a problem—theft on the grand scale of a Nero, petty theft on the scale reflected by this tale.[36]

A Bronze Donkey. Dedicated by the the Ambrakiots to commemorate victory in a night battle with the Molossians. Pausanias tells the tale: "The Molossians were waiting in ambush for the Ambrakiots one night when a donkey being driven in from the fields went running after a she-donkey with every kind of lecherous violence and hoarse cries, and what with the man driving the donkey giving a series of ugly yells at the same moment, the Molossians were terrified and jumped out of their hiding-place. So the Ambrakiots saw what was up and set on them in the dark, and won the battle."[37]

An earthy dedication, from the heart.

The E. A wooden E, depicted on coins as hanging high between the central columns of the temple. Ancient and of uncertain origin, venerated, a highlight of the guides' tour of Delphi—"something worth seeing," as Plutarch put it[38]—and subject to interpretation. Plutarch dedicated to it one of his most engaging dialogues, in which a group of learned gentlemen develop no fewer than seven alternative explanations of its meaning. To this day, it prompts speculative forays ranging in character from dismissive (it was an ancient representation of the tripod that somehow got turned the wrong way round) to richly grounded in the history of religious ideas.[39]

Plutarch opens his dialogue with the thought that Apollo simplifies the practical problems of *life* through the oracle, but also poses intricate puzzles for the *minds* of those who love knowledge in order to "create in their souls a craving for knowledge that leads onward to the truth."[40] The mysterious E exemplifies, in his view, this aspect of Apollo's mission. Some of the explanations brought forth in Plutarch's leisurely dialogue are scholastic, for example, "E" is the fifth letter of the alphabet, thus providing hidden testimony to the fact that the Seven Sages really numbered only five, with two interlopers forcing their way in who were not worthy of the honor. And some are clever but unconvincing, for example, "E" was pronounced "EI" by the ancients, and "EI" meant among other things "if," a word that naturally figured in many inquiries at the oracle—people wished to know if they would win in battle, if they should marry, and so on.

Plutarch's discussants toy with further possibilities derived from the theory of numbers until one of them suggests, in effect, that they have fallen into the trap of thinking without listening. EI, he says, means "Thou art": ". . . an address and salutation to the god. For the god addresses each of us as we approach him here with the words 'Know thyself' as a form of welcome, and we reply to him 'Thou art,' an expression that is true, free from deception, and the only one that suits him alone: the assertion of Being."[41] There ensues from these words one of the finest set pieces in Plutarch, a stately yet felt statement of the precariousness of our lives and the eternal grandeur of divine Being. The following only begins to suggest the beauty of the passage:

> The fact is that we really have no part in Being, but everything of a mortal nature is at some stage between coming into existence and passing away. Dead is the man of yesterday, for he is passed into the man of today; and the man of today is dying as he passes into the man of tomorrow. Nobody remains one person, nor is one person. What, then, really is Being? It is that which is eternal, without beginning and without end, to which no length of time brings change. God is. He, being One, has with only one "Now" completely filled "Forever." Under these conditions, we ought to greet Him with the words "Thou art."[42]

The speaker adds that "Know thyself" is a reminder to acknowledge our human limitations, while "Thou art" is spoken with awe and reverence to That Which Is.

This was Delphi—all of this: a world's fair in perpetual session where nations competed with one another through breathtakingly rich pavilions and triumphal sculpture; a visual archive of myth and story; a wax works of sorts, where current celebrities' images were enshrined and then forgotten; a sacred place where genuine piety placed its golden harvests and its holy images; a gathering of philosophers who wandered, as do we all, from proud self-exhibition to utter sincerity and penetration. And at the very center persisted the abiding mystery that here God spoke to human beings as if to intimates, or very nearly.

11

"Hasten, Teiresias, Believe!"

The speaker is Clement of Alexandria (ca. C.E. 150–215), Greek author of *An Exhortation to the Greeks,* sainted mystic and theologian. Pressing conversion from the ancient religion of the gods to Christianity, he admonishes the entire oracular tradition through one of its legendary heroes, the blind seer of Thebes, Teiresias:

> Come to me, old man, come thou too! Quit Thebes; fling away thy prophecy and Bacchic revelry and be led by the hand to truth. Behold, I give thee the wood of the cross to lean upon. Hasten, Teiresias, believe! Thou shalt have sight. Christ, by whom the eyes of the blind see again, shineth upon thee more brightly than the sun. Night shall flee from thee; fire shall fear thee; death shall depart from thee. Thou shalt see heaven, old man, though thou canst not see Thebes.[1]

Clement is curiously tender toward the memory of Teiresias, but his message is clear. These words from an era when Christianity was new and insecure set the pitch for a chapter in which the tale is dark: the fall of the Delphic oracle and its sister institutions. Within the "pagan" world itself, the lapse of Delphi into a provincial religious center, no longer the Center of the World, was occasioned by the shift of worldly power from Greece to Rome, by changing customs, and not least by the force of ideas: the rational critique of Cicero, the droll mockery of the comic poet Lucian, the venom of a Cynic pamphleteer survive to evoke a gradual change of mind within the "pagan" world itself. Not far behind were zealous Christian officials, monks and congregants, and authors who attacked not just the material existence of the oracular temples but their history, their governing concepts, their intimate mystique. The temple was a purveyor of deception, the Pythia a demon's whore. In the transition from the ancient religion of the gods to the new dispensation, "pagan" prophecy was singled out as a particularly important target because it appeared to compete with the biblical prophets and with the teachings of Christian revelation. Hear Isaiah, not Apollo; mark the Word of Jesus, not the false counsel of a demon. The smoke of sacrifices rising above temples impressed traditional believers as a revitalizing purge of their world; for Christians, it was a stench.[2]

We live in the Christian era, in the Anni Domini, the years of our Lord. Our calendrical fulcrum is the birth of Jesus in a small but turbulent backwater of the Roman Empire. Whether with Christians one regards him as Messiah, or with Jews as reformer, or with Muslims as a revered precursor of Mohammad, his advent marks a watershed in human experience. Few among us are indifferent to the Gospel message of love, the stern teachings from the Mount, the endlessly fruitful parables, the sacred narrative that winds its way from Bethlehem to Calvary. Strange, then, but essential to our enterprise, to experience the thoughts and emotions of Christians in late antiquity as if we were traditional believers, "pagans." This was not a kind word. Cognate with our "peasant," French *paysan*, it refers in early use to a person living in the unconverted countryside where the religion of the gods persisted. More figuratively, it may also refer to a spiritual "civilian," one who has not left home to enlist as a soldier of Christ. We shall more acutely experience the disappearance of Delphi if we stand with the pagans. They are good company and, as we shall see, they, too, debated the value of oracles. On the Christian side, many of the authors whom we will encounter are still read today for their religious insights or historical knowledge, but their polemics against the ancient religion are rarely exercises either in good manners or in impartial thinking. This is the tough part of their authorship.

Eusebius, fourth-century bishop and author of the first history of the Roman Catholic Church, believed that he could date the death of the gods with some precision. It occurred in the lifetime of Jesus, and the event was recounted—although in Eusebius's view not properly understood—by Plutarch. The following is the tale on which Eusebius based his obituary, told by a participant in one of Plutarch's Pythian Dialogues.

Great Pan is Dead

I have heard the word of a man who was not a fool nor an impostor. The father of Aemilianus the orator, to whom some of you have listened, was Epitherses, who lived in our town and was my teacher in grammar. He said that once upon a time in making a voyage to Italy he embarked on a ship carrying freight and many passengers. It was already evening when, near the Echinades Islands, the wind dropped, and the ship drifted near Paxi. Almost everybody was awake, and a good many had not finished their after-dinner wine.

Suddenly from the island of Paxi was heard the voice of someone loudly calling Thamus, so that all were amazed. Thamus was an Egyptian pilot, not known by name even to many on board. Twice he was called and made no reply, but the third time he answered; and the caller, raising his voice, said, "When you come opposite to Palodes, announce that Great Pan is dead." On hearing this, all, said Epitherses, were astounded and reasoned among themselves whether it were better to carry out the order or to refuse to meddle and let the matter go. Under the circumstances Thamus made up his mind that if there should be a breeze, he would sail past and keep quiet, but with no wind and a smooth sea about the place he would announce what he had heard. So, when he came opposite Palodes, and there was neither wind nor wave, Thamus from the stern, looking toward the land, said the words as he had heard them: "Great Pan is dead." Even before he had finished there was a great cry of lamentation, not of one person, but of many, mingled with exclamations of amazement.

As many persons were on the vessel, the story was soon spread abroad in Rome, and Thamus was sent for by Tiberius Caesar. Tiberius became so convinced of the truth of the story that he caused an inquiry and investigation to be made.[3]

"Great Pan is dead." It is one of the most piercing cries of antiquity, addressed to what seems an empty shoreline. Yet even as the words leave the pilot's mouth a crowd of unseen listeners begins to wail. By some unexpected transposition, one can feel oneself among them, whoever they are. And then, Eusebius had a point: the tale is so final and resonant that it evokes meanings beyond its small scale, as if capturing in miniature the relentless shift in world view from the religion of the gods to Christianity. For his part, Eusebius drily commented that the tale reveals "the date of the overthrow of the daemons" in the reign of the emperor Tiberius, when our Saviour is "recorded to have been ridding human life from daemons of every kind."[4] By "daemons," Eusebius meant the gods and their attendants.

THE CRITIQUE FROM WITHIN: PAGANS AGAINST THE ORACLES

As Christian apologists were well aware, they were not the first to doubt or vilify oracles. The development of intellectual disciplines in the sixth through fourth centuries—philosophy, history, empirical science—was paralleled by a critique of tradition that led some thoughtful people to view the oracular process as a dubious inheritance. From Socrates in the fifth century B.C.E. to Plutarch in the first century C.E. and even to the philosophical emperor Julian in the fourth, it is clear that intellectual acuity did not *require* irreverence; Delphi remained for them, as it did for many, the Center of the World where a god advised the human race. If Herodotus toward the beginning of the fifth century B.C.E. gives enthusiastic accounts of Delphic messages rendered, and wrestled with by their recipients, Thucydides toward the end of that century does not linger overlong on oracular matters. He narrates objectively the many consultations sought by combatants and victims in the Peloponnesian War—these things were part of the fabric of his time—but he tips his hand here and there as to what he really thinks.

The first such occurrence is more a matter of tone than of direct critique, and it is full of Thucydides' startling lucidity. He is recounting the first plague in Athens—recurrent plagues weakened the disrupted city as much as military defeats. "At the beginning the doctors were quite incapable of treating the disease because of their ignorance of the right methods. Nor was any other human art or science any help at all. Equally useless were prayers made in the temples, consultation of oracles, and so forth; indeed, in the end people were so overcome by their sufferings that they paid no further attention to such things."[5] The tone here is new; its dry realism—masking, one senses, a very real compassion—conveys the vision of a world in which events have outrun any real or imagined contact with the divine. There is another, more explicit passage. Later in his History (as briefly noted in an earlier chapter), Thucydides reviews the chronology of the war and recalls that oracles at the outset had predicted it to last twenty-seven years, the number to which he also arrives through an analysis of periods of active war, treaties entered into and broken, and a shaky truce. "For those who put their faith in oracles," he remarks, "here is one solitary instance of their having been proven accurate."[6] Plato himself, who preserved for Delphi an authoritative role in his ideal state, did not shy away from the notion that oracles could be deceptive. In one of the dialogues he imagined a world ruled by wisdom; in such a world, he wrote, "you may suppose that prophecy will be a real knowledge of the future, and will be under the control of wisdom, who will deter deceivers and set up the true prophets in their place as revealers of the future."[7]

The claims of traditional belief and the counterclaims of rationality are quite fully worked out in the writings of Cicero (106–43 B.C.), the Roman statesman, author, and lover of nearly all things Greek. Despite the tale (see chapter 1) that associates him with Delphi, in his extended essay *On Divination* he writes of the oracle as a remote institution, little if at all consulted. Other means of piercing the darkness of human affairs are far more familiar: augury in the Etruscan manner, state consultation of the Sibylline Books (again, chapter 1), astrology, the reading of signs such as bird flight, private consultations with charismatic seers—these things are of much more moment for Romans of his era.[8] On the other hand, the pronouncements of the Delphic oracle were so vividly recorded in literature and so embedded in Greek political and military history, which educated Romans knew well, that Cicero has Delphi in mind as he writes. Despite the objectivity with which he gathers arguments and anecdotes for and against divination, his personal perspective is compactly conveyed in an aside referring to Cato, his younger peer in Roman politics: "Cato used to say that he wondered how one soothsayer could keep a straight face when he met another."[9] While Cicero was suitably aware of the difference between a soothsayer of uncertain credentials and a venerable institution, if pressed he might well have said that both relied on credulity and superstition, and in this sense were the same.

For our purposes, we need no more than taste the conflicting arguments in *On Divination.* Cicero gives his brother Quintus the task of defending divination of all time-honored kinds, while he assigns to himself the task of undermining it. One of Quintus's most heartfelt arguments will echo among later pagan authors as they defend oracles against Christian attack—not I think because they "lifted" the argument from Cicero but because they revered in all sincerity the ancient ways which, in their view, had nurtured the achievements of Greco-Roman civilization. It is coolly reflected in the opening of *On Divination*, not pressed home with the passion that Quintus later displays:

> There is an ancient belief, handed down to us even from mythical times and firmly established by the general agreement of the Roman people and of all nations, that divination of some kind exists among men; this the Greeks call *mantiké*—that is, the foresight and knowledge of future events. A really splendid and helpful thing it is—if only such a faculty exists—since by its means men may approach very near to the power of the gods.[10]

In the extended plea that soon follows, Quintus often returns to the notion of the antiquity and universality of divination. "There is, I assure you, nothing new or original in my views; for those which I adopt are not only very old, but they are endorsed by the consent of all peoples and nations."[11] While Quintus cannot explain why divination works, he nonetheless offers literally hundreds of historical anecdotes that demonstrate just when and how consultation with an oracle or augurs has advanced public or private affairs. His reasoning is quite touching: he points out that while he cannot explain, for example, why a particular root or leaf has medicinal virtue, the fact that it is so has long been known, and one would be a fool to disregard the medicine in time of need simply because one can't explain its activity. About the Delphic oracle specifically, he has intriguing things to say:

> Everybody knows the oracular responses which the Pythian Apollo gave to Croesus, to the Athenians, Spartans, Tegeans, Argives, and Corinthians. Chrysippus has collected a vast number of these responses, attested in every instance by abundant proof. I will urge only this much: the oracle at Delphi never would have been so much frequented, so famous, and so crowded with offerings from peoples and kings of every land, if all ages had not tested the truth of its prophecies. For a long time now that has not been the case. Therefore, as at present its glory has waned because it is no longer noted for the truth of its prophecies, so formerly it would not have enjoyed so exalted a reputation if it had not been trustworthy to the highest degree. Possibly, too, those subterranean exhalations which used to kindle the soul of the Pythian priestess with divine inspiration have gradually vanished in the long lapse of time; just as within our own knowledge some rivers have dried up and disappeared, while others have changed their course into

> other channels. But explain the decadence of the oracle as you wish, since it offers a wide field for discussion, provided you grant what cannot be denied without distorting the entire record of history, that the oracle at Delphi made true prophecies for many hundreds of years.[12]

We are in the first century B.C.E. and it is clear that Delphi enjoys no prestige in Rome. This will change. The chaotic emperor Nero (reigning C.E. 54–68) cared enough about the Pythian Games to arrange for his personal victories both in athletics and in music, and admired the art at Delphi enough to plunder hundreds of objects for transport to Rome. Plutarch, who grew up during Nero's reign, renewed the interest of the educated public in Delphi through his widely appreciated writings. The refined emperor Hadrian (reigning C.E. 117–136) sponsored a general revival and enrichment of Delphi that would have surprised Plutarch, who acknowledged the decline of oracles and thought of them in his era as poor but honest, and best left that way. The passage from St. Clement with which we began this chapter, written toward the end of the second or early third century, points the way toward the end—an end that has no specific date, no known and decisive event to mark it. The Delphi of the mind—the literary record—preserves two inquiries, one certainly of the mid-fourth century, the other likely to be fourth century, to which unnamed Delphians, perhaps a remnant of priests, report by letter that the oracle is no longer available. A little later, we shall listen in on those inquiries and answers.

When Quintus is quite through defending oracles and all traditions of divination, the famed trial attorney Cicero responds at length in an effort to sweep away his brother's claims. The gist of his argument is evident in the following passage, where he uses the rhetorical device of addressing Apollo directly:

> Chrysippus filled a whole volume with your oracles; of these some, as I think, were false; some came true by chance, as happens very often even in ordinary speech; some were so intricate and obscure that their interpreter needs an interpreter and the oracles themselves must be referred back to the oracle; and some so equivocal that they require a dialectician to construe them. However, the main question is this: Why are Delphic oracles not uttered at the present time and have not been for a long time? And why are they regarded with the utmost contempt? When pressed at this point their apologists affirm that "the long flight of time has gradually dissipated the virtue of the place whence came

> those subterranean exhalations which inspired the Pythian priestess to utter oracles." One might think that they are talking about wine or brine, which do evaporate. When did the virtue disappear? Was it after men began to be less credulous?[13]

Clearly the battle between traditional devotion and meticulous rationality was already well under way, and in good hands, by the first century B.C.E. The conflict between pagans and Christians over oracles was of another order: not a battle between tradition and reason that would allow for accommodation in practice, but a battle between two opposing "truths." This is a different thing, with fewer rules of engagement. Cicero and Quintus were brothers, members of the same household. Temple and church were not the same household.

The poets of the succeeding Augustan era, which marked the transition to imperial rule, reflect in their own way the depleted prestige of the ancient institution of oracles. Oracles appear in their verse as a convenient, often charming metaphor for wisdom and authority. For example, Ovid in his *Art of Love* urges on the suitor for a woman's love:

> . . . Bear patiently with a rival, and victory
> Will be yours, you'll triumph in the end.
> Take this not as mere human opinion, believe it rather
> Prophetic utterance.[14]

In a graphic discussion, he comically evokes the approval of the great oracles of the past upon his recommendations to women seeking the most flattering positions for intercourse:

> . . . Sex has countless positions—
> An easy and undemanding one is to lie
> On your right side, half-reclining. Neither Delphi
> nor Ammon
> Will tell you more truth than my Muse.[15]

Lest we think these turns in Ovid a special case, we can find the same in the erotic verse of his contemporary, Sextus Propertius. He, too, took pleasure in the sudden change in magnitude from the impersonal grandeur of oracles to the personal trials of lovers:

> The priestess-oracles of Zeus
> cannot speak with more authority

than I can
as to which girl
will snare which bachelor.[16]

Of his own difficulties in love affairs, he would ask:

. . . for what lying oracle
am I not a prize catch?
And what old woman has not heard
my turning dreams ten times?[17]

These sophisticated lines suggest something of the attitudes that Plutarch could presuppose among the urbane readers to whom he addressed his Pythian Dialogues, the philosophical exchanges set at Delphi which we began to explore in chapter 4. The oracle's local reputation was no doubt secure, but in the world at large he could assume nothing of the kind. Further, famous oracles of the past had dropped away: "A great drought of prophecy has spread over the land," Plutarch wrote, memorably, in one of those dialogues.[18] Recovering some of his thoughts will serve our purpose.

FRAGMENTS OF CONVERSATION FROM DELPHI

Kleombrotos of Sparta, a philosopher and traveler, has joined a group of congenial friends at Delphi. He had recently returned from the oracle of Zeus at Ammon, in Libya, about which his friends have heard that the divine influence there, once so strong, is now weak. Another of the company, Demetrios, remarks that they needn't look so far afield for signs of decay—in their own region of Boeotia, and at Delphi too, decay had set in. "What need to speak of others," he asks, "when in Boeotia, which in former times spoke with many voices (*polyphonon*) because of its oracles, the oracles have now failed completely?"

> *Demetrios*: Nowhere now except in the neighborhood of Labadeia has Boeotia anything to offer those who would draw from the well-spring of prophecy. As for the rest, silence has come upon some and utter desolation upon others. And yet at the time of the Persian Wars many had gained a high repute. There have been also more recent manifestations than these at these oracles, but now the oracles are no more; so that it is well worth while, here in the precinct of the Pythian god, to examine the reason for the change.

(They take seats in the Lesche, the elegant meeting house on the temple grounds which we encountered in chapter 4. Others are already gathered. Demetrios explains the topic he and his friends hope to introduce for a discussion in which all are welcome to participate. Suddenly a Cynic philosopher—Cynics were deliberate "outsiders" who could be expected to rail at society's follies—springs up from his place and strikes the ground with his staff.)

Cynic: *Iou, iou,* a difficult matter to decide and one requiring much investigation! It is indeed a wonder, when so much wickedness has been spread over the earth, that Divine Providence has not gathered up its oracles and departed! I propose that you discuss how it happens that the oracle *here* has not also given out, and Herakles for a second time, or some other god, has not wrested away the tripod which is constantly being occupied with shameful and impious questions that people put to the god, some of whom try to test him as though his wisdom were an affectation, while others put questions about treasures or inheritances or unlawful marriages. So Pythagoras is proved to be utterly wrong in asserting that men are at their best when they approach the gods. Those sicknesses and emotions of the soul which it would be good to conceal in the presence of an older man, they bring naked and exposed before the god.

(The others try to calm him.)

Lamprias: Whether the god be the sun or the lord and father of the sun and of all that lies beyond our vision, it is not likely that he should deny his words to people of the present time because of their unworthiness, when he is responsible for their birth and nurture and their existence and power to think. Nor is it likely that Providence, like a benign and helpful mother, who does everything for us and watches over us, should cherish animosity in the matter of prophecy only, and take it away from us after having given it to us at the beginning. Come, sit down again and make a "Pythian truce" with evil, which you are accustomed to berating every day, and join us in seeking some other reason for the decline of oracles.

(The Cynic leaves without a word—perhaps Plutarch's way of telling us that extreme attitudes are not going to uncover much truth. There is quiet for a moment. Then Ammonios launches the argument that Apollo Himself has reduced the number of oracles because conditions have changed in Greece; fewer are needed.)

Ammonios: Greece has far more than its share in the general depopulation which the earlier discords and wars have brought about throughout much of the inhabited world. Today the whole of Greece could hardly muster three thousand men-at-arms. The god's abandonment of many oracles is nothing more than his way of responding to the desolation of Greece.

> For who would profit if there were an oracle in Tegyrae, as there used to be, or at Ptoum—where during some part of the day one might *possibly* meet a human being pasturing his flocks? And regarding the oracle here at Delphi, the most ancient and most famous when Greece had grown strong in cities and the place was thronged with people, today there is one priestess and we don't complain, for she meets every need. There is no reason, therefore, to blame the god. The exercise of the prophetic art which continues at the present day is sufficient for all, and sends all away with their desires fulfilled. It would be a surprise if the god allowed his prophecies to run to waste like water.
> *Lamprias*: My contention is that no prophetic shrine or oracle is ever abolished by the will of God. He creates and provides many other things for us, and upon some of these Nature brings destruction. While the god gives many fair things to mankind, he gives nothing imperishable—as Sophocles puts it, "the works of gods may die, but not the gods."[19]

And the company concludes this part of their conversation with the thought that, while the gods or their attendant daimons may abandon oracles, they may also return when the time is ripe, retune the strings of the great instrument, and resume the oracular function.

In another Pythian Dialogue, Plutarch authorizes a follower of Epicurean philosophy to cast the doubts of his school on the oracle. His name is Boethus, and he speaks powerfully of the role of Chance and the variety of events:

> *Boethus*: My good sir, what kind of an occurrence can there be that is not a debt owed by Time to Nature? What is there strange and unexpected round about land or sea or cities or men which one might foretell and not find it come to pass? Yet this is not precisely foretelling, but telling; or rather it is a throwing and scattering of words without foundation into the infinite; and oftentimes Chance encounters them in their wanderings and accidentally falls into accord with them. Infinity brings all things to pass. These prophets of the type of the Sibyl and Bakis toss forth into the gulf of time, as into the ocean depths with no chart to guide them, words and phrases at haphazard, which deal with events and occurrences of all sorts; and although some come to pass for them as the result of chance, what is said at the present time is equally a lie, even if later it becomes true.[20]

The argument could have been made by Cicero responding to his brother's traditional faith, and indeed it was. Priest of Delphi and a sincere believer,

Plutarch does not leave matters in the hands of an Epicurean doubter. His essential response to all such is reasoned argument—but at very last a resolute assertion of value, take it or leave it:

> We act as if we were anxious and fearful lest the place here lose the repute of its three thousand years, and some few persons should cease to come here, condemning the oracle as if it were the lecturing of some popular speaker. We try to appease and win over the man who complains, instead of bidding him take his leave for all time.[21]

You will recall the memorable scold delivered by Plutarch's Cynic. His target was the poor quality of inquirers at the oracle—reason enough, in his view, for Apollo to withdraw from contact with them. Plutarch's contemporary, the philosopher Epictetus, draws attention to another dubious matter: the quality of priests. To be named priest of certain temples and religious institutions conferred worldly prestige. In the era of Epictetus, men whom he knew to be anything but thoughtfully pious

> get themselves appointed priests and prophets! Priests and prophets of whom? Of gods that do not exist! And they themselves consult the Pythian priestess—in order to hear lies and to interpret the oracles to others! Oh what monstrous shamelessness and imposture![22]

Epictetus protested; several generations later, Lucian preferred to laugh. "What is your opinion, Tychiades, about that sort of thing—I mean oracles, prophecies, outcries of men under divine possession, voices heard from inner shrines, or verses uttered by a maiden who foretells the future? Or course, you doubt that sort of thing also?"[23] The tone is urbane, world-weary, splittingly ripe. In Lucian's comic dialogues, the gods are chatty, often testy, all too human. Their exchanges could be taken verbatim from the sitting rooms of a stuffy club, or from the comedies of Oscar Wilde, who knew his Lucian. In *Zeus Rants*, the cynical Momus tirelessly pokes fun at Lord Apollo, who behaves like the spoiled scion of a family business:

> *Momus*: My admirable friend, since you claim to be a prophet and have collected large fees for such work, even to the extent of getting ingots of gold once upon a time, why do you not give us a timely display of your skill?
> *Apollo*: How can I do that when we have no tripod here, no incense or prophetic spring like Castalia?

> *Momus*: There now! You dodge the test.
> *Zeus*: Speak up, my boy, don't give this libeler a chance to insult your profession by saying that it all depends on a tripod and water and incense, so that if you didn't have those things you would be deprived of your skill.
> *Apollo*: It would be better, father, to do such business at Delphi or Colophon where I have all the necessaries at hand, in the usual way. However, I will try.
> *(Stage business is implied as Apollo goes dramatically into trance.)*
> *Zeus*: What in the world are you going to say, my boy? These preliminaries are terrifying! Your color is changed, your eyes are rolling, your hair stands on end, your movements are frenzied, everything about you suggests demoniacal possession and gooseflesh and mysteries![24]

In another dialogue, Apollo is an overworked executive with far-flung subsidiaries to look after:

> *Zeus:* Plague take all philosophers who say that bliss is to be found only among the gods! If they but knew all that we endure. Apollo has taken up a very active profession, and has been deafened almost completely by people besetting him with requests for prophecies. One moment he has to be in Delphi; the next, he runs to Colophon; from there he crosses to Xanthus, and again at full speed to Delos or to Branchidae. In a word, wherever his prophetess, after drinking from the holy well and chewing laurel and setting the tripod ashake, bids him appear, there is no delaying—he must present himself immediately to reel off his prophecies, or else it is all up with his reputation in the profession.[25]

There is a good deal more of this sort of fun in Lucian's writings. All of these texts, not excluding those of our Delphic priest, Plutarch, demonstrate that the passionate inquiry, abiding mystery, and awe associated anciently with Delphi and other oracles were slowly vanishing in the first centuries of our era. Traditional believers maintained the oracle, inquirers still presented themselves in all sincerity, and authors in the vast Roman Empire could count on readers to understand at once their allusions to Delphi. The oracle was certainly intact as an institution through the second century, and Porphyry would write his lost *Philosophy of the Oracles* in the third, but we begin to lose sight of Delphi in this era—except in the bitter polemics of Christians against pagans and pagans against Christians, for whom the Delphic oracle remained a central symbol of all that was good, or bad, in the traditional pre-Christian religious life.

CHRISTIAN VOICES

"The stupidity of custom":[26] the blunt phrase is from Clement of Alexandria, never one to mince words. It captures the Christian rejection of the *ethos*, the *synetheios*, the *nomos*—the cultural climate, shared customs, and order of life—of the Greco-Roman world to the extent that climate, customs, and order required acknowledgment of the traditional gods. "Custom is truly nonsense."[27] Good, and what else is nonsense? "The mysteries are mere custom and vain opinion."[28] The gods? "The most part of the stories about your gods are legends and fictions."[29] Interesting—there seem to be exceptions. What of the ancient, trusted way of life? "You say it is unreasonable to overthrow a way of life handed down to us from our forefathers. Why then do we not continue to use our first food, milk, to which our nurses accustomed us from birth?"[30] Is there anything positive at all in the old ways? "Let us shun custom; let us shun it as some dangerous headland, or threatening Charybdis, or the Sirens of legend. Custom strangles man; it turns him away from truth; it leads him away from life; it is a snare, an abyss, a pit, a devouring evil."[31]

This is Clement, speaking not just for himself but for many who felt called to that radical disruption, Christianity. "I bring the sword," said Jesus; it was now in Clement's hand. He did not dismiss the gods as mere illusion. They were worse: "How can the shadows and daemons any longer be gods, when they are in reality unclean and loathsome spirits?"[32] Thank God, their delusive oracles were finally silenced—or so Clement thought. The passage where he most clearly expresses his convictions is well worth hearing:

> Do not seek after godless sanctuaries, after the mouths of caverns, the Cirrhaean tripod *[i.e., Delphi]*. The Castalian spring, at least, is all silent. So is the spring of Colophon; and the rest of the prophetic streams are likewise dead. Stripped of their absurd pretensions, though none too soon, they are at last thoroughly exposed; the waters have run dry together with the legends attached to them. Relate to me the unprophetic prophecies of that other form of divination—I should rather say hallucination—the oracles of Apollo, Clarian, Pythian and Didymean, and those of Amphiarius and Amphilocus; and, if you will, devote to destruction along with them the soothsayers, augurs and interpreters of dreams. At the same time, take and place by the side of the Pythian Apollo those who divine by flour, and by barley, and the ventriloquists still held in honor among the multitude. Yes, and let the sanctuaries of Egypt and the Tuscan oracles of the dead be delivered

> over to darkness. Homes of hallucination in very truth they are, these schools of sophistry for unbelieving men, these gambling-dens of sheer delusion. Your Phoebus is a lover of gifts but not of men.[33]

For Clement, the Delphic oracle is no more noble than a village fortune-teller, a ventriloquist holding forth in the marketplace for a few coins. In place of the institutional traditions and enduring folkways inventoried in this passage, Clement offered something alien to them but, from his perspective, incomparably truer: "Will you listen to a giver of oracles? You have the whole company of the prophets, who are joined with Moses in this sacred fellowship."[34]

Yet the Delphic oracle is singled out for attack; Clement cannot quite dismiss it as one among many delusions. Like other adversaries of the oracle, he turns its own legends against it. At this point in our experience of Delphic tales, we can listen to his attack quite knowledgeably:

> I can at once prove to you that man is better than these gods of yours, the daemons; that Cyrus and Solon are better than Apollo the prophet. Your Phoebus betrayed his friend Croesus, and, forgetful of the reward he had received (such was his love of honor), led the king across the river Halys to his funeral pyre. This is how the daemons love; they guide men to the fire! But do thou, O man of kinder heart and truer speech than Apollo, pity him who lies bound upon the pyre. Do thou, Solon, utter an oracle of truth. Do thou, Cyrus, bid the flaming pyre be quenched. Come to thy senses at the eleventh hour, Croesus, when suffering has taught thee better. Ungrateful is he whom thou dost worship. He takes the reward of gold, and then deceives thee once again. Mark! it is not the daemon, but the man who tells thee the issue of life. Unlike Apollo, Solon utters no double-meaning prophecies. This oracle alone shalt thou find true, O barbarian. This shalt thou prove upon the pyre.[35]

Clement's attack is fascinating in its strategy of asserting the superior wisdom and compassion of the *human* participants in the saga of Croesus. Herodotus would have been floored to learn that his tale could be interpreted as an indictment of the greed and pitilessness of Lord Apollo.

Clement is writing in the later second and early third centuries, not a time when Christians could command armies or even local militias, but his words presage the era, not distant, when undeclared war against the temples would break out across the eastern Mediterranean. He was, in spirit if not deed, a firebrand: "If you wish to cease from folly," he advised, "the fire shall be your guiding light. Fire it was that burnt up the temple in Argos together with its priestess Chrysis, and also that of Artemis in Ephesus. The temple of Apollo at Delphi was first caught by a storm and then utterly destroyed by the 'discerning fire.' "[36] His assertion is untrue, unless Clement is misremembering the destruction of the sixth-century temple by earthquake, replaced by the temple now surviving as a ruin. Although untrue, it conveys his conviction—and perhaps his intuition of the future. Clement is more valued today for his luminous mystical vision than for his fiery polemics. But standing with the pagans, we see the fire, not the light.

Origen (ca. 185–ca. 254) was Clement's student at an important Christian school in Alexandria and later for a time became its master. He cast a long shadow over early Christian history: Origen's richly speculative thought offered alternatives that elicited fierce support and opposition for centuries, until a mid-sixth century council condemned him utterly. His contribution to the attack on the religion of the gods was a book, *Against Celsus*, carefully preserved although much else of his authorship was destroyed over time by fellow Christians who thought him a heretic. *Against Celsus* presents us, not for the last time, with what amounts to a dual authorship. The first author is Celsus, target of Origen's polemic and author of the first surviving philosophical critique of Christianity, written ca. 178–180. Celsus' book must have had staying power with pagan audiences and uncommitted Christians because Origen was moved to respond to it some sixty years later, toward the end of his life, and in doing so included such long verbatim extracts that Celsus' book can be reconstructed. No independent manuscript survives; the Christian heirs to antique literature experienced their fiduciary responsibility only intermittently. We have, then, two books nested, and for this reason we will begin to hear the voice of the pagan resistance.

Celsus takes up and intensifies the theme we first encountered in Quintus, Cicero's pious brother. The oracles have been a just and compassionate guide throughout the unparalleled development of Greco-Roman civilization; have helped states and individuals, punished evildoers, maintained an atmosphere of the miraculous that encouraged human enterprise. You will see that we ourselves, at this point in our knowledge of Delphic tales, could have written this passage from Celsus. His sources, while greater than our own, are in large measure the Delphi of the mind—the literary record. He has read what we have read, and he uses that material to defend ancient values. "What need is there," asks Celsus,

> to collect all the oracular responses which have been delivered with a divine voice by priests and priestesses, as well as by others, whether men or women, under divine influence? All the wonderful things that have been heard issuing from the inner sanctuary? All the revelations made to those who consulted the sacrificial victims? And all the knowledge that has been conveyed to men by other signs and prodigies? To some the gods have appeared in visible forms. The world is full of such instances. How many cities have been built in obedience to commands received from oracles; how often, in the same way, delivered from disease and famine! Or again, how many cities, from disregard or forgetfulness of these oracles, have perished miserably! How many colonies have been established and made to flourish by following their orders! How many princes and private persons have, from this cause, had prosperity or adversity! How many who mourned over their childlessness have obtained the blessing they asked for! How many have turned away from themselves the anger of demons! How many who were maimed in their limbs have had them restored! And again, how many have met with summary punishment for showing want of reverence to the temples—some being instantly seized with madness, others openly confessing their crimes, others having put an end to their lives, and others having become the victims of incurable maladies! Yea, some have been slain by a terrible voice issuing from the inner sanctuary.[37]

Following his strategy of point and counterpoint, Origen sets to work at once to respond to these claims on behalf of the Christian community. His first argument questions Celsus' sources and asserts the value of the prophetic and miracle-working traditions of Judaism and Christianity:

> I know not how Celsus brings forward these as undoubted facts, while he treats as mere fables the wonders recorded and handed down to us as having happened among the Jews, or as having been performed by Jesus and His disciples. Why may not our accounts be true, and those of Celsus fables and fictions?

Events no less great than those sponsored by Delphi and other oracles were set in motion by the biblical prophets:

> Through the commands pronounced by the prophets cities were founded, men were cured, and plagues were stayed. Indeed, the whole Jewish race went out as a colony from Egypt to Palestine, in accordance with the divine oracles.

And then, in Origen's view the integrity of the Delphic oracle leaves something to be desired:

> It is related of the priestess of Apollo that she at times allowed herself to be influenced in her answers by bribes; but our prophets were admired for their plain truthfulness.

So far Origen is temperate in criticism. He goes much farther. He, too, has read, as we have, the quarrel among pagan authors and schools concerning the value of oracles—"we could quote passages to show that even among the Greeks themselves there were some who utterly discredited the oracles"—but he brings this to mind only to preface a more passionate argument:

> Let it be granted that the responses delivered by the Pythian and other oracles were not the utterances of false men who pretended to a divine inspiration. And let us see if we cannot convince sincere inquirers that there is no necessity to attribute oracular responses to divinities, but that they may be traced to wicked demons—to spirits at enmity with the human race, which wish to hinder the soul from rising upwards, from following the path of virtue, and from returning to God in sincere piety.[38]

The first and most compelling proof Origen offers is a stridently sexual version of the Pythia's trance while she presided from the tripod. He will not be the last to project the oracular process as a spooky seduction:

> It is said of the Pythian priestess, whose oracle seems to have been the most celebrated, that when she sat down at the mouth of the Castalian cave, the prophetic spirit of Apollo entered her private parts. And when she was filled with it, she gave responses which are regarded with awe as divine truths. Judge by this whether that spirit does not show its profane and impure nature by choosing to enter the soul of the prophetess by means of what no modest man would ever see or speak of. And this occurs not once or twice, which would be more permissible, but as often as she was believed to receive inspiration from Apollo.

Perhaps it is worthwhile to remember at this point that Origen's personal response to the temptation of sexuality in his youth was to castrate himself. While this act does not condemn, it does alert us to the repulsion he must have experienced as he pondered the image of Apollo's ineffable coupling with His priestess. Having set in place this image, sure to trouble men and women seeking in all sincerity to tread a somewhat ascetic Christian path, Origen goes on to apply to the Delphic oracle the gender bias of his time, place, and religious community. Apollo is again the loser: His choice of a priestess—of a *woman*, and not even a very distinguished woman (Origen knows his Plutarch)—provides further proof that Apollo is demon, not god:

> If Delphian Apollo were a god, would he not have chosen as his prophet some wise man? Or if such was not to be found, then one who was endeavoring to become wise? How came he not to prefer a man to a woman for the utterance of his prophecies? And if he preferred the latter sex, as though he could only find pleasure in the breast of a woman, why did he not choose among women a virgin to interpret his will? But no; the Pythian judged no wise man, no man at all, worthy of the divine possession, as they call it. And among women he did not choose a virgin, or one recommended by her wisdom, or by her attainments in philosophy. He selects a common woman. Perhaps the better class of men were too good to become the subjects of the inspiration.

He is not quite done demolishing the Delphic oracle. Measuring the difference between the biblical prophets and what he knows of Delphi, he finds fault with yet another fundamental aspect of the oracular process: *enthousiasmos*. Its passion, its apparent disorder, are so many signs of demonic activity:

> It is not the part of a divine spirit to drive the prophetess into such a state of ecstasy and madness that she loses control of herself. He who is under the influence of the Divine Spirit ought to be the first to receive the beneficial effects, and these ought not to be first enjoyed by the persons who consult the oracle. That should be the time of clearest perception when a person is in close intercourse with the Deity. If the Pythian priestess is beside herself when she prophesies, what spirit fills her mind and clouds her judgment with darkness, unless it be of the same order with those demons which many Christians cast out of persons possessed?

Thus Origen: a man of immense conviction and intellect, an influential teacher across the patchy but growing Christian community, for whom the Delphic oracle was in all respects an object of revulsion. Had he referred more objectively to the biblical prophets, he would have recalled passionate encounters between Jehovah and His prophets: not all episodes were as crystalline, as quietly illuminated, as Origen would have his readers believe. But he was not arguing for Jesus from a secure position; he was a soldier of Christ in a time of war, when his religion was still subject to persecution.

His vision of Delphi endured, and surfaced more than a century later in the writings of St. John Chrysostom (ca. 347–407), born decades after the emperor Constantine issued the historic edict of tolerance in the year 313, which gave official sanction to Christianity. In St. John's era, however, debate and periodic violence between Christians and pagans were far from over, although the traffic in violence had now reversed direction and flowed for the most part from Christian hotheads to pagan defenders of temples and shrines. While pagans and Christians now served side by side in the government and in many other functions, the struggle for the minds of men and women, and for worldly influence, continued.

The early churchmen were combatants. John Chrysostom—John the Golden-Mouthed, famed as a preacher—was educated in Antioch by the resolutely pagan orator, Libanius, whom we shall meet. John lived for some years as a hermit, returned to Antioch to preach, and was named Patriarch of Constantinople in the year 398. His probity and outspokenness earned him powerful enemies in the Christian leadership and court who managed, within a few years of his accession, to have him censured for incorrect views, removed from office and exiled, and ultimately coerced into a harsh winter trek that ended his days. John's comments on oracles, and Delphi specifically, reproduce with further emphasis two of Origen's primary themes: the contrast between *enthousiasmos* and the lucid bearing of the true prophet, and the darkly erotic scenario that joins Apollo with His priestess.

While we now have the taste of these themes, it is worthwhile to verify that they had become the common property of Christian apologists. John categorizes the Delphic oracle with all other types of "soothsaying," institutional and maverick, when he writes: "This is peculiar to the soothsayer, to be beside himself, to be under compulsion, to be pushed, to be dragged, to be haled as a madman. But the prophet not so. With sober mind and composed temper and knowing what he is saying, he uttereth all things."[39] One of the ironies of the preferred Christian attitude of composure and lucidity is that these traits would have been regarded by thoughtful pagans as Apollonian.

He grants to men and women
Healing from grievous sicknesses;
His is the harp. He gives to whom he will
The Muse, and brings into the heart
Law, that thinks not of battle.[40]

These lines from Pindar, written some nine centuries before John Chrysostom, reflect the essential tranquillity of the realm of Apollo, at the center of which was the dutiful life of the Pythia. But that was long ago, and the matter at hand is to enforce the new revelation by discrediting the old revelatory process. John continues:

> I am compelled now to bring foward and expose another disgraceful custom which it were well to pass by, because it is unseemly for us to mention such things; but that you may more clearly know [the shame of those who consult soothsayers] it is necessary to mention it. The Pythoness is said, being a female, to sit at times upon the tripod of Apollo astride, and thus the evil spirit ascending from beneath and entering the lower part of her body, fills the woman with madness, and she with dishevelled hair begins to play the bacchanal and to foam at the mouth, and thus being in a frenzy to utter the words of her madness. I know that you are ashamed and blush when you hear these things.

THE DETECTION OF IMPOSTORS

It was a small violence to chronology to skip forward from Origen in the first half of the third century to John Chrysostom in the later fourth, but the identity of argument across the gap was worth experiencing. Living a productive life in that long interval was a key Christian author, Eusebius (ca. 260–ca. 340), bishop of Caesarea, first historian of the Church, sometime advisor to the emperor Constantine, relentless adversary of the religion of the gods. In his book arguing the superiority of Judeo-Christian religious culture over pagan religious culture, he predictably mounts a fierce attack on "the antiquated seats of delusion,"[41] the oracles. However, he unpredictably enlists the help of an irascible pagan author, the Cynic philosopher and controversialist Oenomaus, whose unconstrained attack on oracles Eusebius must have had in his library and read with a sense of profound affinity. Dating to about the year 120 C.E., Oenomaus' tract, *The Detection of Impostors*, became the focus of controversy in the mid-fourth century when Eusebius cited it at length, while the pagan emperor Julian took Oenomaus to task for his indiscriminate fury. We meet Oenomaus in the pages of Eusebius, and again in Julian.

Eusebius begins his attack with observations of his own concerning what he takes to be the contrived and deceptive character of the Apollo oracles at Delphi, Kolophon, Branchidae, and elsewhere. Setting up a fictive "prudent man" and speculating about his opinions, Eusebius writes:

> The poems and compositions of the oracles, he would say, are fictions of men not without natural ability but extremely well furnished for deception, and are composed in an equivocal and ambiguous sense, and adapted, not without ingenuity, to either of the cases expected from the event.[42]

The content of oracular messages, Eusebius continues, is based not on divine inspiration but on research. No ancient author gives a more detailed version of this "explanation" of oracles, an explanation adopted in essence by some modern scholars, although without Eusebius' censure:

> [The temple officials] associate with themselves in their jugglery many confederates from without, who make inquiries about those who arrive, and the wants of each, and what he has come to request. Also, they conceal within their temples many secret shrines and recesses inaccessible to the multitude. The darkness helps their purpose not a little, as do the anticipatory assumption, the superstition of those who approach, and the opinion which has prevailed among them from the time of their forefathers.
>
> To this must be added also the silliness of mind of the multitude and their feeble, uncritical reasoning, and on the other hand the cleverness and craftiness of those who are constantly practising this mischievous art, prophesying obscurely and darkening the sense of their oracles by equivocations and indistinctness of expression, in order that no one may understand what is foretold, but that they may escape detection by the uncertainty of their statement. . . . The authors of the oracles are not gods nor yet daemons, but the delusion and deceit of human impostors.[43]

Eusebius is not prepared to declare that the gods were mere fantasies, however much he condemns oracular messages as human contrivance. Like many of his fellow Christians, he took the view that "those who have been honored among the heathen as gods in every city and country district were not gods nor yet good daemons, but the very contrary."[44]

While Eusebius goes on to restate many of the arguments we have already encountered, he fares into a zone of originality when he convenes Oenomaus to assist him. Oenomaus had had some serious scrapes with oracles—had inquired several times and been bitterly disappointed as many times. With his Cynic predisposition to cry foul, he sat down to pen a furious diatribe against oracles. These strident discourses were a specialty of the Cynic school. Their carping tone and tolerance of the notion that the end justifies the means are already familiar to us from the passionate Christian authors we have met; they were heirs to the tradition.

The saving grace of Oenomaus is that he can be funny. He fumes perfectly. As it happens, Oenomaus went to the oracle of Apollo at Klaros in a time of personal difficulty and put his question. This was the response he received, followed by his commentary:

> *In the land of Trachis lieth*
> *Thy fair garden, Herakles,*
> *Where all flowers forever blooming,*
> *Laden with perpetual dews,*
> *Are culled all day, yet ne'er diminish.*

> Impotent fool that I was, I became elated by the "Herakles" and the "garden of Herakles in its bloom," dreaming of an easy life because of the blooming garden. Then, on inquiring further, I was told by someone that he had heard that this very answer had been given from you *(i.e., Apollo)* to one Kallistratos, a merchant of Pontos. When I heard this, what do you think was my indignation? I would no longer accept the oracle. It appeared that none went without his share in the oracle, neither robber nor soldier, neither lover nor mistress, neither flatterer, nor rhetorician, nor sycophant.[45]

Oenomaus also made his way to the famed oracle of Apollo at Kolophon, where he received the following answer—his commentary appended as before:

> *When a man large stones projects from a widely whirling sling,*
> *With the blows he slays grass-eating geese unutterably great.*

> Now who will interpret for me what in the world is meant by these "grass-eating geese unutterably great"? Or the "widely whirling sling"? Will Amphilokos, or the god of Dodona, or will you at Delphi, if I should come there? Will you not go and hang yourself with your "widely whirling sling," and take your unintelligible verses with you?[46]

There is much else in the team play of Eusebius and Oenomaus that we would enjoy, but the gist is now clear. Eusebius finds his partner shortsighted in one respect only: "The plain speaking of Oenomaos in the *Detection of Impostors* is not free from Cynical bitterness. For he will not admit that the oracles proceed from a daemon, much less from a god, but says that they are frauds and tricks of human impostors."[47] In all other respects he felt that he had a firm ally in attacking "the feebleness both of the givers and receivers of [oracular] responses."[48]

To honor Eusebius, who has the real distinction of writing the first history of the Church, let us give him the opportunity to comment on all that has come before. "We have sufficiently exposed the character of the oracles," he writes in summary, and

> our Saviour has exhibited in the teaching of His Gospel an excellence worthy of God and at the same time beneficial to man; for by it alone, and by no other teaching, deliverance from the daemoniacal phantoms, which had from the beginning overshadowed and afflicted the whole life of man, was secured for all.[49]

"TO ALL INTELLIGENT MEN THE END OF THE TEMPLES WAS PAINFUL INDEED."

The fourth century has endless intricacies.[50] For our purposes we need principally two milestones: the years C.E. 313 and C.E. 392. The first marks Constantine's edict of tolerance for Christianity—the conversion into public policy of his adoption of the religion of Jesus Christ. The second marks the passage into law, by the emperor Theodosius, of a total prohibition against the celebration of pagan rites in temples and homes. In the interval between these dates, legislation and vandalism gradually eroded the autonomy, wealth, and security of temples across the Roman Empire, although matters stood very differently in different parts of the empire as the great transition unfolded. In some cities and regions, coexistence of pagans and Christians proved possible; in others the conflict was bitter. However, from the moment of Constantine's adoption of

Christianity as his personal religion, the triumph of Christianity over the religion of the gods was sealed. Enormously able and energetic, Constantine defined his era, set the future in motion. "We resolve to grant Christians and all other men freedom to observe whatever religion they think fit, so that the divinity, who has his abode in heaven, be propitious and benevolent as well for us as for any of those living under our rule. . . . No cult [shall be] deprived of due honors."[51] Words of truly great meaning, ending the persecution of Christians—and opening the way, as the century progressed, to unanticipated violence.

At mid-century the establishment of Christianity slowed, and even appeared to reverse direction, through the concerted activity of a figure regarded by his Christian contemporaries as Julian the Apostate. Among thoughtful pagans later narrating his brief life, he had quite another name: *theotatos Ioulianos*,[52] godlike Julian. A nephew of Constantine born in 332, Julian belonged to a branch of the family that had been repressed in the power struggle that followed Constantine's death. His life spared, he was dispatched to provincial obscurity to be raised by Christian and pagan tutors. Although instructed in Christian doctrine and surprisingly well versed in biblical knowledge, he was drawn both to the ancient temple rites and to the richly philosophical mysticism that had emerged in later antiquity out of Platonism. He pursued his study of philosophy in Ephesus and Athens, where his classmates included future leaders of the Christian church. Constantius II, son of Constantine and sponsor of the assassination of Julian's father, found it convenient in 355 to call Julian away from his studies to serve as Caesar in Gaul and Britain. The immediate needs were military, and perhaps Julian was intended to die in line of duty in northern Europe. Instead, he distinguished himself as a military strategist and earned the devotion of his troops. One has the impression of another Marcus Aurelius. Like Marcus, he was willing not just to tolerate but to master his military obligations at the frontier of the Empire. Like Marcus, even while in the field he read and wrote into the night.

In the year 360, Constantius attempted to exercise authority over Julian and his army. In response, the troops rebelled and acclaimed Julian Augustus—Constantius' equal and rival. Accepting their charge, Julian marched toward the inevitable trial of strength with Constantius resident in Constantinople, but the unexpected death of Constantius left him uncontested emperor of East and West. Sixteen months later Julian himself was dead, mortally wounded on campaign in Persia.

Rarely causing violence to Christians but never favoring them, Julian did what he could as emperor to reinstate the ancient religion.

> I am a follower of King Helios. And of this fact I possess within me, known to myself alone, proofs more certain than I can give. But this at least I am permitted to say without sacrilege, that from my childhood an extraordinary longing for the rays of the god penetrated deep into my soul.[53]

This is his powerfully idealistic voice. Julian's devotion was directed to the visible sun, and far beyond to a metaphysical sun, source of life and goodness, of which all the gods were fractions and aspects. In practice he took a strenuous view of philosophy. "The true short cut to philosophy is this," he wrote:

> A man must come competely out of himself and recognize that he is divine, and not only keep his mind untiringly and steadfastly fixed on divine and stainless and pure thoughts, but he must also utterly despise his body and think it, in the words of Heraclitus, "more worthless than dirt."[54]

With scarcely any alteration, Julian's thinking here could find its place in the letters of St. Paul or the teachings of the ascetic Desert Fathers. In Julian's era, Christian monastics had already begun to absent themselves from the political mêlée of Christianity "in the world" to retire into the solitude of rural Egypt. The finest forces arrayed on each side of the conflict between pagans and Christians were much like each other.

We can glimpse something of Julian's reverence for ancient truth and ways in his angry rejection of our now familiar combatant, Oenomaus, whom Christians had appropriated to their cause. Oenomaus struck Julian as a traitor not only to the whole of Greco-Roman tradition but to his own Cynic lineage, for which the moderately ascetic emperor had an affinity:

> This is his aim, to do away with all reverence for the gods, to bring dishonor on all human wisdom, to trample on all law that can be identified with honor and justice, and more than this, to trample on those laws which have been, as it were, engraved on our souls by the gods, and have impelled us all to believe without teaching that the divine exists, and to direct our eyes to it and to yearn toward it; for our souls are disposed toward it as eyes toward the light.[55]

Julian's accession as emperor was greeted with relief among his highly placed pagan contemporaries. Libanius, once his teacher, now a dedicated supporter, evoked in an address to Julian his heartfelt vision of renaissance, in which the ancient landscape and society are returned to themselves—and tells us that Julian was regarded by his friends as another Pythia, an oracle:

> Now would be the time to desire life and to offer sacrifices for a longer span, for now we can truly live, when the breezes of happiness waft over the earth, when there reigns one human of body and divine in soul, when on the altars fire surges up and the smoke of sacrifice purges the air, when men feast gods and gods consort with men. Confident in the reliance to be placed in the powers above, [our emperor] leads the world more wisely under their guidance. He does not wait for the oracles from heaven but establishes himself in place of the Pythia and refuses to gaze upon the lofty brow of seers or to make so great a duty dependent upon the will of others. Thus it happens that you both wait and proceed when the time is ripe.[56]

By Julian's reign, serious steps had been taken against pagan religious institutions and practices. Animal sacrifice and divination had been forbidden, although not with uniform success throughout the empire. In 357–58, laws were promulgated to criminalize sorcery and divination: "Let the curiosity to know the future be silenced for all forever."[57] Many temples had been closed or converted to other uses, some vandalized or quarried for architectural elements incorporated into new churches. Oracular temples were scarcely functioning, if at all. That Julian had thought carefully about the status of oracles is evident from his writings. Friendly toward the Jewish faith and its prophetic tradition—and using these things as admired points of reference in his critique of Christianity—he acknowledged that in his era all types of ancient prophecy had declined. His own practice of communion with the will of the gods was not an impiety under present circumstances but a divine gift:

> The spirit that comes to men from the gods is present but seldom and in few, and it is not easy for every man to share in it or at every time. Thus it is that the prophetic spirit has ceased among the Hebrews also, nor is it maintained among the Egyptians, either, down to the present. And we see that the indigenous oracles of Greece have also fallen silent and yielded to the course of time. Then, lo, our gracious lord and father Zeus took thought of this, and that we might not be wholly deprived of communion with the gods has granted us through the sacred arts a means of inquiry by which we may obtain the aid that suffices for our needs.[58]

The "sacred arts" may mean divination in the old Etruscan manner, by reading the organs of sacrificial animals, but there could be something else here, hinted already by Libanius when he described Julian as "establishing himself in place of the Pythia"—something more personal and secret. Late pagan literature has examples of strictly personal oracular activity that occupied to some degree the place once occupied institutionally by the great oracular temples. It is as if the oracular function retreated from temple to home, from public ceremony to private devotion. Eunapius, pagan author of a *Life of Julian*, evokes this migration in his description of a gifted young man, the son of his teacher Chrysanthios:

> His kinship and affinity with the gods was so unceremonious and familiar that he had only to place the garland on his head and turn his gaze upwards to the sun, and immediately deliver oracles which were always infallible and composed after the fairest models of divine inspiration."[59]

What could be these "models of divine inspiration," if not messages from Delphi and other oracles known to the circle of Chrysanthios, as they are known to us, through Herodotus, Plutarch, and other authors? By the mid-fourth century, the "Delphi of the mind" on which we have been relying throughout this book was the only one available.

Julian is said to have attempted to set things right at Delphi. Learning that Christians had been buried near Kastalia, the stream used for centuries to establish ritual purity, Julian ordered the removal of those tombs.[60] Further, according to tradition—now Christian, not pagan—he attempted to inquire at Delphi. The result was "the last oracle." We do not know what he asked, but tradition records the oracle's answer to his emissary:

> *Tell the emperor that my hall has fallen to the ground.*
> *Phoebus no longer has his house nor his mantic laurel*
> *Nor his prophetic spring. The water has dried up.*[61]

The Christian scholars by whom Julian's writings were partially preserved added what must be a legendary footnote to his short life. As he lay dying of battle wounds, he is said to have acknowledged the defeat of the religion of the gods: "Thou hast conquered, Galilean."

These traditions were gathered up in a poem by Algernon Charles Swinburne, the late Victorian poet now overshadowed by his greater contemporaries. Drippingly Romantic, "The Last Oracle" nonetheless evidences the nostalgia for ancient times and things that gathers around the figure of Julian. The lines are addressed to Pythian Apollo:

Years have risen and fallen in darkness or in twilight,
    Ages waxed and waned that knew not thee nor thine,
While the world sought light by night and sought not thy light,
    Since the sad last pilgrim left thy dark mid shrine.
Dark the shrine and dumb the fount of song thence welling.[62]

For some years after Julian's death in 363, pagans and Christians managed to live in reasonable harmony, despite occasional violence against pagans and their religious institutions. However, in about the year 379, Julian's friend and teacher Libanius found it necessary to petition the devoutly Christian emperor Theodosius for the restoration of oracles. "The oracles should once more perform their previous function," pleaded Libanius,

> and give advice to those who ask what they should do to improve their position. There would be no need of human counsel or counselor, since the decision about our welfare would come from the gods themselves. However, the oracles are silent and have made the world an unhappier place for it.[63]

A few years later, Libanius again addressed the emperor in what appears to be an open letter circulated to a small, influential audience. *For the Temples* is an eloquent petition "about the temples and the need for them not to be abused as they are now." Libanius assumes statesman-like roles of tutor, counselor, and friend to the court as he reviews the past, but he expresses sheer fury against the "black-robed tribe who eat more than elephants." These were monks, as he perceived them. In his era, they had already become a force in public life. Libanius is worth hearing out in some detail. The voice is valedictory. He remembers everything: the old order of society, the sense of repose that he and others used to experience in the temples, the reliance of Greece and Rome upon inspired seers, the overwhelming success of their civilization, which cannot have been wholly unrelated to reverence for the gods. But there is nothing to be done, and he knows it:

> [Constantine] thought it to his own advantage to recognize some other as a god. For all that, he made absolutely no alteration in the traditional forms of worship. Though poverty reigned in the temples, one

> could see that all the rest of the ritual was fulfilled. You have neither ordered the closure of the temples nor banned entrance to them. From the temples and altars you have banished neither fire nor incense nor the offerings of other perfumes. But this black-robed tribe, who eat more than elephants and, by the quantities of drink they consume, weary those that accompany their drinking with the singing of hymns, who hide these excesses under an artificially contrived pallor—these people, Sire, while the law yet remains in force, attack the temples with sticks and stones and bars of iron, and in some cases, disdaining these, with hands and feet. Then utter desolation follows, with the stripping of roofs, demolition of walls, the tearing down of statues and the overthrow of altars, and the priests must either keep quiet or die. After demolishing one, they scurry to another, and to a third. Such outrages occur even in the cities, but they are most common in the countryside.
>
> Temples, Sire, are the soul of the countryside: they mark the beginning of its settlement, and have been passed down through many generations to the men of today. In them the farming communities rest their hopes for husbands, wives, children, for their oxen and the soil they sow and plant.
>
> If they prate to me of the teachings of the scriptures they profess to obey, I will counter them with the despicable acts they have committed. In estate after estate shrine after shrine has been wiped out by their insolence, violence, greed, and deliberate lack of self-control. No one has sacrificed any victim, yet the temples, great and small alike, in which the weary used to find repose, have all been demolished, and those who have suffered this loss are like shipwrecked mariners, swept from the ships in which they sailed.
>
> These people who now claim to discourse upon heaven and its occupants—let any of them tell me which it was the Romans followed when from such small and humble beginnings they attained supreme power. Was it the god of these people? Or was it the gods with temples and altars, from whom they heard, by means of seers, what they should or should not do?[64]

His words scarcely require commentary. While from our vantage point we are aware of the grandeur of Christian teaching and of the person of Jesus, it does us no harm to be aware of the misery and violence visited upon pagans and the great "ships" in which they had sailed for so many centuries—among them, the temple at Delphi.

In a curious parable inscribed on the record of things, the people of Nicaea were among the very last to send a question to Delphi. It was in their city (modern Isnik), in the year 325, that Constantine convened the first Ecumenical Council, which began to define the church, its doctrines and its boundaries, as we know them today. According to Eusebius, it was also from Nicaea—date uncertain, veracity uncertain—that the city leaders dispatched emissaries to Delphi to ask whether they should continue to send offerings as in years past to Apollo at Delphi. It would surely not be good history, but acceptable storytelling, to imagine that on the road from Nicaea the city's emissaries to the oracle hurried unremarked past church officials riding solemnly toward the Council. The response given to Nicaea was not a proper oracular message at all, but more in the nature of an authoritative letter:

> It is not possible to renew the spoken oracle at Pytho.
> Already made dim by length of time,
> It has donned the keys of unprophetic silence.
> But offer to Phoebus, as is the custom,
> The sacrifices prescribed by the oracle.[65]

In the year 391, Theodosius closed all temples in Rome: "No one is to go to the sanctuaries, walk through the temples, or raise his eyes to statues created by the labor of man."[66] In the following year, an edict prohibited all forms of pagan worship across the empire, both in temples and in homes. One was not permitted even to offer incense to a divinity, to decorate a tree with ribbons, or to improvise an altar "with bunches of torn-up grass." In the year 397, the reuse of construction materials from temples was authorized for public works such as road and bridge repairs. In 435, an edict ordered the destruction of all temples "if there are any still untouched."[67]

Writing in the reign of Theodosius, the pagan teacher Eunapius summoned simple eloquence: "To all intelligent men the end of the temples was painful indeed."[68]

12

Know Thyself

Know thyself: *gnothi sauton*: γνῶθι σαυτόν. "Know thyself" retains the force of a voice speaking, and in its brevity carries silence with it. Although understood by many of the ancients as the point of departure for all philosophy, it was not an abstraction—it was, and surely remains, a voice addressed singularly to each person. In ancient times it was inscribed "somewhere," as Socrates says, on the temple at Delphi; scholars now think just within the temple porch.[1] No ancient author helps us imagine the experience of mounting the Sacred Way through the animated crowd, passing into the silence of the temple, and coming upon the inscription, no doubt large and deliberately presented. Its call to action implies a precarious position, as if we do not know ourselves. Many pilgrims to the temple must have been shaken by it.

In Pliny's time, the first century C.E., the inscription may have been brightened with gold leaf.[2] But by then it had long since risen from the wall to become the common inheritance of all Greece, all Rome. Today it is the only fragment of Delphic wisdom that floats freely among us, lighting here and there in the reflections and communications of psychologists, ministers, writers, teachers, seekers—and occasionally germinating, still a fertile seed. Its simplicity gives it some of the powers of a talisman, protecting its owner from unnecessary complexity, reseating him or her in the essential.

"Know thyself" is a voice speaking, but who is the speaker? "The 'Know thyself' descends from heaven,"[3] wrote Juvenal the satirist, striking a memorably sober note. Of this much the ancients were sure: Apollo is the source, and beyond Him all heaven. But the ancients were willing to tolerate uncertainty as to who first discovered these words in his mind or on her lips. Perhaps they came to one of the Seven Sages as a divine inspiration—to Bias or Thales or Chilon—or perhaps they were first spoken by one of the early priestesses at Delphi, Phemonoe or Phanothea. Perhaps the words predate these legendary figures; the matter was unclear. Even that master of precision, Aristotle, was willing to stand back: "Let the question of its origin," he wrote, "lie in dispute."[4]

The ancients were unanimous on one point: to know oneself is difficult. From start to finish, the tradition surrounding the commandment asserts its difficulty. Thales, one of the legendary Seven Sages, was once asked: "What is difficult?" "To know oneself," he replied. "And what is easy?" he was asked. "To give advice to another."[5] Much the same thought survives in a fragment from the mid-fifth century playwright, Ion:

> "Know thyself" is quickly said. How to do this,
> Among the gods Zeus alone understands.[6]

From the era of Ion to late antiquity, the presumption of difficulty remained intact. Commenting on the wisdom of the Seven Sages from his vantage point at the turn of the fourth century C.E., Iamblichus echoed the long tradition:

> [The Seven Sages] did not investigate what was simply good, but especially good, nor what is difficult, but what is particularly so—namely, for a man to know himself. So also they considered not what was easy, but what was most so, namely, to continue following habits.[7]

Even in the early Christian rephrasing of ancient wisdom, the notion of difficulty survived. St. Basil of Caesarea, one of Julian's critics, captured it through the metaphor of the eye, which looks out most vigilantly but "cannot see itself."[8] We are anatomically unsuited for self-knowledge.

The ancients were impressed by the compactness of the commandment. We still have the term "laconic," given to few words, recalling the region of Lakonia controlled by Sparta. Plato viewed "Know thyself" as typically Spartan in brevity, and he described the Seven Sages as "admirers and disciples of Spartan culture. Their wisdom may be viewed as belonging to the same category of pithy and memorable dicta."[9] Centuries later, Plutarch likened "Know thyself" and other brief sayings of the Seven Sages to "streams forced into a narrow channel": the words lose their transparency, "but if you will investigate what has been written and said about them . . . , you will not easily find more extensive writings on any other subject."[10] He had a second metaphor for the sayings: they were seeds. "How many philosophic inquiries have they set on foot, and what a horde of discourses has sprung up from each, as from a seed!"[11] Dio Chrysostom, an author most attentive to Delphic heritage, went so far as to suggest that the condensed sayings of the Sages were "even more divine" than the Pythia's answers, "for the response which is made to each for himself he hears and then goes his way—such responses are not dedicated and thereby made known to all mankind—but the maxims of the Seven Sages have been appointed for the common use of all."[12]

The first references to "Know thyself" in literature are simple, like the phrase itself, yet immensely evocative. Whatever it is to "know oneself" goes uncodified in the earliest surviving texts but is evoked in a way that encourages exploration. To know oneself is implicitly understood as process, a way of living and being distinct from the body of self-knowledge that might accumulate; the action of knowing remains primary, and so one always has unfinished business. The early texts convey with noble simplicity a sense of direction toward self-knowledge rather than narrow formulations of what that knowledge must be. This openness and relative absence of definition could not endure unchanged. As the Greek philosophical tradition developed, the inherent tension between wonder and precision, inquiry and system, developed with it. The verbal simplicity and practical difficulty of "Know thyself" invited commentary and discussions of method; how could it be otherwise? As we examine this tradition, rooted in Delphi but reaching out across the ancient world, we are almost sure to find ourselves in turn delighted, moved, exasperated—and again moved, by the long meditation that survives in ancient texts. This chapter is not a comprehensive survey, but if all goes well it should reflect the tradition in some of its most vital phases and provide food for thought.

As already observed, the tradition begins with the Seven Sages, fragments of whose compact thought were recorded by later authors. Their passage through the seventh and early sixth centuries is poorly documented, more legend than history. Plato tells us that they came together at Delphi and, in the course of their deliberations, dedicated a number of inscriptions ever after associated with Delphi.[13] It is quite certain that three maxims of the Sages were inscribed on the temple—Know thyself, Nothing too much, and this more obscure one: Make a pledge and destruction is near. Some students of these matters—not the present generation of scholars—have asserted that a maxim from each of the Sages was inscribed at Delphi. If this was so, visitors to the temple would have been confronted with dryly objective observations, for example: Practice is everything, and Most people are bad.[14] But Plutarch doesn't mention this even in dialogues that take up the first three, and he would know.

I HAVE SEARCHED MYSELF: HERACLITUS

The tradition enters literature more concretely with the fragments of Heraclitus, whom we have encountered. Flourishing in about 500 B.C.E., he is known to us through extraordinarily eloquent and suggestive excerpts recorded by other writers. Gathered in a book of fragments, they are one of the most powerful testimonies to early thought; they create, for at least some people today, a sense of passionate kinship with a man known, after all, through a handful of words. The fragments arise from the same spiritual universe as "Know thyself"; they speak the same bare language. Heraclitus directly cites the commandment in what amounts to a comment on it, but he is most engaging in fragments where one senses him responding to it, making it his own.

To grasp something of Heraclitus' approach, we will need to remember that his teaching was a call to attention, to wakefulness: the pattern of the world, both what is forever fixed in it and what forever changes, can become apparent only to a wakeful person. In the largest statement we have from him, he puts great weight on the concept of the Logos, typically left untranslated because no single word in modern languages does it justice:

> Although this Logos is eternally valid, yet men are unable to understand it—not only before hearing it, but even after they have heard it for the first time. That is to say, although all things come to pass in accordance with this Logos, men seem to be quite without any experience of it—at least if they are judged in the light of such words and deeds as I am here setting forth. My own method is to distinguish each thing according to its nature, and to specify how it behaves; other men, on the contrary, are

> as forgetful and heedless in their waking moments of what is going on around them as they are during sleep.[15]

What is the Logos concept at this point in human experience, long before it entered Christian scripture? Scholars, of course, debate its meaning—some in recent years taking a reductive view, as if the Logos were merely Heraclitus' "account" of things, others viewing it as a term of religious philosophy. Philip Wheelwright's brief, thoroughly paradoxical paraphrase captures much: "a transcendental and universal Other who speaks as it were."[16] My own working paraphrase shies away from the "who," the trace of a transcendent person admitted by Wheelwright; I cannot help but conceive the Logos as the luminous order of things, everywhere hidden and present, both a power and a pattern.

Heraclitus projects a world in which the hiddenness of the Logos and the complexity of the character of things can best be met and deeply apprehended by probing, insistent attention. In the aristocratic society to which he belonged, he asserted a radically new definition of superiority having nothing to do with lineage and wealth. The person of outstanding worth is reverently aware of the Logos shaping all things and meticulously attentive to what Heraclitus called "particulars"—the details of all things experienced.[17] The scope is vast, from the very highest level to the most close and evident.

In this context, we can perhaps more acutely hear his three surviving observations relating to "Know thyself":

> It pertains to all men to know themselves and to be temperate.
> I have searched myself.
> You could not discover the limits of soul, even if you traveled every road to do so; such is the depth of its meaning.[18]

These fragments have been commentated at length by many devoted scholars over the years—all to the good. Yet if one allows them to work their spell, one tends to enter into the state Heraclitus valued: something more like attentiveness or wakefulness than before. In this sense, they do not invite commentary, and one has to break the spell to check whether there is anything here about which we could usefully learn through taking our distance and putting the analytical mind back to work.

In the first fragment, Heraclitus joins two of the Delphic commandments: Know thyself, and Nothing too much, with the implication that a temperate or balanced way of life results from knowing oneself. This conjunction is later echoed with some variation by Plato, Plutarch, and others,[19] an indication that the view was widely accepted. The ancient ideal of temperance, balance, or right thinking (*sophrosyne*) is powerfully evident in a poem surviving from the seventh-century warrior-poet, Archilochos, whom we have already encountered:

> Soul, soul,
> Torn by perplexity,
> On your feet now!
> Throw forward your chest
> To the enemy;
> Keep close in the attack;
> Move back not an inch.
> But never crow in victory,
> Nor mope hangdog in loss.
> Overdo neither sorrow nor joy;
> A measured motion governs man.[20]

Sophrosyne is obviously not a formula for a dull life, but certainly for one endowed with a better chance of preserving flexibility and inner freedom.

"I have searched myself." Heraclitus, and the entire tradition that followed, projects response to the commandment as an activity, a challenging exercise—a search. Heraclitus asserts the accomplished maturity of his own search, but thereby invites us to undertake no less. He asserts to inspire, not to crush.

"You could not discover the limits of soul. . . ." The Greek word translated by "soul" is *psyche*, meaning not only mind-and-sensibility, as it does in our time, but the essence of what we are: the word "soul" comes closer than any. Heraclitus's commitment to vigilance and respect for detail is brought to bear in an inner world of unlimited scope. "I have searched myself," he reports—but knows that he has not reached the limits of soul and cannot.

By the mid-fifth century, there is a persuasive sign that "Know thyself" had become a touchstone of Greek thought, not an empty cliché but something more like a shared value providing guidance. In *Prometheus Bound*, perhaps the last play of Aeschylus (d. 456), Oceanus comes as a sympathetic advisor to the rocky crag where Prometheus is suffering the horrible punishment imposed by Zeus. Oceanus is speaking:

> Know yourself and reform your ways to new ways,
> For new is he that rules among the Gods.[21]

He counsels Prometheus to be humble before Zeus—Prometheus has talked too freely, too arrogantly for his own good. Implicitly drawing on the thought of Thales with which this chapter began, Oceanus drives his point home:

> You are by nature better at advising
> Others than yourself.[22]

"Know thyself" in this application has quite definite meanings: know your own measure and limits, know your place.[23] As the Delphic commandment was assimilated in Greek society, it acquired various practical meanings that coexisted with the more spiritually charged meanings we have begun to encounter. The commandment was not only an invitation to inward exploration; it was also a basis for behavior in society, and as such we shall come across it quite frequently. Once the Athenian orator Isocrates felt that he had demolished his adversary in a debate on the Spartans. " My opponent," he complacently observed, "had experienced the force of the inscription at Delphi and come to know both himself and the nature of the [Spartans] better than before."[24] There is no spiritual hush over this remark; it reflects a very public man.

I DIRECT MY INQUIRIES TO MYSELF: SOCRATES

The most supple discussion of self-knowledge in Plato occurs in the *Phaedrus*, where Socrates and his friend Phaedrus take refuge from the midday heat along the banks of a river.

> *Phaedrus*: You see that tall plane tree over there.
> *Socrates*: To be sure.
> *Phaedrus*: There is some shade, and a little breeze, and grass to sit down on, or lie down if we like.
> *Socrates*: Then make for it.
> *Phaedrus*: Tell me, Socrates, isn't it somewhere about here that they say Boreas seized Orithyia from the river?. . . .
> *Socrates*: No, it was about a quarter of a mile lower down, where you cross the sanctuary of Agra; there is, I believe, an altar dedicated to Boreas close by.
> *Phaedrus*: I have never really noticed it, but pray tell me, Socrates, do you believe the story to be true?
> *Socrates*: I should be quite in the fashion if I disbelieved it, as the men of science do. I might proceed to give a scientific account of how the

> maiden, while at play with Pharmacia, was blown by a gust of Boreas down from the rocks hard by, and having thus met her death was said to have been seized by Boreas, though it may have happened on the Areopagus, according to another version of the occurrence. For my part, Phaedrus, I regard such theories as no doubt attractive, but as the invention of clever, industrious people who are not exactly to be envied, for the simple reason that they must then go on and tell us the real truth about the appearance of centaurs and the Chimera, not to mention a whole host of such creatures, Gorgons and Pegasuses and countless other remarkable monsters of legend flocking in on them. If our skeptic, with his somewhat crude science, means to reduce every one of them to the standard of probability, he'll need a deal of time for it. I myself have certainly no time for the business, and I'll tell you why, my friend. I can't as yet "know myself," as the inscription at Delphi enjoins, and so long as that ignorance remains it seems to me ridiculous to inquire into extraneous matters. Consequently I don't bother about such things, but accept the current beliefs about them, and direct my inquiries, as I have just said, rather to myself to discover whether I really am a more complex creature and more puffed up with pride than Typhon, or a simpler, gentler being whom heaven has blessed with a quiet, un-Typhonic nature. By the way, isn't this the tree we were making for?
> *Phaedrus*: Yes, that's the one.[25]

Plato artfully raises the topic of self-knowledge in an ordinary setting at a casual pace, and that must be no small part of the intended message: these seemingly high matters must be approachable here and now or they cannot be worth all that much. Self-knowledge is both the highest of values and an issue that can be profitably explored while searching for a cool spot at midday. Answering Phaedrus, Socrates makes clear that the unfinished work of knowing oneself renders many pursuits trivial by comparison. He confesses that he does not yet know himself—and by this admission sets a standard that later generations, to our own time, have been unable to forget or entirely overlook. For if the purest model of wisdom in the fullness of his maturity "cannot as yet know himself," then the teaching is unmistakable: none of us knows ourselves. In this he joins Heraclitus, who proposes a journey without end.

Socrates' examples of self-knowing catch one's attention: he questions whether he is "more puffed up with pride than Typhon, or a simpler, gentler being." The realm of inquiry is not the mind but instead impulse and feeling. While other Platonic dialogues make clear that knowledge of one's own mind is very much a part of full response to the Delphic commandment, here Plato emphasizes what today we would call the "unconscious": unobserved feeling, attitude, behavior. The dialogue moves briskly on from this point to other concerns—it is not explicitly dominated by the question of self-knowledge—but Socrates' reflections have sense and warmth that can provide a lifetime of encouragement to those, in any age, to whom the Delphic commandment speaks.

While Delphi may speak to all, not everyone is listening. Socrates had a special friendship with Alcibiades, a much younger man who occupies a uniquely ambiguous place in the pageant of Athenian history. Clever, handsome, wealthy, connected, shameless, fun-loving, seductive, Alcibiades had but one vulnerability: toward Socrates. The old sage was the only person who befriended in him something that he himself disregarded, and the only person who disregarded the charisma by which all other men were enslaved. There was a pebble in Alcibiades' sandal: Socrates. There was no place to grab one man: Socrates. "He makes me admit," Alcibiades once said, "that while I'm spending my time on politics I am neglecting all the things that are crying for attention in myself. So I just refuse to listen to him."[26]

Alcibiades was for the most part a loyal follower of the Delphic commandment as Socrates, with grim wit, once reformulated it: "By no means know thyself."[27] To fully accomplish this, Socrates suggested that three categories of self-ignorance would do: a man "may think himself richer than his property makes him"; may think himself "taller and more handsome and physically finer in general" than he is; and, more commonly, may be deluded concerning what Socrates calls "possessions of the soul"—think himself virtuous when he is not, wise when he is not. Knowing oneself is, in part, a matter of seeing through vanity to whatever the truth may be. Not too surprisingly, a Platonic dialogue brings together Socrates and Alcibiades for a discussion dedicated quite substantially to the question of self-knowledge. Many scholars consider the dialogue spurious—written not by Plato but by an imitator—but in antiquity it was unreservedly accepted as genuine and served later authors as a point of departure for their own investigations of self-knowledge.

The concept that allows Socrates to introduce the question of self-knowledge is "taking pains over oneself."[28] "We may be taking no pains over ourselves," he hazards, "although we think we are." By bluntly stating the possibility, even the likelihood, of unconscious negligence, Socrates draws both Alicibiades and the rest of us into conversation. The first point of truth he establishes is that taking pains over something means applying a specific skill or art to it: the shoemaker takes pains over shoes by applying his knowledge of shoemaking. He then asks: "Whatever kind of art can we use for taking pains over ourselves?" Alcibiades, depicted in the dialogue as a young man just readying himself for political life, replies simply: "I cannot say." Socrates continues that we could not know what makes a shoe better without knowing shoes, from which it follows that we could not know the art that makes a better human being without knowing what we ourselves are. At this point, Delphi is not far:

> *Socrates*: Well, and is it an easy thing to know oneself, and was it a mere scamp who inscribed these words on the temple at Delphi; or is it a hard thing, and not a task for anybody?
> *Alcibiades*: I have often thought, Socrates, that it was for anybody; but often, too, that it was very hard.
> *Socrates*: But, Alcibiades, whether it is easy or not, here is the fact for us all the same: if we have that knowledge, we are likely to know what pains to take over ourselves; but if we have it not, we never can.[29]

Through a series of distinctions, Socrates now drives toward understanding what is authentically self. Everything—possessions, skills, the body itself—is soon perceived as external to an inner reality, *psyche* or soul, which is the true object of self-knowledge. "He who enjoins a knowledge of oneself bids us become acquainted with the soul." It is this lofty premise that made *Alcibiades I* so precious to late antique pagans drawn to mysticism, and to some of their Christian peers (for example, Basil's metaphor of the eye must owe a debt to this dialogue). From this perspective, the meaning of "Know thyself" is not at all the one we encountered in *Prometheus Bound*—know your place and limits. But the conversation is not over:

> *Alcibiades*: Your advice seems to me good, Socrates, but try to explain in what way we can take pains over ourselves.
>
> *Socrates*: Well, we have taken a step ahead, for there is pretty fair agreement now as to what we are, whereas before we were afraid that, without knowing it, we would take pains over something other than ourselves. . . . The next step is to understand what it means to take pains over the soul.[30]

In answer to his own question, Socrates returns to the Delphic commandment as the basis for a fairly elaborate "thought-experiment":

> *Socrates*: Suppose that instead of speaking to us as a whole, [the oracle] said to our eye "See thyself," how should we understand its meaning?

From this intriguing question he moves through a rather crabbed reasoning to the effect that the eye would then need to look into a reflective surface such as a mirror—just such a surface as exists within the eye itself: the eye of another person reflects our own image back to us. This reflective part of the eye he regards as most perfect and draws an analogy with the most perfect part of the soul: wisdom. "This part of the soul," he concludes, "resembles God, and whoever looks at this and comes to know all that is divine will gain thereby the best knowledge of himself."[31] The reasoning and work with metaphor are not especially deft, but four key concepts have nonetheless been joined into a pattern, and that is surely worth retaining: the soul, wisdom, the divine, and self-knowledge. As we look further in the tradition surrounding "Know thyself," we will see that it moves between this essentially religious view of self-knowledge and a more ethical, behavioral view—between an approach to inwardness and an approach to action.

Socrates says at one point in the dialogue: "Ah, my remarkable friend, listen to me and to the Delphic motto, Know thyself." This much has been accomplished. On the other hand, we have not yet encountered anything resembling method: to urge us to look to the divine part of the soul for self-knowledge is a statement of values not method. But Plato, and Socrates before him, are not in reality evasive: the whole of their teaching maps human being, and our relation with the gods and with one another, in answer to the Delphic commandment and the needs of life. And as Plato well knew, to the teaching in words one has to add the example of Socrates as he lived and met circumstances. No one was more sensitive to his example than that great sinner, Alcibiades. Once he was reminiscing about a military campaign in which both he and Socrates were soldiering:

> He started wrestling with some problem or other about sunrise one morning, and stood there lost in thought, and when the answer wouldn't come he still stood there thinking and refused to give it up. Time went on, and about midday the troops noticed what was happening, and naturally they were rather surprised and began telling each other how Socrates had been standing there thinking ever since daybreak. And at last, toward nightfall, some of the Ionians brought out the bedding after supper—this was in the summer, of course—partly because it was

> cooler in the open air, and partly to see whether he was going to stay there all night. Well, there he stood till morning, and then at sunrise he said his prayers to the sun and went away.
>
> And now I expect you'd like to hear what kind of a show he made when we went into action. . . . Do you know, Socrates saved my life, absolutely singlehanded. I'd been wounded and he refused to leave me, and he got me out of it, too, armor and all.[32]

There are more than a few hints about method here, almost unbearably rigorous. But we asked.

Xenophon's account of Socrates offers the richest understanding of self-knowledge as the basis for external welfare. You will remember that Xenophon was a pupil of Socrates who led a diverse and successful life as a military leader and occasional author. The title of this book, *Have you been to Delphi?*, derives from a dialogue he recalled between Socrates and an ambitious young man, Euthydemus, who had amassed a splendid collection of the writings of sages and poets but had not yet acquired much practical experience. When in the course of the conversation Socrates had rather cornered the young man, he circuitously raised the question of self-knowledge to show the way on:

> *Socrates*: Tell me, Euthydemus, have you ever been to Delphi?
> *Euthydemus*: Yes, certainly—twice.
> *Socrates*: Then did you notice somewhere on the temple the inscription "Know thyself"?
> *Euthydemus*: I did.
> *Socrates*: And did you ignore the inscription, or did you pay attention to it and try to consider who you were?
> *Euthydemus*: Indeed I did not, because I felt sure that I knew that already—for I could hardly know anything else if I did not even know myself.[33]

After a bit more maneuvering, Socrates was able to confront the young man with the many ways in which self-knowledge is the basis for good living, positive reputation, and communal welfare. The passage deserves a reading:

> "Isn't [it] obvious," said Socrates, "that people derive most of their benefits from knowing themselves, and most of their misfortunes from being self-deceived? Those who know themselves know what is appropriate for them and can distinguish what they can and cannot do; and,

by doing what they understand, they both supply their needs and enjoy success, while, by refraining from doing things that they don't understand, they avoid making mistakes and escape misfortune. Self-knowledge also enables them to assess others; and it is through their relations with others that they provide themselves with what is good and guard against what is bad for them. Those who do *not* know themselves and are totally deceived about their own abilities are in the same position whether they are dealing with other people or any other aspect of human affairs. They don't know what they want or what they are doing or what means they are using; and, through making gross mistakes about all these, they miss the good things and get into trouble. People who know what they are doing succeed in their activities and become famous and respected. Those who are like them gladly associate with them, while those who are unsuccessful in their affairs are anxious for those men to make decisions for them and to represent their interests, and pin to them their hopes of prosperity, and for all these reasons regard them with special affection. But those who don't know what they are doing make bad choices and fail in whatever they attempt, and so not only suffer loss and retribution in respect of these actions, but damage their reputation in consequence, get themselves laughed at, and live despised and unhonored. You can see, too, that any States which have gone to war with stronger ones through not knowing their own capability either lose their territory or exchange freedom for slavery."[34]

In this passage we are far from the spirituality of Heraclitus and of the phases of Plato we have explored. On the other hand, we are not far from good and usable views. Xenophon, the military man, preserved a thoroughly practical version of Socrates on self-knowledge, and there is no reason to doubt that his master, who cared so much to educate the young to live soundly and govern well, said something like this on some occasion—or perhaps many—much like this one.

By the calendar, we have now reached the first part of the fourth century B.C.E. We would probably agree that a diverse, whole, and challenging understanding of self-knowledge has been achieved within the tradition. It looks deep within to uncover and benefit from what is most central in the soul; it looks pragmatically to the external world in order to manage personal and communal affairs with lucidity and without illusion. Is the remainder of the tradition—the many centuries between Plato and the transitional late antique pagan and Christian thinkers—essentially a footnote to this understanding? Or did the tradition surrounding "Know thyself" refresh itself and find new perspectives?

WHAT ENEMY HAVE I LEFT?

"Know thyself" can be understood as the primal, irreducibly simple summons to inner life, to the construction of relationship with oneself. But we have also seen that it can be understood as the basis for astute conduct. Each of these perspectives was developed and in some ways intensified as the tradition continued after Socrates. The later fourth-century playwright Menander conveyed with serene sophistication one possible reworking of the theme: "In many ways the saying 'Know thyself' is not well taken. It would have been more practical to say: 'Know other people.' "[35] His easy freedom to critique and even reverse the divine commandment lets us know that hereafter "Know thyself" will have to fend for itself, so to speak, in an increasingly cosmopolitan society. For those within that society who could hear the message of Delphi but had no persuasive idea of how to go about "knowing themselves," there was still a means, offered by society itself. An anonymous text, probably of the third century B.C., shows the direction *into* society to discover oneself:

> It is very hard, as some of the Wise have declared, to know oneself—we are unable to contemplate ourselves from within ourselves. And because we are unable to know ourselves, we do unwittingly the very things for which we find fault with others. However, just as when we wish to see our face we look into a mirror, when we wish to know ourselves we can acquire that knowledge by looking at our friend. For our friend is a second self.[36]

This anonymous author of this book of ethical guidance makes a leap from the ancient conviction about the *difficulty* of knowing oneself to his own certainty that we *cannot* "contemplate ourselves from within ourselves." The balance between Plato's inwardness and Xenophon's enlightened action is apparently lost on this author, who no doubt reflected the thoughts of many in his era. One of the most common subversions of any discipline is to think "impossible" where the discipline itself asserts merely, but truthfully, that it is difficult. On the other hand, this anonymous author's awareness of how useful friends can be to one another in a search for self-knowledge is a contribution to the tradition of response to Delphi. Many centuries later, Epictetus echoed this theme and endowed it with characteristically vigorous common sense. "If one instructed a singer in a chorus to 'know himself,'" he asked, "would he not heed the order by paying attention both to his fellows in the chorus and to singing in harmony with them? Yes. And so in the case of a sailor? or a soldier?

Does it seem to you, then, that man has been made a creature to live all alone by himself, or for society?"[37] However much one may wish to "contemplate oneself from within oneself," and may need to do so in order to draw closer to the unwearied depths of human nature, Epictetus reminds us of the innumerable occasions when self-knowledge cannot be isolated from taking action together with others.

The question of faultfinding was blatantly evident to the ancients. Plutarch put it in extreme form: "Upon no one is the god so likely to have enjoined 'Know thyself' as upon him who is going to find fault with another."[38] On the other hand, the commandment directs us toward honest assessment of our own faults—and this theme becomes more engaging than it promises to be at first sight. Addressing the urbane society of his era, Plutarch linked the Delphic commandment to preserving integrity and good sense:

> If, in obedience to the god, we learn that the precept "Know thyself" is invaluable, and if at the same time we carefully review our own nature and upbringing and education, how in countless ways they fall short of true excellence, we shall not readily let flatterers walk over us. If Truth is divine, then the flatterer is in all likelihood an enemy to the gods and particularly to the Pythian god. For the flatterer always take a position against "Know thyself" by creating self-deception.[39]

Plutarch's contemporary, Dio Chrysostom, carried the question of self-examination still further in a fictional dialogue between his perennial hero, Diogenes the Cynic, and Alexander the Great. Before setting out on his campaign of world conquest, Alexander is visiting Corinth, where he finds Diogenes, the fiercely independent philosopher who fascinates Alexander in the same way that Socrates fascinated Alcibiades:

> *Alexander*: If I capture Darius and the kings of the Indians to boot, there will be nothing to prevent my being the greatest king that ever lived. What enemy have I left, if I capture the peoples I have mentioned?
> *Diogenes*: The most difficult of all to conquer, one who does not speak Persian or Median as Darius does, I presume, but Macedonian and Greek.
> *Alexander*: Who is this enemy of mine in Greece or Macedonia?
> *Diogenes*: Why, you don't know?—you who think that you know more than anyone else?
> *Alexander*: In that case, will you please tell me? Do not conceal it.
> *Diogenes*: I have been trying to tell you for a long time, but you do not hear that you are yourself your own bitterest foe and adversary as long

> as you are bad and foolish. And this is the man of whom you are more ignorant than of any other person. For no foolish and evil man knows himself, otherwise Apollo would not have given as the first commandment,"Know thyself!"—regarding it as the most difficult thing for every man.[40]

This is a wonderfully satisfactory text, and certainly one of the earliest formulations of the truth—and truism—that one is one's own worst enemy. Despite the loss of so much ancient literature, we are beginning to get a sense for what Plutarch called "the horde of discourses" written by the ancients in response to the Delphic commandment. There were so many aspects to discover and open out for others.

Universal dissemination of the commandment in ancient society naturally meant that it would become, for many, a commonplace rather than revered counsel, and this in turn permitted the vastly entertaining poets and satirists of the Augustan era and the Empire to turn it to their purposes. Ovid, in *The Art of Love*, gives a demonstration. He describes himself as reciting certain lines about the erotic frenzy of mares in heat when suddenly

> Apollo abruptly
> Materialized beside me, thrumming a chord
> On his gilded lyre, bay in hand, bay wreathed about his sacred
> Hair (to poets he will sometimes appear
> In visible form). "Preceptor," he told me, "of wanton
> Love, come, lead your disciples to my shrine,
> Show them the world-famous sign, that brief commandment:
> *Know yourself.* Only with true
> Self-knowledge will a man love wisely, pursue the matter
> By exploiting the gifts he's got.
> If nature's made him handsome, let him flash his best profile;
> If smooth-skinned, he should recline
> Bare-shouldered. The brilliant talker can fill in those awkward
> Silences; the good singer should sing,
> The good drinker—drink. . . .
> Such was Apollo's counsel,
> Counsel to be obeyed: this god speaks truth.[41]

Lucian, the second-century satirist whom we have met before, memorably took his turn at this sort of thing in a dialogue that brings together in the afterlife three of the wealthiest men who have ever lived, Croesus,

Midas, and Sardanapolus. They are regretting the lives they used to lead when Menippus, an early satirist and honored predecessor of Lucian, interrupts: "Bravo, go on. You keep up your whimperings, and I'll accompany you with song, with a string of Know-thyself's for my refrain. That's the proper accompaniment for such lamentations."[42] But Lucian, the Jonathan Swift of his era, was not just an entertainer—he was immensely observant and capable of extreme refinement. In what amounts to a very early essay in dance criticism, he returns us to the initial premise of this part of our discussion: one can look to others for self-knowledge, one can develop through self-knowledge the ability to play one's role in society with something more like insight and forbearance. "In general," Lucian wrote of what must have been a dance drama,

> the dancer should be perfect in every point, so as to be wholly rhythmical, graceful, symmetrical, consistent, unexceptionable, impeccable, not wanting in any way, . . . keen in his ideas, profound in his culture, and above all, human in his sentiments. In fact, the praise that he gets from the spectators will be consummate when each of those who behold him recognizes his own traits, or rather sees in the dancer as in a mirror his very self, with his customary feeling and actions. Then people cannot contain themselves for pleasure, and with one accord they burst into applause, each seeing the reflection of his own soul and recognizing himself. Really, the Delphic admonition "Know thyself" realizes itself in them from the spectacle. When they go away from the theater they have learned what they should choose and what avoid, and have been taught what they did not know before.[43]

One senses from Lucian's easy reach for "the Delphic admonition" just how embedded it was in ancient culture—never at any great distance from thoughtful people, always a point of reference, sometimes an inspiration.

SHAKE YOURSELF UP

The question of method has been hovering at the edge of this conversation with the ancients. Surely, despite loss of texts and our distance from the ancient world, some sensible hints on method have survived, which we can grasp. Some pages ago we heard Iamblichus define the difficult and the easy—to know oneself, to live habitually—and it is no error to read this as practical advice. Like the emperor Julian, whom we will meet again in this section, Iamblichus suggests that authentic self-knowledge must be won at the cost of seeing through conventional patterns of thought and behavior. But the call to practice is nowhere stronger than in the teaching of Epictetus, the former slave who gathered pupils around him first in Rome, later in the eastern empire in the second century C.E. Epictetus had a hard, impatient edge combined with penetrating practicality: his teaching concerns living, he urged his pupils along like an inspired cattle-driver. He was—and is—not safe to be around.

While Epictetus taught a certain tranquillity of mind, he pushed his pupils into life to see for themselves whether they had anything like personal calm that could survive the first sharp blow. Using the metaphor of the theatrical chorus, which he found especially fertile in lessons, he mocks the man who can only perform when surrounded by others and counsels us to "walk around by ourselves"—and bear the consequences:

> As the good chorus-singers in tragedy cannot render solos, but can sing perfectly well with other voices, so some men cannot walk around by themselves. Man, if you are anybody, walk around by yourself, and talk to yourself, and don't hide in the chorus. Let yourself be laughed at sometimes, look about you, shake yourself up, so as to find out who you really are.[44]

This is method: one must expose oneself and observe what happens next. But self-exposure, as Epictetus taught, is not recklessness: his pupils were well prepared by his teaching. Although to explore his teaching in depth goes beyond sensible boundaries for this chapter, it is fair to say that his insights on receiving impressions from life—harsh or sweet—without being subjugated by them, and his emphasis on observant intelligence and quiet will gave his pupils a perspective from which to face and benefit from the vicissitudes of life.

Epictetus converted the challenge of knowing oneself into a practical program. His pupils mustn't have gotten much sleep. One of his notions was to start with small things and work your way up to large ones. He issued this particular challenge in the form of an imaginary conversation with a terrified person:

> "But the tyrant will chain—" What? Your leg. "But he will cut off—" What? Your neck. What, then, will he neither chain nor cut off? Your moral purpose. This is why the ancients gave us the injunction, "Know thyself." What follows, then? Why, by the gods, that one ought to practice small things, and beginning with them pass on to the greater.

> "I have a headache." Well, do not say, "Alas!" " I have an ear ache." Do not say, "Alas!" I am not saying that it is impermissible to groan, only do not groan in the center of your being.[45]

This, too, is method. To know oneself is to preserve a sense of self despite outer difficulties—to let nothing, even great pain, displace it. But we are not required to begin with major challenges, headaches will do.

There is another element of method in Epictetus; call it thorough thought. Speaking with a man who aspired to follow the demanding path of the wandering Cynic philosopher, Epictetus passed in review the difficulties of that life of material poverty and deliberate unconventionality, and concluded with this counsel: "Think the matter over more carefully, know yourself, ask the Deity, do not attempt the task without God."[46] To know oneself must mean here to take one's own measure, to assess who one is and what, at base, one wishes. This inward measuring participates in a larger circle of reflection and prayer.

We should not take leave of Epictetus without recalling another aspect of the abrasive, strangely liberating realism of his approach to self-knowledge. "Why are the words 'Know thyself' carved on the front of [Apollo's] temple," we have already heard him ask, "although no one pays attention to them?"[47] You may remember from chapter 3 that Apollo at Delphi represented for Epictetus the very model of duty fulfilled despite outward obstacles: the temple would be there, and Apollo ready to speak within it, even if humankind passed by without noticing. The thought must mirror his experience as a teacher.

There was a point of method about which the ancients could not reach a unanimous view. Some, like the Roman statesman and philosopher Cicero, believed—surely on the basis of experience—that far-reaching study of all kinds of knowledge would eventually lead the knowledge-seeker to the quest for self-knowledge. It is as if a gap would be discovered and imperiously demand attention. Others, echoing Socrates in that wonderful riverside conversation, believed that wide-ranging speculative study lured one away from the intensity and modesty of focus on oneself. "What sort of thing am I?" is a very different question from "What is the order of the universe?" The first question, according to some of the ancients, promised great and immediate benefits, while the second could lead to a profitless morass. The passages where the issue is taken up need not be quoted here and now,[48] but the gist of the question remains interesting today, when there is a general conviction that science and technology have given us greater powers than we are morally prepared to handle; many people have the queasy sense that knowledge runs ahead of self-knowledge, and that this is dangerous.

On the other hand, there was agreement that impartial self-inventory is essential. Speaking of this, some project a sensitive, exploratory approach to oneself while others propose a tough-minded approach: psychology versus taxonomy, art versus science. These left-brain, right-brain matters were being faced long before us. Philo Judaeus (c. 30 B.C.E.–C.E. 45), an engaging Jewish thinker of Alexandria, equally versed in Greek and biblical knowledge, found in biblical tales allegories of the soul in search of self-knowledge. When Rebecca and Isaac (Gen. 27:41 ff.) send Jacob to her brother Laban to escape the wrath of Esau and to find a wife among Laban's people, Philo finds himself arrested by Rebecca's advice, "Stay with him a while." Philo does not hear mere storytelling, he hears coded counsel to descend into the ordinary world and come to know oneself:

> This mother says, "Child, make thine abode with him," not forever, but "for a few days." This means "Learn well the country of the senses; know thyself, and the parts of which thou dost consist, what each is, and for what it was made, and how it is meant to work, and who it is that, all invisible, invisibly sets the puppets in motion and pulls their strings, whether it be the Mind that is in thee or the Mind of the Universe."[49]

As Philo reads with his very special eyes, Jacob is counseled to make a "precise scrutiny" of Laban, symbol of the outer world. Jacob is not to be caught by his experience but to turn it to advantage while preserving his strength and goodness of character. All of this is a vigorous approach to self-knowledge, not armchair knowledge but the result of confrontation with "the country of the senses" and persevering effort to keep one's balance. One knows oneself, one makes the required inventory of what each part is "and for what it was made, and how it is meant to work," by living fully yet observantly. On the other hand, Philo's language is evocative and somewhat indirect; he seems to want more to inspire a migratory sense of direction toward self-knowledge than to stipulate details of method. Philo was acutely aware of the limitations of human knowledge. He viewed self-knowledge as the proper domain of human beings and, with the reverence of his Jewish faith, retreated from any pretension to "know all." This essential modesty is captured in his comments on Exodus 33:13–24, where Moses asks the Lord to reveal Himself. Philo's sensibility recasts the words of Jehovah in a way that reflects both the psalmist and the sophist:

> The apprehension of Me is something more than human nature, yea even the whole heaven and universe will be able to contain. Know thyself, then, and do not be led away by impulses and desires beyond thy capacity.[50]

Julian, our doomed emperor, was harder than Philo. As you can imagine, he thought a great deal about self-knowledge and heard the Delphic call as acutely as any in his generation. Like some of his predecessors in attempting to understand the task of self-knowledge, he found it helpful to link the irreducibly simple "Know thyself" with another Delphic injunction. Plutarch, as you may recall, related it to the call for moderation: Nothing too much. Julian, touched by the example of Diogenes, linked it with the oracle's legendary advice to Diogenes: Give a new stamp to the common currency. In these rather ambiguous words of counsel, Julian and many others heard a charge to abandon all received and commonly held ideas, and to drive toward facts and truths one can establish for oneself.[51]

The truths of genuine self-knowledge had two quite different "flavors" for Julian: on the one hand a cold inventory, on the other an aspiration to become godlike by uniting inwardly with that in us which is not different from the gods. "In philosophy," he wrote, "the end and the beginning are one, namely, to know oneself and to become like the gods. That is to say, the first principle is self-knowledge, and the end of conduct is resemblance to the higher powers."[52] On the way toward that resemblance, there is much work to do. Julian presents the task of knowing oneself as a meticulous intellectual challenge. His tone is somewhat off-putting—there is nothing here to match the earthy humor of Epictetus—but it is worthwhile to taste how a person of high intelligence in late antiquity viewed the challenge of knowing oneself:

> He who knows himself will know not only about his soul but his body also. And it will not be enough to know that a man is a soul employing a body, but he will also investigate the essential nature of the soul, and then trace out its faculties. And not even this alone will be enough for him, but in addition he will investigate whatever exists in us nobler and more divine than the soul, that something which we all believe in without being taught and regard as divine, and all in common suppose to be established in the heavens. Then again, as he investigates the first principles of the body he will observe whether it is composite or simple; then proceeding systematically he will observe its harmony and the influences that affect it and its capacity and, in a word, all that it needs to ensure its permanence. And in the next place he will also observe the

> first principles of certain arts by which the body is assisted to that permanence, for instance, medicine, husbandry, and the like.[53]

Proceeding systematically. . . . We are far from the simplicity of "Know thyself," but we should cede a few points to Julian. He may exaggerate the need for distinct categories and procedural expertise, but some degree of mapping and method is surely needed, and all of the perseverance that his programmatic approach implies. "Really," remarked Plutarch, "it is possible that if the 'Know thyself' of the oracle were easy for every man, it would not be held to be a divine injunction."[54] Really, we should not be surprised to find challenging methods brought to bear on the task.

BEGINNING AT THE HEARTH

The ancients struggled, as we do, with the eternal paradox of human nature. On the one hand we are what Plato called "featherless bipeds," doomed to die and often living badly. On the other hand our minds encompass the universe and, as Julian has just said, there is that in us "which we all believe in without being taught and regard as divine." The ancient understanding of "Know thyself" could not help but confront this paradox, sometimes emphasizing one side or the other, sometimes reaching for a comprehensive vision that acknowledges both the divine and its precarious dwelling in us. Menander, the fourth-century playwright, shows what it means to acknowledge without illusion our mortal condition:

> When you wish to know yourself—what you are—look at the tombs as you pass along the street. In them lie the bones and the light dust of men—of kings, and tyrants, and wise men, and men greatly exalted by reason of their birth or fame or personal beauty. A common grave claimed them all, mortals that they were. Looking to these things, know yourself.[55]

Yes, of course, but that is not the end of the matter. Cicero continues the long thought some centuries later in an evocation of the mind as it matures, passing from one study to another:

> To the soul occupied night and day in these meditations there comes the knowledge enjoined by the god at Delphi, that the mind should know its own self and feel its union with the divine mind, the source of the

> fulness of joy unquenchable. For meditation upon the power and nature of the gods of itself kindles the desire of attaining an immortality that resembles theirs, nor does the soul think that it is limited to this short span of life.[56]

Yes, but that is not yet the end of the matter. Plutarch resumes the long thought in his dialogue, *The E at Delphi* (see chapter 10), where he interprets the enigmatic wooden E, hanging high in the temple, as meaning "Thou art," and intended to remind us both of imperishable divine being and of frail human becoming:

> [The E] is an address and salutation to the god, complete in itself, which brings him who utters it to thoughts of the god's power. For the god addresses each one of us as we approach him here with the words "Know thyself," as a form of welcome, and we in turn reply to him "Thou art," as rendering unto him a form of address which is truthful, free from deception, and the only one befitting him only, the assertion of Being. The one is addressed in awe and reverence to the god as existent through all eternity, the other is a reminder to mortal man of his own nature and the weaknesses that beset him."[57]

These three passages are surely enough to prepare us for the reflections of late antique thinkers for whom "Know thyself" was a summons to spiritual quest. From their perspective, could one but know oneself, one would know Being, "the fulness of joy unquenchable," and know oneself as Being. While the direct impression of Being may be brief in duration, it reveals the hidden order of things and offers a natural basis for stability—for a life of faith, search, and kindness. One perceives oneself and all others as exiles from Being, yet one knows one's home, and one has confidence that what we live, and how we live, quickens or delays the journey home. From this perspective, to know oneself is not primarily an act of prudence, not primarily preparation for skilled action in the world, but an act of longing and, when fulfilled, an initiation. The language of the Greek mystery rites becomes audible as the ancient conversation continues.

Macrobius, Roman and pagan (ca. C.E. 400), captured quite poignantly the theme of exile and return:

> The one way for a man to know himself is to look back at the first beginnings of his origin and birth, and not seek himself without. For so the soul puts on her own virtues through the consciousness of her nobility, and with these she afterwards tears herself away from the body and is carried back whence she has descended, because she has not

> soiled herself in her bodily state nor been burdened with impurities—nor does she seem ever to have deserted the Heavens, which she has continued to possess by looking to them in her meditations.[58]

Pursuing the same thought a century later, the pagan philosopher Proclus used a beautiful phrase from the Eleusinian mystery, *beginning at the hearth*, by which he (and the mystery tradition) must have meant beginning from the inmost spark that makes us what we are—beginning from the very basis and origin of our lives. "From what point," he asks,

> should we properly begin the purification and perfection of ourselves other than with the command which the God at Delphi gives us? For as an inscription presents itself to those who are about to enter the precinct at Eleusis, forbidding the uninitiated to go within, so surely the Know thyself on the temple front at Delphi showed, I fancy, the way of approach to the divine, and the most effectual road to purification. It says virtually in plain terms to those who can understand that he who knows himself beginning at the hearth is able to be united with god, the revealer and guide of universal truth and of the purified life.[59]

These are late pagan texts, but it will not be lost on us that they could in all essential respects have been written by Christian contemporaries of Macrobius and Proclus: the "sound" of late antique mysticism is unison, or very nearly, among pagans and Christians. We can ask Gregory the Thaumaturge, a pupil of Origen's, to speak from the Christian perspective:

> Certainly the most beautiful task of philosophy is attributed to the most famous seer among the demons as a very wise injunction: "Know thyself." The very soul endeavors to look upon itself as if in a mirror; if it becomes worthy of this communion it contemplates in itself a reflection of the divine intelligence, and it pursues an ineffable path toward divinization.[60]

We began with the idea of paradox: with the cohabitation in us of coarse and fine, base and noble, time-stricken and eternal. There is a drive in these late texts to break altogether free of the human condition, to resolve the paradox in favor of heaven. This makes the texts both touching and, perhaps for many of us, somewhat remote: we would settle for less. But how much less? One possible answer to this question shines through the words of Philostratus, a pagan author of somewhat uncertain date (C.E. 2nd–3rd centuries). "I consider," he wrote,

> that a wise man does nothing in private nor by himself alone; I hold that not even his inmost thoughts can be so devoid of witness that he himself at least is not present with himself. The sage who "knows himself" and has his own conscience as his perpetual companion will never cower before things that scare the many, nor venture on courses which others would engage upon without shame.[61]

Much the same quality—realistic yet upright, transparent enough but grounded—is evident in Gregory's praise of his master Origen: "He taught us to be wise and to be with self, and to wish and try to know ourselves. This indeed is the noblest function of philosophy, which is ascribed to the most oracular of gods, since it is an all-wise command—the Know thyself."[62]

"He taught us." We can detect behind these simple words the disciplined life of a school in which Origen, with due mastery, led his pupils—in part academically, in part experientially—toward what it means "to be with self." Other texts to which we have listened, especially the words of Epictetus as recorded by his gifted pupil Arrian, similarly suggest the intensity and directness of school training. Such texts flow from the teaching/learning experience and reflect that experience to a degree but not entirely: they are not the experience itself. An irretrievably lost oral tradition underlies some of the surviving texts from which we have assembled our understanding of the ancients' approach to "Know thyself." Like music, teachings are performed in the present moment. In some ways the standard term "oral tradition" does not capture what it must have been to study day-to-day with Heraclitus, Socrates, Diogenes, or Epictetus. Their words—their "oration," however informal—can survive as texts but the influence of their persons, the creative pressure they exerted on others by virtue of what they were, survives only in descriptions, which of course are texts themselves. Oral teaching could be more accurately, although eccentrically, described as "incarnate teaching" or "ocular teaching": incarnate, of the body, because the teacher's atmosphere, stance, gesture, and motion communicate without words; ocular because the teacher's vigilant eyes summon students to practice and in their qualities—surely of heightened attention, perhaps of exceptional kindness—they, too, are a source of teaching without words.

If the many texts we have explored in this chapter do not quite show a practical direction toward self-knowledge but only suggest what that direction might be, we have no reason to conclude that the tradition itself was lacking. Making allowance for the loss of so much ancient literature, the record is quite full and satisfactory. As Dio Chrysostom said, the Delphic commandment was addressed to all without exception, not only to the fortunate pupils of gifted teachers, but also to men and women in rags, in crowns, in street clothes. We are at no greater disadvantage than the average pilgrim.

KNOW THE MOMENT

At Olympia, many days' travel from Delphi, there was an altar dedicated to a minor but compelling god, Kairos.[63] In the Olympic setting, the god's name translates as "Opportunity." A number of texts tell us that seizing the unpredictable moment of opportunity in a frantic chariot race or wrestling match often spelled the difference between victory and defeat. The god Kairos belonged at Olympia—and everywhere, including Delphi, where the ancients celebrated themselves and their gods through athletic contests. "The moment gives the crown,"[64] sung Pindar in an ode to a victor at the Delphic games; and in another praise song he congratulated a charioteer for handling his reins cleverly "in the nick of time."[65] "Know the moment" was Olympic wisdom, just as "Know thyself" was Delphic wisdom. Both sayings were attributed to the Seven Sages—Pittakos was traditionally given rights to "Know the moment."[66] But I have already altered the saying by the shift from "Know the opportunity"—literally opportunistic advice applicable to the games and to the game of life—to the more general "Know the moment." This alternative translation is equally legitimate but suggests experience beyond the games. Hippocrates, for example, made the comparison, in medical practice, between the passage of time and the moment of opportunity:

> Time (*kronos*) is that wherein there is opportunity (*kairos*), and opportunity is that wherein there is no great time. Healing is a matter of time, but it is sometimes also a matter of opportunity.[67]

Looking a little further, we can find, as so often, a wickedly sophisticated use of the term in later poetry, for example, a homoerotic epigram by Strato that converts ancient wisdom into droll seduction:

> "Know the moment" said one of the Seven Sages;
> For all things, Philippos, are more loveable
> In their prime. A cucumber, too, is a fruit

> We honor at first when we see it in its garden bed,
> But after, when it ripens, it is food for swine.[68]

Hippocrates prepares us better than witty Strato for the powerful mutation of the word *kairos* when it enters the vocabulary of the Gospels and the first generations of Christian authors. For them *kairos* is not even remotely the moment of opportunity, to be seized and exploited, but rather the privileged moment when the will of God makes itself known, be it through suffering or through joy. Mark 1:15: "The time is fulfilled and the kingdom of God is at hand." In the Greek of the Gospels, this quality of time is *kairos*, not *kronos*.

Noticing this mutation from the *kairos* of athletes and physicians to the *kairos* of spiritual dimension, I found myself linking the wisdom of Olympia and Delphi: as if to know oneself and to know the moment are each other's completion. As you recall, a number of our source authors linked "Know thyself" with other counsel—Plato and Plutarch with "Nothing too much," Julian with the oracle's advice to Diogenes. It may make sense for us to do the same. But why?

The sources need no correction in their own time; they are what they are. On the other hand, it is not completely evident that "Know thyself" is sufficient counsel for those who feel, even today, addressed by Socrates when he asks, "And did you try?" "Know thyself" is incomparably valuable advice—yet it can lead to what philosophers call solipsism and to what the rest of us are likely to experience as narrowly self-involved human beings. It was not meant to sponsor great preoccupation with one's petty self or petty preoccupation with one's greater self. It was meant to inspire vigorous self-assessment as a preface and companion to authentic inwardness. It was meant, as well, to lay the groundwork for lucidity in the conduct of one's own affairs and of affairs of state. But like all good things, it is easily diverted into odd channels. Those who "know themselves" may know nothing but themselves, and their self-absorption rather spoils them.

To know the moment, in all possible senses, provides the balance. It suggests vigilant attention to the course of events and to one's own possible contributions to general welfare. It suggests the value of striking deep roots in the present moment, in which all things unfold, without disregarding needs to ponder the past and envision the future. It divides us as we are in reality divided, between a rich capacity for inwardness and a no less complex and rewarding presence in the world. "Know thyself" and "Know the moment" are addressed to us as if we are here and whole to receive them. Apollo and the Seven Sages are confident that we can integrate the call to ourselves and the call to participate.

STERNO TRIPODOS: THE TRIPOD WITHIN

India was the edge of the world which later Greeks could acknowledge: Alexander had marched to it with his troops and others, causing less turmoil, had profited from their encounters with Indian thinkers. Greeks detected in India signs of a mature and serious view of life, different but respectable. The late antique biography of Apollonius of Tyana—is it biography, fiction, or both?—sends that saintly pagan to India where he comes upon a circle of impressive philosophers with whom, in effect, he compares notes. In the course of their exchange, the topic of divination naturally comes up. The leader of the Indian brotherhood provides a striking account of their practice:

> We foresee of our unaided selves and foretell to others things they know not. This I regard as the gift of one thoroughly blessed and endowed with the same mysterious power as Delphic Apollo. The ritual insists that those who visit a shrine to obtain a response must purify themselves first, otherwise they will be told to "depart from the temple." Consequently I consider that one who would foresee events must be healthy in himself, and must not have his soul stained with any sort of defilement nor his character scarred with the wounds of any sins; so he will pronounce his predictions with purity, because he will understand himself and the sacred tripod in his breast (*sterno tripodos*).[69]

The concluding phrase is arresting. Does it suggest a point of rest for our thoughts about Delphi? In late antiquity the waning of the great institutional oracles made room for a personal approach to divination. Apollonius's Indian friend takes this pattern to the ultimate point when he reports that an individual who has lived well and understands himself can discover the "tripod within," an extraordinary source of knowledge. In some respects it would be fitting, and convenient, to apply this thought to the Delphic institution as a whole. The argument would unfold as follows: What *really* occurred at Delphi over the centuries was communion with oneself and a sharing of guidance that ranged from high wisdom to road maps. The Pythia drew from herself, the attending priests interpreted by their own best insight, the questioners summoned their most resolute attitude before the mystery of Delphi, and when all went well the result was a quite spectacular enactment of truth-seeking and the uncovering of truth. All participants felt that they were in touch with the mind of God, and this creative fiction provided a rush of momentum, lasting a thousand years and serving people well.

The argument has merit. It captures the dimension of psychological inwardness that was a part of the Delphic experience, if not for state embassies on official business, then for individuals on private business and for the temple personnel. It promises that we have not lost touch with the essential attribute of the Delphic oracle because "the tripod within" is potentially available to each and all. In this sense the argument annuls history, asserts enduring possibility.

But accepting this perspective and acknowledging the hidden tripod within, can we also be wary of domesticating Delphi, of reducing it to a comfortable scale? In ancient times the oracle was a source of discomfort: its ambiguities were uncomfortable for questioners, its claim to speak the word of God was uncomfortable for rationalists. These discomforts are worth preserving. We still cannot say with certainty where our own natures end and another nature begins, nor can we say with certainty what the proper language of the Other must be. The tripod within may not be one's own. Perhaps the Delphic oracle did quite well, after all, in reaching to the extremity of our natures, and then beyond to discover a spoken word full of paradox and truth.

The early Greek hymns typically end
with a sign of verve and continuity, addressed
to the god or goddess to whom the hymn is dedicated.
The words, and their meaning, still live:

I will remember you and another song.

Afterword

Delphi and Nechung: A Dialogue with Lobsang Lhalungpa on Parallels Between the Delphic Oracle and the Chief State Oracle of Tibet

A Tibetan lama and scholar now living in the United States, Lobsang Lhalungpa has translated into English numerous Tibetan works on religious doctrine and meditative practice. He is also a major participant in the formation of the Tibetan-language curriculum for Tibetan schools in north India. Mr. Lhalungpa is the son of the Chief State Oracle of Tibet who served in approximately 1912–18. In addition, his uncle was an attendant of a Chief State Oracle in the 1940s. He is thus intimately familiar with the institution. In his brother's company during the years before the Chinese invasion, he travelled widely in Tibet to explore its many regional oracles and other living religious traditions. Editorial intervention in this recorded dialogue has been restricted to clarifying meanings and condensing much of the Delphic side of the exchange.

RL: The fragmented nature of our possible knowledge of Delphi makes one ask whether there is—or was—a comparable institution in another cultural setting, about which knowledge is more complete. And the Chief State Oracle of Tibet comes to mind.

It is too much to expect a close identity between Delphic and Tibetan "oracular cultures," but Delphi was arguably the Chief State Oracle of its time and place, and the best book on Tibetan oracles,[1] to which you contributed very centrally, indicates surprising parallels. It could be helpful to explore the Tibetan phenomenon in general and to look at those things in Tibet that occupy the gaps in the Delphic record. The Tibetan analogues cannot be assumed to reveal anything definite about Delphi, but they should at least indicate the *kinds* of things that occupy those gaps in a fully developed oracular culture.

What was the purpose of the Tibetan State Oracle, and what sorts of questions were asked of it by state officials?

LL: Let me say first that there were three recognized state oracles, among which the Chief State Oracle was best known. The Chief State Oracle resided at Nechung Monastery, which served as his institutional base and where he was head of the monastery. For this reason, the Chief State Oracle was ordinarily known as the Nechung Oracle. Now, regarding official questions: they came from two main sources, the Dalai Lama and high government officials such as the Council of Ministers. The questions usually concerned the general well-being of the country. Because the Tibetan economy is primarily agricultural, there were always inquiries about rainfall, good weather, bad weather, and such. There were also questions about the well-being of ordinary people and about international relations, especially with China. China has always been a problem for Tibet.

When the Cabinet ministers went to Nechung Monastery, they would take with them a prepared questionnaire. One of the secretaries would read it aloud in front of everybody while the oracle sat on his throne and listened. Question number one would concern the health and long life of His Holiness: Do you foresee any obstacles to his health, and if so what should be done? The second question would concern the general well-being of the people: Would there be continuous economic development—not quite development, but stability? Will there be an epidemic? And the third question: if there was a specific problem arising from the Chinese attempt to interfere with Tibet or any problem of this order, they would specifically ask about it. For example, in my youth Chiang Kai Shek was trying to use Western Chinese warlords to invade Tibet. In such an instance, the question would be raised: Is there anything we can do? What should we do?

The Oracle would whisper the answer to each question to his secretary, who was holding a blackboard on which he would quickly write down the answers.

The Cabinet usually visited the monastery at least once during the Tibetan New Year season, which falls in early spring according to the lunar calendar. At another time of year there was a big government-sponsored festival honoring the Chief State Oracle, and the Ministers would go there again. The Oracle went into trance and they would put a number of questions. After that solemn event there were festivities, the monks at the monastery would stage dances and hold a celebration.

If there was an emergency—usually it would concern problems with China—the Cabinet would suddenly arrive at the monastery. For this reason, the Chief State Oracle had to be ready at all times. He would go into trance and answer the questions. In cases where a question was of a delicate nature, the consultation was done not in the assembly hall but rather in a private shrine with just the concerned ministers in attendance, perhaps three or four, with the Oracle and his secretary.

When the Dalai Lama is alive, the Chief State Oracle is officially and personally attached to him, and His Holiness can call upon him at any time. The State Oracle would go to the palace, whether the Potala winter palace or Norbulingka summer palace, and meet with His Holiness in his private residence or in one of the shrines. In front of His Holiness he would go into trance, and his Holiness would personally discuss things with him. At such a time, only the Dalai Lama's personal staff, no more than two or three, would be present—no high officials. For this reason, virtually nobody would know what questions His Holiness had on his mind—it was just between the two of them. If the Dalai Lama felt that the issues were unusually sensitive, he would even ask his few attendants to go out.

RL: Were there periods when the Chief State Oracle was not as important as in other periods, or was it always considered quite important?

LL: In many matters, foreign and domestic, the Chief State Oracle was not consulted—the issues at hand were discussed at various official levels and decided at those levels. If the Cabinet could not reach a decision independently, they would call the National Assembly and put the question before it to decide. In a majority of cases, whatever the problem, the government had to handle it through ordinary deliberations. The domain of the Chief State Oracle was clearly restricted to the types of questions I mentioned earlier. Even so, it was held in very high esteem. Owing to the Dalai Lama's personal association with it, it was very prestigious and influential.

RL: Were there opportunities for individuals to ask it questions?

LL: Usually, the Chief State Oracle was not allowed to attend to private individuals' requirements or requests. Nobody could go to Nechung Monastery and ask the officiant to please go into trance. However, next to Nechung Monastery there is a big Gelugpa monastery, Drepung, which was my monastery. Given the historical association between Nechung and Drepung, there was a special arrangement whereby the Council of Abbots of Drepung Monastery—its chief governing body—could go to Nechung once or twice a year to consult the Chief State Oracle. Other than that, the Oracle is neither required nor permitted to attend to private or ordinary requests. His role is clearly specified and he confines himself to those things that are required of him.

RL: In the Delphic record, there are hints about the difference between the priestess's own words and the recasting of those words into poetic form or a more coherent statement by the attending priests. Is there a parallel?

LL: For the Tibetan oracles, be it the Chief State Oracle, lesser State Oracles, or ordinary oracles, the questions were usually asked by people directly, or they would bring questionnaires to which the oracle would answer through his secretary. The secretary would listen to what the oracle told him, write down exactly what he heard, transfer the whole thing to the questionnaire, impress the oracle's seal on it, and return it to the questioner. So, obviously, the secretary did not exercise any interpretive role. He just transcribed.

RL: Are the Oracle's words in ordinary language or in highly colored language?

LL: Interestingly enough, there were two different modes. Most ordinary oracles spoke in a simple local dialect, whatever it was. But the Chief State Oracle and some of the high oracles—there were quite a number of them—often answered in versified form. Some of the Chief State Oracles are known for their poetic answers. Others were less poetic, but they all tended to be. I have compared some of the sayings or answers of Chief State Oracles. One was so eloquent, so beautiful—really poetic. Others were poetic, but not to the same degree. Individual traits do come out.

RL: The secretary who transcribes the Oracle's words does so without interpreting their poetry?

LL: He *cannot* interpret. He has to write down exactly what he hears. If he has a doubt, he whispers, "What did you say?" and the oracle repeats. He just writes it down—that we always observed. There were many, many different oracles and their temples for ordinary people, and we used to go to watch and listen to people asking questions. Sometimes, instead of submitting questionnaires, you could go to the oracle and whisper in his ear if you didn't want others to hear you—you whisper and he whispers back. In such cases, the secretary has nothing to do with it. The answer is direct.

RL: Legends and myths about the origin of the Delphic oracle narrate how Apollo came to Delphi, overcame the dragon that ruled there, established himself, appointed his priests, and so on. Are there comparable origin tales for the Chief State Oracle?

LL: Almost in every case, there is a story or legendary account of the origin of a particular institution or its presiding spirit. In the case of Nechung, here is the legend. In the eighth century, when the great Indian master Padmasambhava was invited to Tibet, he came by way of Nepal, and all along the way, according to legend, he encountered obstacles originating from spiritual forces. In each encounter, he finally conquered his adversary and put it under vow to serve as the guardian of the land, or the region or village. From then on, this spirit was recognized by the locality and installed at a special temple, and from time to time the spirit or a member of his retinue would visit a person of their choice, who would go into trance and then attend to the needs of the villagers.

The Chief State Oracle has a somewhat different foundation legend. The famous first Tibetan monastery, Samye, was complex—at one and the same time a monastery, an academic institution, a meditation center, and a center for translation. While Padmasambhava was helping to build it, he recognized that the work of this institution must be protected. It needed a guardian. Already, he had encountered so many obstacles and conquered them. He knew that in one of the most remote areas of northeastern Tibet—presently, I think, Chinese Kiangsu state—there were some old Tibetan Bönpo monasteries, protected by a very powerful guardian named Pehar. And he decided that he had to bring that particular guardian to Samye and put him under vow to reside there, to protect the institution, and in general to protect the Buddhadharma. And so he asked the king to send an expedition to that region. The king immediately organized a military expedition with the King's son at its head.

Before they left, Padmasambhava gave them blessings. And the account says that just before they left, through his tremendous power Padmasambhava produced an image of a powerful Buddhist guardian—everybody saw it—and this guardian entered into the flag they were carrying. This was the assurance that they were under the protection of a very powerful guardian as they entered the realm of Pehar. The expedition successfully reached the chief Bönpo monastery, where they obtained several precious items. As they made their way home with them, Pehar followed, and so Pehar came to Samye. Padmasambhava was waiting for him there. He immediately put Pehar under vow.

There is a saying that when Padmasambhava brought him under vow, Pehar manifested as a terrifying figure to challenge him and tried to destroy him, but Padmasambhava was a super wizard who could not be conquered. So Padmasambhava overcame him, put his scepter—his *dorje*—on the head of his adversary, and said, "You are under vow, and now you will be the protector of this temple and of the Buddhadharma across the land." From then on, Pehar had a special temple in the monastery, and the monks were required daily to propitiate and worship him. This was the origin of Nechung.

RL: There is almost no information about the selection of the Delphic priestess, apart from a few inscriptions indicating family ties. While I'm sure the process was very different in the Tibetan setting, it is worth asking how the medium was selected.

LL: In the case of the Chief State Oracle, each time there was a vacancy at the seat of the oracle, neither the Dalai Lama nor the Tibetan government could choose a candidate. Somebody in one of the monasteries would be chosen by the guardian Pehar himself, and the selection would become evident through signs. By signs I mean that a particular monk would from time to time suddenly go into trance. He himself would have no control over the event. He was forced—his body was used, and he would go into trance. People around the monastery would know, they would say: this person seems to have a visitation, and they would report to His Holiness or to the government. Naturally, the man had to be tested first. This was the general method of choosing the Chief State Oracle.

I can give a specific example—my own father. At the beginning of the century, probably 1910 or so, he was at one of the colleges of Drepung Monastery and studying to be a learned *geshe*, a doctor of Buddhist doctrine. At that time there was a vacancy at Nechung Monastery, there was no oracle, and his Holiness was waiting for the signs. My father was a young monk, very brilliant in his studies. His teacher told him that if he continued to work seriously, he could be a very good and learned monk, and that was his personal desire: he wanted to complete his studies and become a teacher. But suddenly he couldn't study as diligently as before because every now and then he became possessed and went into trance. His teacher said, "Well, now comes the obstacle to your religious training and career." And the teacher wouldn't tell anybody. They tried to keep the situation a secret between the two of them. But word spread to other monks and monasteries, and His Holiness was continuing to look for signs. He had already written to three big monasteries, requesting that if anybody were to show signs of becoming an oracle, this should immediately be reported to him.

In the event, the second Chief State Oracle told His Holiness that there was a monk by the name of Gyaltsen Tharchin who was destined to be the next Chief State Oracle. There could not have been a clearer indication. The Dalai Lama again wrote to the monasteries, which replied that there was such a monk, "where we don't know, but in one of the monasteries." Then the monastery leaders looked for him and heard from various sources that there was indeed a young monk who went into trance every now and then. They were delighted and immediately reported the news to His Holiness. The next thing that happened was that suddenly a host of people came on horseback and took him to the palace. There His Holiness immediately put him on the throne and, with monks chanting, he was installed as Chief State Oracle. He had to go into trance right in front of His Holiness. This is how he was recognized and installed at the Nechung Monastery.

During the 1940s, there was another Chief State Oracle, a friend of my father's, also a monk, who was chosen in the same way. There was a vacancy, and this monk was suddenly going into trance every now and then. Finally everybody knew. At that time the Dalai Lama was still a minor, and so his Regent brought the monk to the palace, tested him, and recognized him as Chief State Oracle. When oracles are associated with monasteries, the selection process is much as I have described. But there are also lay oracles—married men and married women—in which case the selection is based on family ties, from father to son or mother to daughter. The father would choose one of his sons, the elder or whomever he thinks most appropriate. They would go through the ceremony, and if the son responded by going into trance, he would then be confirmed as the next oracle.

RL: Another area in the Delphic record where there is a complete gap concerns training—there is nothing at all about the training of the priestess.

LL: Strictly speaking, there is no training at all because the person—the medium himself—is neutral in the sense that he is not directly involved in the process of oracular activity. But in the case of high oracles, the medium is generally required to go through Buddhist training, especially training in advanced yoga concerned with controlling inner energies, chakras, and the nervous system. People would commonly say that the Chief State Oracle, or any oracle, must have a special kind of energy within his body, and a sensitive nervous system, so that a powerful spirit can possess him and function appropriately. The medium's body is the spirit's base during the oracular session. If the base is very sensitive, then the functioning of the oracle will be much more genuine. There was, then, the belief that the oracle must spend his time doing yoga and purifying himself, and must lead a pure life—must be very religious, very spiritual. Were he to lead an ordinary, sensual life, then even if he was once reliable, he would deteriorate and become almost a useless oracle.

RL: Were there examples of deterioration?

LL: People—villagers, for instance—would say, "Well, in my family's case, what this oracle told us was true. But there have been many cases where what he said was not true." Then there would be doubts about the oracle. Where there were more and more doubts, the oracle would not last very long.

There is an interesting reason why each oracle had to be spiritual and pure. His body was dedicated to a particular force or spirit, who often had been put under a religious vow by a powerful religious figure such as Padmasambhava. Therefore the force or spirit is itself a Buddhist, following its Buddhist vow under an obligation to protect. In keeping with this, the oracle's body should not be available or used by any other forces. To exclude this possibility, the person must be pure; if he is pure, he has his own special strength and there is no opportunity for other forces to use this body. The Chief State Oracle is required to devote himself continuously to meditational practices so that he keeps his body exclusively for a particular guardian, Pehar.

There are some interesting stories about how another powerful spirit used the body of the Chief State Oracle during the 13th Dalai Lama's time. The oracle was often consulted by the government, but there was a suspicion that each time he went into trance, the prediction or guidance he gave was not quite accurate or authentic. In many cases, it was misleading. Therefore, they thought that the guardian himself did not come—somebody else was managing to use the Oracle. Now, not long before, a very powerful lama had been involved in a plot against the Tibetan government. Finally, the plot was discovered and the lama was arrested with a number of others. Either he was killed or he died, and when he died, they treated him like a criminal: his body was taken to a particular place and buried under a black stupa to indicate that an evil person lay underneath. But as soon as the construction was over, the whole thing cracked, indicating that he could not be constrained in this way. And so came that very powerful spirit, which used the medium. They all talk about this. I heard this story from many older Tibetans.

RL: One trustworthy author on Delphi said that "we give these women—the oracular priestesses—a lot of trouble by watching over them to keep them chaste and pure." They were sheltered from contact with strangers and lived very dedicated lives. There are clear parallels.

LL: The life of the Chief State Oracle was very isolated. He was not supposed to socialize, to meet too many people, but he had a palatial house, a host of servants, everything provided. In that setting, he was to lead a very pure religious life. But, you know, there were many women oracles, some famous, all lay women, married. The institutional connection with Nechung, a monastery of celibate monks, accounts for the fact that the Chief State Oracle was always male.

I have visited some of the female oracles. One was periodically consulted by the high officials, the government, and the monastic council. Her temple was not very far from the Nechung temple—you just had to go a little higher. She was very famous in Tibet. The system of transmission there was hereditary, from mother to daughter. When my brother and I visited her in 1944 or thereabout, the daughter came out and asked which we wanted to consult. The mother already had a number of years in office, so we said that we would like to talk to the mother.

RL: Can we explore the behavior of the medium in trance? The key term from the Greek material is *enthousiasmos*, which gives us our "enthusiasm." The state of the Delphic priestess in trance is reported to have been very intense, agitated, physically restless. Socrates described it as a divinely inspired madness. The book to which you contributed implies a surprisingly exact Tibetan parallel to the state of *enthousiasmos*.

LL: I have observed a number of oracles going into trance. Among the high oracles—the powerful ones such as the first Chief State Oracle, the second and third, and other high oracles recognized by monasteries and well known—the process was quite similar. On the designated day, the oracle would come to the temple and put on his ceremonial warrior's costume, but not the helmet, and would take his seat on a high throne while monks chanted to the accompaniment of an orchestra. In front of the oracle would be a big incense pot, with incense burning in it. It all made a very serene atmosphere—the monks chanting, the musical instruments playing. . . .

The monks serving him would attentively wait for the signs that he was entering into trance. As he was sitting there, you could actually watch the development take place. At first, there was this man sitting in a meditative state, with closed eyes, breathing very calmly and serenely, with no movements, facial or otherwise. Just sitting there. . . . And the chanting goes on and on and on. There are certain chants, all in verse: such and such a powerful deity, by such and such a name, with all your powers, come now, today, visit this medium—and so on. At a certain point you can see the signs coming through.

First, there are some facial movements—you can see the muscles moving, and little by little, his complexion becomes reddish. And the whole face becomes radiant. At the same time, his hands begin shaking, his legs begin to shiver; now he is panting. There is tremendous energy bubbling out—you can see this. At that point he is probably semiconscious. Suddenly the signs become very strong, and the monks sense that he has entered into full trance. He is almost in violent movement. Two monks then bring the big helmet, put it on his head, and strap it tight—so tight. Because the pure gold helmet is so heavy, two monks have to handle it. One of my uncles was an attendant to the Chief State Oracle during the 1940s, and I used to watch him tie the helmet. "Why," I once asked, "do you tie it so tightly?" "Well," I remember him answering, "that is the time when he is in full trance, it won't hurt him. But if you don't know the time, if you do it too early, the man will die—we would suffocate him."

When all this has happened, the Oracle is still shaking, moving violently, but suddenly he calms down a little and gets up in his heavy costume. His attendants give him a bow and arrow, a sign of warrior status. He comes down the steps from the high throne, moves backward, and faces the big shrine behind the throne, which houses a statue of Padmasambhava. He dances a beautiful dance, then bows three times in front of Padmasambhava. Then he moves forward, returns to his seat, and begins to receive the ministers who have been standing there, waiting in line. One by one, they go to him to receive his blessing first, and then they return to their respective places. One of the secretaries stands up and reads the questionnaires.

Entering trance takes perhaps ten minutes and, as you see, it is a violent process. Then he calms down a little, but from that point on you see that he is not a normal person. In his facial expression, his eyes, there is no normal movement. His eyes are turned upward, his mouth is wide open, his tongue is twisted upward. This situation prevails even when he speaks—he speaks to his secretary but as soon as he finishes speaking he resumes that mouth position. Very often he would remain in this state until all questions had been answered, and then suddenly he would drop. That is the moment when his attendants quickly untie his helmet. They carry him on a stretcher, in an unconscious state, to a back room where there is a bed on which they lay him and wait for his return to consciousness. It takes an hour for him to recover fully.

So it is not so easy. I think the person probably suffers during the time when he is still semiconscious.

RL: You said that in a sense there is no training, apart from yogic training, because the connection with Pehar is direct. On the other hand, when the Oracle rises, descends the steps, and bows to the shrine of Padmasambhava, isn't this learned behavior? It strikes me as a ritual act which the Oracle could have seen the previous Oracle do or may have been instructed to do.

LL: Tibetans always say that the Oracle himself has no role whatever in what he does and says. Sometimes a particular family would ask the temple to organize an oracular session. After the Oracle came out of his trance, he would rest a while and then join the family for conversation. Often in such instances, he would ask the members: "What did *he* say?"—by which he meant the guardian or spirit presiding over the Oracle. Generally, the belief is widespread that oracles in trance are completely unconscious. They also say that if the Oracle plays a role, that means he is not in full trance and is faking.

RL: Why is the Oracle's helmet heavy? Does its weight serve a purpose?

LL: There is a purpose. The moment the Oracle's body is possessed, his powers, strength, energy multiply many times over; therefore, he can carry the heavy helmet. But if the Oracle were to fake, and a lot of oracles fake, he could not carry the helmet.

I'll just tell you one story. There were many, many oracles in Tibet, not all of them honest. And the 13th Dalai Lama felt quite disturbed about the way the oracles misused their name and power. He ordered the Chief State Oracle at the Nechung Monastery to bring all of the important oracles from different regions to Nechung to have them undergo a personal test. This was organized in 1932, when I was a child and actually saw all of these different oracles gathering there. A commission was formed, and everybody had to appear before it to explain and demonstrate what he or she was doing. One old woman went into trance before the commission. She was very impressive, she answered questions very well. The commission was very pleased. And then she took off her hat and said, "You see, this is how I make my living. I wasn't in trance, I was making it up." She was so honest—and she had fooled the commission. People can do all kinds of things.

RL: Do local oracles, of the kind this woman pretended to be, go through a violent process as they enter trance?

LL: The signs of possession are typically mild. There was one particular woman I visited who was very interesting. She had her own temple and a number of members visiting her; she was known for her healing power, and she would provide answers and predictions at the same time as she treated people. My brother and I spent a day at her temple to observe. People visited her, offered their respect, brought gifts, and she would be sitting on a high throne, without any visible sign of trance. I asked the members, "Is she in trance?" "Yes," they said. I was surprised, because she looked so normal, so ordinary. She would smile at everybody and talk in a normal voice.

I didn't have a question for her, but toward evening she was visited by monks from the big monasteries—monks of the kind we call *dabto*, comparable to Japanese samurai. These were martial monks with a code of honor, respecting everybody and rescuing people in trouble. They had been drinking beer, and some of them were drunk. How could they return drunk to their monasteries? Other monks took one of them to the lady and said, "He's drunk." She picked a few rice grains out of a silver bowl, put them in her palm, uttered some mantras, rubbed them, and told the monk: "Take this with some more drink." So the monk then drinks *more*, to take the medicine. He rests a few minutes, gets ups, and walks away. He's steady.

RL: Did your father live a long life?

LL: Yes, he lived into his late seventies, but he was Chief State Oracle for only five or six years. He didn't serve very long.

I only once saw him go into trance at our house. Something upset him tremendously and he began to faint. I was in my room.

I ran to him, felt that something terrible was happening, and asked my stepmother to come quickly. Father was lying on his bed. I felt his heartbeat and pulse, and he was all right. I asked for a box of sacred pills, crushed some, mixed them into tea water, and put it in his mouth. Suddenly, he began to talk. "Quickly," he said to me, "there are two holes in the top of my skull. Press them." He used to shave his head as monks do. The holes were signs or impressions of the *dorje*. I found them and pressed. Slowly, he calmed down. As he calmed down, he got up but was still in trance. He blessed the house, then suddenly went back and lay down for a time. And then he was normal.

He told me why he had asked me to press those points. When Padmasambhava put Pehar under vow, he placed his scepter on Pehar's head. There resulted this sign, which ever after has indicated whether the Oracle is being visited by the real guardian or by a false one. In my father's case, the double sign indicated that the real one had possessed his body.

This sign offers an important verification when high government officials consult the Chief State Oracle about the location of the reincarnation of the Dalai Lama. When we were searching for the present Dalai Lama, the Chief State Oracle came to the palace and most of the officials were dismissed; only the Regent, the Chief State Oracle, and four cabinet ministers were present. When the Oracle was in trance, he was asked to take off his helmet. He took it off and showed his head to the Regent: the sign was there. Then he put the helmet on and answered their questions. They would not ask their questions until they had seen the sign.

One of the main functions, though a very rare one, of the Chief State Oracle was the discovery of the authentic Dalai Lama. In every case, from my great uncle's time, my father's time, up to recent times, whenever the Oracle encountered this question, the answer was correct. During the 1940s, when we were looking for the Dalai Lama's reincarnation and I was a small boy, the government was consulting all the great lamas and oracles, and doing many things to find out where he was to be found. During the first phase of the search, every time the Chief State Oracle was brought to the palace and went into trance, he would get up and dance and then face the east and bow down three times. This was the first indication that the search party should go east and nowhere else.

Sure enough, later on, when it came to more precise predictions, he gave the names and everything else needed. But early on, he was giving signals. Sometimes he would throw a scarf to the east.

Everybody was satisfied with the Chief State Oracle's contributions.

RL: The Delphic priestess in trance sat upon a tripod, with a cauldron serving as her seat—in effect, her sacred furniture was borrowed from simple cooking utensils. In addition, some ancient authors say that a special smoke or vapor rose from a chasm beneath the tripod and that this vapor contributed to her trance state. Archaeologists have found nothing to justify these assertions. On the other hand, one trustworthy author asserts it as common knowledge that from time to time the most wonderful fragrance came from the inner shrine. My suspicion is that the Delphic officiants may have used incense in a special way, not unlike what you have described.

LL: For the Chief State Oracle, they used very good incense containing all kinds of fragrant herbs; the best contained twenty-five different ingredients. Besides that, they used raw pine resins, which, if you don't burn too much, gives off a sweet fragrance. These things are always burned in front of the Oracle as the process gets underway. Finally the whole temple is saturated with incense.

RL: Was there more incense for that service than for ordinary services?

LL: Incense is burned as a part of regular offerings, but not much, just a few sticks. During Oracle functions, they burn a great deal.

RL: On the other issue—the tripod and cooking cauldron—some scholars have referred to Siberian shamanism, where an initiatory experience of the apprentice shaman may involve a realistic vision of his body being butchered and boiled, and then restored whole to him, as if reborn and renewed. On this reading, the Pythia is sacrificed: her ordinary person is consumed so that the god can speak through her. Is there a comparable symbology in Tibet?

LL: I don't recall anything similar. To purify themselves, Oracles receive Buddhist empowerments—purifications that empower them to carry on advanced practices. Other than that, I haven't seen or heard anything requiring the Oracle to be used as a sacrifice, even symbolically.

RL: From the Greek record it is clear that many people had faith in the genuineness of their oracles, and that some witnesses were publicly skeptical. Within Tibetan tradition, is there the same interplay between faith and doubt?

LL: Tibetans are very religious; they *would* believe in many kinds of prophetic indications. Yet individually they are cautious. Families were adherents of a particular oracle or institution, and family members attached to a particular oracle would go there regularly for consultations. Even if they had nothing to ask, they would still take part in ceremonies and festivities. But there were always skeptics who would say, "Well, we can ask, but we don't know what kind of answer we will get, correct or incorrect." They would ask, in any case. The questions do not always concern weather or things of that order, but very specific matters. If a person was a merchant, he might ask, "I have so many hundred bales of wool already gathered. Should I sell now, or should I wait until prices go up?" They come with these very practical questions. The oracle has to say, "Sell now," or "Sell six months from now." And if the answer turns out to be wrong, next time the merchant won't ask.

RL: The Delphic oracle became subject to doubt during the Persian Wars because the oracle often seemed to favor capitulation to the Persians. People began to doubt its patriotism, and its prestige was at least briefly tarnished after the Greek victory.

LL: The nearest parallel that comes to mind occurred when we were facing the threat of invasion by the Chinese Communist army. The Chinese had already declared that Tibet was part of China, and they intended to "liberate" the country. It was a very, very, nervous time. Long before that, there had been signs in China that the Nationalist government was falling and that the Communists would soon be in power. At various times the Council of Ministers and Regent would ask the Chief State Oracle concerning the future course of events. Every time the answer was very angry—that everything from now on would be very bad, that affairs would steadily deteriorate, that nothing could save Tibet. This answer came so clearly and so often, although he wouldn't reveal whether the country would be completely dominated by China. But in many respects he said that the situation was hopeless. They would ask what should be done. Nothing.

RL: The oracle at Delphi was famous in its time for a trait that was rather useful politically: the ambiguity of its answers. People, and whole communities, would go to great lengths to interpret its most ambiguous answers, which often enough dealt with matters of war and peace. Are there examples of that kind of ambiguity in the State Oracle?

LL: Ambiguity showed up in the Oracle's answers when he replied in symbolic language rathern than directly and precisely. Such symbols were subject to interpretation. To some very vital questions the answers were given in metaphors, similes. "If you ride a blue horse, you will escape"—things of this kind. In one instance, certain tribes of Mongols invaded Tibet and pursued the Regent of the fifth Dalai Lama. The Regent asked the Chief State Oracle what to do. The answer was a set of verse stanzas, one of which was more or less "Ride the blue horse, go quickly." The Regent could not understand what was meant. Much later, it was interpreted that he was to cross the river Kyichu and go well beyond it to escape. This never occurred to him. He didn't go, and the Mongols arrested and killed him.

There is another story about ambiguity. An expectant mother in a village once went to her local oracle and asked whether she would have a girl or a boy. She very much wanted a boy. "Girl, no. Boy," replied the oracle. She went off, delighted. Some months later, after delivering a girl, she returned to the oracle's personal aide, who had been in attendance. "The oracle was wrong!" The aide protested the oracle's innocence. "It said: 'Girl. No boy!' "[2]

There was a high oracle, called Karmashar, associated primarily with the Gelugpa monastery of Sera. Its temple was in Lhasa. Every summer we had a special festival called Consecration of the Universe. At that time, all of the oracles had their own special festivals and went into trance. Their temples and monasteries organized the activities, and the members would come to visit and honor them. Apparently, this was an ancient custom dating to an era when warriors honored the warrior gods for their victories and supplicated them for help in the next war. In any case, this oracle would go into trance and then give a prediction for the country—and expressed everything in symbols, almost twenty different symbols. They were very strange: for example, years before the Second World War, the same oracle revealed a series of prophetic symbols showing the head of a dragon in a tiger's mouth, with the tiger's tail in a bull's mouth. This was later interpreted to mean the wars between China and Japan, and Japan and the United States. People usually had a pretty clear idea of their meaning. The Lhasans talked about these things. Everybody paid attention to the predictions. People copied, studied, and discussed them.

RL: Does the Tibetan Chief State Oracle still exist?

LL: Yes, the institution. Actually, nothing is left in Tibet, everything is gone: temples, monks, and institutions completely wiped out. They are not allowed even to talk about these things. But in India, we have at least the major oracles still functioning, and two oracles attached to the Dalai Lama. These young oracles are occasionally consulted. In India there are also two or three others, formerly associated with different monasteries. A segment of the oracular institution has survived.

I want to mention one further thing. As I said before, the spiritual guardian presiding over an oracle is a Buddhist himself; he is an initiate and a practicing Buddhist. For this reason, he may not be there very long. When he achieves his enlightenment he will not come down. Then somebody else will take his place.

Notes

NOTES, PREFACE

1. Elie Wiesel, *Sages and Dreamers* (New York: Summit Books, 1991), 160.

NOTES, CHAPTER 1

1. Adapted from Dio Chrysostom, "Diogenes or On Servants," *Discourses*, trans. J. W. Cohoon (LCL, 1944), vol. 1:10.21–28.

2. Plutarch, *Lives*, trans. B. Perrin (LCL, 1949), vol. 7:3.3–5, 5.1–3.

3. Philip Wheelwright, trans. and commentary, *Heraclitus* (Princeton: Princeton University Press, 1959), 19. Hereafter cited as Wheelwright, *Heraclitus*.

4. W. O'Neill, trans. and commentary, Proclus, *Alcibiades*, vol. 1 (The Hague: Martinus Nijhoff, 1965), 5.

5. Plutarch, *Obsolescence of Oracles*, 421A, from *Moralia*, trans. F. C. Babbitt (LCL, 1957), vol. 5. Hereafter cited as Plutarch, *Obsolescence*.

6. Abridged from Strabo, *Geography*, trans. H. L. Jones (LCL, 1954), vol. 3:7.7.10. Hereafter cited as Strabo, *Geography*.

7. Ibid., 9.3.6.

8. Pausanias, *Guide to Greece*, 2 vols., trans. with an introduction by Peter Levi, rev. ed. (Harmondsworth, Eng.: Penguin, 1979, 10.5.3. Hereafter cited as Pausanias, *Guide to Greece*.

9. Ibid., 6.3.8.

10. Ibid., 8.8.3.

11. Ibid., 10.25.1.

12. Readers interested in the archaeological survey of Delphi will find extensive bibliography in H. W. Parke and D. E. W. Wormell, *The Delphic Oracle*, 2 vols. (Oxford: Blackwell, 1956); and in Joseph Fontenrose, *The Delphic Oracle: Its Responses and Operations, With a Catalogue of Responses* (Berkeley: University of California Press, 1978).

13. There are of course exceptions: the scholarly work of Georges Roux, Pierre Amandry, and others is both exacting and religiously sensitive. See Georges Roux, *Delphes: Son oracle et ses dieux* (Paris: Les Belles Lettres, 1976); and Pierre Amandry, *La mantique Apollinienne à Delphes* (Paris: Boccard, 1950).

14. Edouard Schuré, *The Great Initiates: A Study of the Secret History of Religions* (1st ed. Paris: 1889); (San Francisco: Harper and Row, 1961), 266, 285.

15. See, for example, Claude Bragdon, *Delphic Woman: Twelve Essays* (New York: Alfred A. Knopf, 1936).

16. Rex Warner, trans., Thucydides, *The Peloponnesian War* (Harmondsworth, Eng.: Penguin Classics, 1954), 1.9. Hereafter cited as Thucydides.

17. Julian, "To Sallust," from *The Works of the Emperor Julian*, trans. W. C. Wright (LCL, 1913), vol. 2:250C. Hereafter cited as Julian.

18. See C. G. Jung, *Letters 1951–1961*, ed. Gerhard Adler in collaboration with Aniela Jaffé, Bollingen Series, vol. 2 (Princeton: Princeton University Press, 1973–75), 611. For a photograph of the inscribed doorway, see *C. G. Jung: Word and Image*, ed. Aniela Jaffé, Bollingen Series (Princeton: Princeton University Press, 1979), 137.

19. Plutarch, *The Oracles at Delphi No Longer Given in Verse,* 403E, from *Moralia,* trans. F. C. Babbitt (LCL, 1957), vol. 5. Hereafter cited as Plutarch, *The Oracles.*

20. Porphyry, *Of the Philosophy to be Derived from Oracles*, cited in Eusebius, *Preparation for the Gospel*, trans. Edwin Hamilton Gifford (Oxford: Clarendon Press, 1903), 157, 144a.

21. Stanley Lombardo and Diane Rayor, trans., *Callimachus: Hymns, Epigrams, Select Fragments* (Baltimore and London: The Johns Hopkins University Press, 1988), 9.

22. See Strabo, *Geography*, 9.3.12.

23. Based primarily on Dionysius of Halicarnassus, *Roman Antiquities*, trans. E. Cary (LCL, 1978), vol. 2:4.62.1–4, with material from another telling in Dio Cassius, *Dio's Roman History*, trans. E. Cary (LCL, 1954), vol. 1.

24. Cited from Ariel Gluklich, "Images and Symbols in the Phenomenology of the Dharma," *History of Religions* 29, 3, (February 1990): 259.

25. Isocrates, "Oration to Archidamus," in *Isocrates*, trans. G. Norlin (LCL, 1928), vol. 1:31.

26. On the Center, see Mircea Eliade, *Patterns in Comparative Religion* (New York: New American Library, 1954), 231–33; and *idem*, *The Sacred and the Profane: The Nature of Religion* (New York: Harcourt Brace, 1959), chap. 1.

27. Pausanias, *Guide to Greece,* 10.16.2.

28. Plutarch, *Obsolescence,* 409E–410A.

29. C. M. Bowra, trans., *The Odes of Pindar* (Harmondsworth, Eng.: Penguin 1969), Pythian VI, l. 3, 26. Hereafter cited as Pindar.

30. Strabo, *Geography,* 9.3.6.

31. Plutarch, *Obsolescence,* 409E–410A.

32. David Grene, trans., Herodotus, *The History* (Chicago: The University of Chicago Press, 1987), 8.144. Hereafter cited as Grene, Herodotus.

33. P. Aelius Aristides, "The Panathenaic Oration," 181D.62–3, 240D.190, in *The Complete Works,* Charles A. Behr, trans. (Leiden: Brill, 1981–86).

34. Scholarly study of ancient Greek athletics is a distinct field. See Wendy J. Raschke, ed., *The Archaeology of the Olympics: The Olympics and Other Festivals in Antiquity* (Madison, WI: University of Wisconsin Press, 1988), which includes Joseph Fontenrose, "The Cult of Apollo and the Games at Delphi," 121–140. See also Sophocles, *Electra,* 699–721, and a late but vivid source, Heliodorus, *An Ethiopian Story,* where there is a credible description of the footrace in armor. B. P. Reardon, ed., *Collected Ancient Greek Novels* (Berkeley: University of California Press, 1989), 424 ff.

35. Attributed to Simonides, *The Greek Anthology,* trans. W. R. Paton (LCL, 1918), vol. 5:9. (Book 13, epigram 14).

36. Pausanias, *Guide to Greece,* 7.17.6.

37. For background, see M. L. West, *Ancient Greek Music* (Oxford: Clarendon Press, 1992); on Delphi, see 288–301.

38. Kathleen Freeman, *Ancilla to the Pre-Socratic Philosophers* (Cambridge: Harvard University Press, 1948), 150.

39. Pausanias, *Guide to Greece,* 10.24.4.

40. Ibid., 9.23.1–4.

41. *Lyra Graeca,* trans. J. M. Edmonds (LCL, 1924, 235), vol. 2.

NOTES, CHAPTER 2

1. *Hesiod, The Homeric Hymns, and Homerica,* trans. Hugh G. Evelyn-White (LCL, 1974); Homeric Hymn to Pythian Apollo, ll: 247–53. Hereafter cited as *Hymns.*

2. Xenophon, *Memorabilia,* trans. E. C. Marchant (LCL, 1959), 1.1.6–9.

3. *Hesiod and Theognis,* trans. Dorothea Wender (Harmondsworth, Eng.: Penguin, 1973), 125; G. Roux, *Delphes,* 162n, interprets Theognis' admonition as laying out the code that governs an official deputy seeking an answer at Delphi on behalf of his city.

4. Xenophon, *Anabasis,* trans. Carleton L. Brownson (LCL, 1968), vol. 3:3.1.4–8.

5. Epictetus, *Encheiridion,* trans. W. A. Oldfather (LCL, 1956), vol. 2:32.

6. Adapted from Epictetus, *Discourses,* trans. W. A. Oldfather (LCL, 1956), vol. 1:2.7.1 ff.

7. Epictetus, *Encheiridion,* 32.

8. Adapted from *The Greek Anthology* (LCL), vol. 5:14.73.

9. Athenaeus, *The Deipnosophists,* 5.219A, trans. C. B. Gulick (LCL, 1951), vol. 1.

10. Dio Chrysostom, "In Athens, About His Banishment," *Discourses* (LCL), vol. 2:13.9–12. Dio's tale of Diogenes, with which this book began, conveys another fragment of the code for questioners in its warning to "know oneself" before undertaking to know a god by inquiring at an oracle.

11. Grene, Herodotus, *The History,* 2.171; see also 2. 65. In his dialogue *The E at Delphi.* Hereafter cited as Plutarch, *The E*), Plutarch withholds information about the drawing of lots, the process by which the Pythia ordered the sequence of inquirers on a given day at the temple (see 391D).

12. Pausanias, *Guide to Greece,* 1.14.3–4.

13. Grene, Herodotus, *The History,* 7.111.

14. Iamblichus, *Life of Pythagoras,* trans. Thomas Taylor, 1st ed., (London: 1818; reprint Rochester: Inner Traditions International, 1986), 94.

15. Adapted from Herodotus, *The History,* 4.131–32.

16. Ibid., 4.163–64.

17. Ibid., 9.33–35.

18. Aeschylus, *Prometheus Bound,* ll. 661–62, trans. David Grene, in *The Complete Greek Tragedies,* David Grene and Richmond Lattimore, eds., vol. 2 (Chicago: The University of Chicago Press, 1959). Hereafter cited as Grene/Lattimore.

19. Plutarch, *The E* 385C.

20. Adapted from Plutarch, *The Oracles,* 407D.

21. Adapted from Herodotus, *The History,* I.68; the translation of the oracle is by Peter Levi in Pausanias, *Guide to Greece,* 16n.

22. Pausanias, *Guide to Greece,* 8.11.10.

23. Ibid., 2.7.6, with Peter Levi's note.

24. Ibid., 1.37.6–7.

25. Dio Chrysostom, "The Rhodion Oration," *Discourses* (LCL), vol. 3:95–98.

26. Lucian, *Zeus Rants,* trans. A. M. Harmon (LCL, 1929), vol. 2:28.

27. Lucian, *Dialogues of the Gods,* trans. M. D. Macleod (LCL, 1961), vol. 7:244.

28. Iamblichus, *Life of Pythagoras,* 86.

29. Ibid., 127.

30. Wheelwright, *Heraclitus,* fr. 24, p. 29.

31. Porphyry, *Of the Philosophy,* cited in Eusebius, *Preparation for the Gospel,* p. 158, 144C.

32. Adapted from *The Contest of Homer and Hesiod,* 315, 326, in *Hesiod, The Homeric Hymns, and Homerica* (LCL, 1974).

33. For a summary of sources, see Alice Swift Riginos, *Platonica: The Anecdotes Concerning the Life and Writings of Plato* (Leiden: E. J. Brill, 1976), 141–45; this telling is drawn from Riginos as well as Plutarch, *On the Sign of Socrates*, trans. P. H. deLacy and B. Einarson, *Moralia* (LCL, 1959), vol. 7:579A–D.

34. Plutarch, *The E*, 386E.

NOTES, CHAPTER 3

1. Robert Graves, *The Greek Myths*, 1-vol. ed. (Mt. Kisco, NY: Moyer Bell Ltd., 1988); copyright notices of 1955, 1960, reflect the original 2-vol. ed. and its 1960 revision.

2. See esp. Walter Burkert, *Greek Religion*, trans. John Raffan (Cambridge: Harvard University Press, 1985).

3. Plutarch, *Whether an Old Man Should Engage in Public Affairs*, 792F, in *Moralia*, trans. H. N. Fowler (LCL, 1949), vol. 10.

4. Grene, Herodotus, *The History*, 1.47.

5. Pindar, Pythian IX, ll. 44–49.

6. *Oxford Classical Dictionary*, 2nd ed., s.v. "Apollo."

7. Pindar, Pythian III, ll. 27–30.

8. *Idem*, Olympian VI, ll. 37–38.

9. *Idem*, Pythian XI, ll. 7–9.

10. Strabo, *Georgraphy*, 9.3.11.

11. *The Greek Anthology* (LCL), vol. 5:14.71.

12. Ibid.

13. Diogenes Laertius, *Diogenes*, 6.42, in *Lives of the Eminent Philosophers*, trans. R. D. Hicks (LCL, 1958), vol. 2.

14. Plutarch, *Isis and Osiris*, 378D, in *Moralia*, trans. F. C. Babbitt (LCL 5).

15. Epictetus, *Discourses* (LCL), vol. 2:3.1.17.

16. *Hymns*, To Delian Apollo, ll. 133–34:332–33.

17. Adapted from Diodorus Siculus 16.91, trans. C. Bradford Welles (LCL, 1963), vol. 8.

18. *Hymns*, To Delian Apollo, l. 1:324–25.

19. Apollonius of Rhodes, *The Voyage of Argo*, 4.575 ff., trans. E. V. Rieu, 2nd ed. (Harmondsworth, Eng.): Penguin, 1971.

20. Pindar, Pythian V, ll. 63–68.

21. Diodorus Siculus 16.26, in the translation offered by Giulia Sissa, *Greek Virginity*, trans. Arthur Goldhammer (Cambridge: Harvard University Press, 1990), 34–35. Sissa's work is especially rewarding. See Plutarch, *Obsolescence*, 433C.

22. See Pausanias, *Guide to Greece,* 10.5.3–5.

23. *Hymns,* To Pythian Apollo, ll: 388–544, with abridgment and occasional paraphrase; see also Euripides, *Iphigenia in Tauris,* 1234 ff. The poetic project of the anonymous bard includes accounting for the ancient name Pytho by which Delphi was originally known. In the ancients' opinion, the name arose from the verb *pytho,* to cause to rot.

24. *Hymns,* To Pythian Apollo, ll: 388–544, with abridgment and paraphrase.

25. Plutarch, *The E,* 388E–389B.

NOTES, CHAPTER 4

1. Plato, *Symposium,* 201C ff., trans. Michael Joyce, in *The Collected Dialogues of Plato,* Edith Hamilton and Huntington Cairns, eds., Bollingen Series (New York: Pantheon Books, 1961). (This edition hereafter cited as Hamilton/Cairns). In a note to the author, C. R. Beye remarks that scholars regard Diotima as a fictional creation. From my perspective, essentially that of the Delphi of the mind, her presence in widely read literature as an archetype of the all-wise priestess retains significance.

2. Iamblichus, *Life of Pythagoras,* 27.

3. Plutarch, *The E* 385C. Evidence collected by G. Roux, *Delphes,* 92n, suggests that at earlier periods women may have been permitted to consult the oracle. See Euripides, *Ion,* ll: 226–29.

4. Plutarch, *The Oracles,* 402E.

5. Plato, *Phaedrus,* 244B–C, trans. R. Hackforth in *The Collected Dialogues,* Hamilton/Cairns.

6. Plato, *Timaeus,* 71E–72A, trans. Benjamin Jowett, in *The Collected Dialogues,* Hamilton/Cairns.

7. Readers interested in the theme of a "higher" dementia and the traditional map of the mind will value Ananda K. Coomaraswamy's essay, "Manas," in *Metaphysics,* Roger Lipsey, ed., *Coomaraswamy: Selected Papers,* vol. 2, Bollingen Series (Princeton: Princeton University Press, 1977), 209–219.

8. Plato, *Ion,* 534C–D, trans. Lane Cooper, *The Collected Dialogues,* Hamilton/Cairns.

9. Plato, *Phaedrus,* 242C.

10. Plato, *Symposium,* 203A.

11. We have been exploring these three dialogues for some time: *The Oracles, Obsolescence,* and *The E.*

12. Adapted from Plutarch, *The Oracles,* 404E–F.

13. Plutarch, *The Dialogue on Love,* 759B, from *Moralia,* trans. E. L. Minar, F. H. Sandbach, and W. C. Helmbold (LCL, 1961), vol. 9.

14. Ibid., 763.

15. Adapted from Plutarch, *The Oracles,* 438A.

16. See G. Roux, *Delphes,* 71ff.

17. Lucan, *De bello civili,* 5.165–193, trans. Fontenrose, *The Delphic Oracle,* 209.

18. Pausanias, *Guide to Greece,* 10.12.1.

19. Wheelwright, *Heraclitus,* fr. 79, p. 69.

20. Pausanias, *Guide to Greece,* 10.12.1.

21. Ibid., 10.12.6.

22. Plutarch, *Obsolescence,* 414E.

23. Ibid., 416F–417A.

24. Ibid., 415A.

25. Ibid., 416F–417A.

26. Ibid., 431A.

27. Ibid., 431C.

28. Ibid.

29. Ibid., 432D–E.

30. Ibid., 433D.

31. Ibid., 434C.

32. Ibid., 435A ff.

33. Ibid., 435E ff.

34. Plutarch, *The Oracles,* 396C–D. For this set of passages, the translations are by Donald Russell in Plutarch: *Selected Essays and Dialogues* (Oxford: Oxford University Press, 1993). Hereafter cited as Russell, Plutarch.

35. Ibid., 397A.

36. Ibid., 397C.

37. Ibid., 404B ff.

38. Ibid.

39. Ibid., 405C–D.

40. Ibid., 408F.

41. Diodorus Siculus, *Greek Virginity,* 16.26.6–27.

42. Georges Roux, *Delphes,* 67–68.

43. This point is made by H. W. Parke, *The Delphic Oracle,* 85–86; see also G. Roux, *Delphes,* 99–100; and Plutarch, *Numa,* 9.6: "... Wherever in Greece a perpetual fire is kept, as at Delphi and Athens, it is committed to the charge not of virgins but of widows past the age of marriage."

44. P. Aelius Aristides, *The Panathenaic Oration,* vol. 1, 83 ff.

45. Plutarch, *Isis and Osiris,* 364E, trans. F. C. Babbitt, *Moralia* (LCL), vol. 5.

46. Aeschylus, *The Eumenides*, ll: 1–34.

47. Euripides, *Ion*, ll: 1367–69, trans. Ronald Frederick Willetts, in *The Complete Greek Tragedies*, vol. 2, Grene/Lattimore.

48. G. Roux, *Delphes*, 142 and 142n, discusses evidence for and against the Pythia's use of the bowl of water for the type of divination known as clairomancy, water gazing. Water divination is practiced in our own time by the priests of the Kogi people, a remote Andean community that has preserved its pre-Columbian culture. See Alan Ereira, *The Elder Brothers: A Lost South American People and Their Message About the Fate of the Earth* (New York: Alfred A. Knopf, 1992).

49. Plutarch, *Whether an Old Man Should Engage in Public Affairs*, in *Moralia*, 784B.

50. Willis Barnstone, trans., *Greek Lyric Poetry*, 1st ed. (New York: Schocken, 1972), 136–37. Tyrrhenia was the Greek term for the Etruscan cities of Italy.

51. Plutarch, *On Brotherly Love*, 489E, in *Moralia*, trans. W. C. Helmbold (LCL, 1957), vol. 6.

52. Euripides, *Ion*, ll: 89–100, in *The Complete Greek Tragedies*, vol. 2, Grene/Lattimore.

53. Ibid., ll: 226–29.

54. Rather than footnote extensively to Roux, *Delphes*, a work lucidly organized by topic, I prefer to acknowledge here that in this section the source for historical facts and speculations specifically concerning the oracular process, unless otherwise attributed, is the appropriate chapter in Roux. Errors of interpretation or emphasis in this section are naturally my own responsibility.

55. See Pausanias, *Guide to Greece*, 7.22.

56. This suggestion is from H. W. Parke, *The Delphic Oracle*, 28–29.

57. Plutarch, *Table-Talk, VII*, 709A, in *Moralia* (LCL), vol. 9.

58. S. Lombardo and D. Rayor, *Callimachus*, Iambics, ll: 9–10, p. 81. See Walter Burkert, *Homo Necans: The Anthropology of Ancient Greek Sacrificial Ritual and Myth*, trans. Peter Bing (Berkeley: University of California Press, 1983).

59. See Plutarch, *The Greek Questions*, 292E–F, in *Moralia*, trans. F. C. Babbitt (LCL, 1957), vol. 4.

60. Plutarch, *Obsolescence*, 431D.

61. Aeschylus, *The Eumenides*, l. 39, in *The Complete Greek Tragedies*, Grene/Lattimore; for other sources see G. Roux, *Delphes*, 97.

62. Strabo, *Geography*, 9.3.5.

63. *Hymns*, "To Hestia," p. 449. This ancient collection preserves what may be a Delphic hymn to Hestia, from which these lines are drawn.

64. Athenaeus, *The Deipnosophists*, (LCL, 1951), vol. 1:2.37 ff.

65. M. L. West, *The Orphic Poems* (Oxford: Clarendon Press, 1983), 147.

66. Plutarch, *Concerning Talkativeness*, 512E, in *Moralia*, trans. W. C. Hembold (LCL, 1957), vol. 6. Citing a line from the saga of Croesus in Herodotus (see chapter 6).

67. From Plutarch, *The Divine Vengeance,* 557C, in *Moralia*, trans. P. H. de Lacy and B. Einarson (LCL, 1959), vol. 7; and Pausanias, *Guide to Greece,* 10.13.

68. Pindar, Pythian VI, l: 15.

69. Adapted from Plutarch, *Alexander* 14, in *Plutarch's Lives*, trans. Bernadotte Perrin (LCL, 1971), vol. 7.

70. Adapted from Apollodorus, *The Library*, trans. James George Frazer, two vols. (LCL, 1921), 1.9.1–2.

71. Pausanias, *Guide to Greece,* 3.4.

72. Plutarch, *Lysander*, from *Plutarch's Lives* (LCL), vol. 4:303–07. See also Thucydides, *The Peloponnesian War,* 5.2; Diodorus Siculus 14.3.

73. Diogenes Laertius, *Diogenes,* 5.91.

NOTES, CHAPTER 5

1. Iamblichus, *Life of Pythagoras*, chap. 28, p. 76.

2. The translation that follows, by Hugh Tredennick, will be found in Hamilton/ Cairns, *Socrates' Defense (Apology),* 20D–23C.

3. Plato, *Laches,* 188A, trans. Benjamin Jowett, in *The Collected Dialogues,* Hamilton/ Cairns.

4. "You could not discover the limits of soul even if you traveled every road to do; such is the depth of its meaning." Wheelwright, *Heraclitus,* fr. 42, p. 58. For discussion, see chap. 12.

NOTES, CHAPTER 6

1. Alan Bullock, *Hitler and Stalin: Parallel Lives* (New York: Alfred A. Knopf, 1992), 680.

2. Aubrey de Sélincourt, trans., *Herodotus: The Histories* (Harmondsworth, Eng.: Penguin Books, 1954), 15. This highly readable translation will be cited throughout the chapter.

3. Plutarch, *The Oracles,* 401E–F.

NOTES, CHAPTER 7

1. Adapted from Pausanias, *Guide to Greece,* 7.5.

2. Adapted from Herodotus, *The History,* 5.114.

3. Strabo, *Geography,* 6.1.9.

4. Adapted from Clement, *Exhortation to the Greeks,* 1.2P, trans. C. W. Butterworth (LCL, 1953), vol. 9.

5. Pausanias, *Guide to Greece,* 10.24.1.

6. Adapted from Plutarch, *Solon,* 4, *Plutarch's Lives,* trans. Bernadotte Perrin (LCL), vol. 1.

7. Plato, *Protagoras,* 343A–B, trans. W. K. C. Guthrie, in *The Collected Dialogues,* Hamilton/Cairns.

8. Diogenes Laertius, *Bias,* 1.83, from *Lives of Eminent Philosophers,* trans. R. D. Hicks (LCL, 1950), vol. 1.

9. Diodorus Siculus 9:6–8.

10. Diogenes Laertius, *Myson,* 9:106–7.

11. Adapted from Herodotus, *The History,* 1:65, with the addition of two lines to the oracular message from Diodorus Siculus, 7:14, and Theodoret of Cyr, *Therapeutique,* 9:10.

12. Xenophon, *Constitution of the Lacedaemonians,* 9, trans. E. C. Marchant (LCL), vol. 7.

13. Adapted from Plutarch, *Lycurgus* 29, *Plutarch's Lives* (LCL), vol. 1.

14. Adapted from Dionysius of Halicarnassus, *Roman Antiquities,* 44.67ff., trans. E. Cary (LCL), vol. 3.

15. Dio Cassius, *Roman History,* pp. 80–81, trans. Earnest Cary (LCL, 1954), vol. 1.

16. Grene, Herodotus, *The History,* 2:172–4.

17. Diogenes Laertius, *Zeno* 7:2.

18. Adapted from Pausanias, *Guide to Greece,* 1:43.

19. Iamblichus, *The Life of Pythagoras,* trans. Kenneth Sylvan Guthrie, in *The Pythagorean Sourcebook and Library,* ed. David R. Fideler (Grand Rapids, Michigan: Phanes Press, 1987), 58–59. Hereafter cited as *Sourcebook.*

20. Cited from a lost work of Aristippus by Diogenes Laertius, *The Life of Pythagoras,* in *Sourcebook,* 147.

21. Iamblichus, *The Life of Pythagoras, Sourcebook,* 61.

22. *Sourcebook,* 131, 143.

23. Ibid.

24. Ibid., 108.

25. Ibid., 109–10.

26. Ibid., 129.

27. Diogenes Laertius, *Diogenes,* 6.2:20–21.

NOTES, CHAPTER 8

1. Plutarch, *Phokion,* 8:3, *Plutarch's Lives,* trans. Bernadotte Perrin (LCL, 1949), vol. 8.

2. Athenaeus, *The Deipnosophists,* 6.261D.

3. Xenophon, *Hellenica,* 4:7, trans. Carleton L. Brownson (LCL, 1950), vol. 1; Plutarch, *Sayings of Kings and Commanders,* 191B, trans. F. C. Babbitt, *Moralia* (LCL, 1931), vol. 3.

4. Adapted from Plutarch, *Aristides,* 11:3–9, *Plutarch's Lives* (LCL, 1958), vol. 2.

5. Ibid., 20:3–6.

6. Plutarch, *The Roman Questions,* 264F–265A, trans. F. C. Babbitt, in *Moralia* (LCL), vol. 4.

7. Pausanias, *Guide to Greece,* 4:15; Diodorus Siculus 8:27.

8. Adapted from Pausanias, *Guide to Greece,* 10:16.4.

9. Lycurgus, *Against Ieocrates,* 83–87.

10. Pausanias, *Guide to Greece,* 8:25.

11. Adapted from Herodotus, *The History,* 1:156–59.

12. Pausanias, *Guide to Greece,* 5:3.

13. Adapted from Nonnos, *Dionysica* 4:285, trans. H. J. Rose (LCL, 1956), vol. 1.

14. Adapted from Herodotus, *The History,* 6:34–35.

15. See Fontenrose, *The Delphic Oracle,* 125 ff.

16. Adapted from Herodotus, *The History,* 1:174.

17. Thucydides, *The Peloponneisan War,* 324.

18. Dionysius of Halicarnassus, 12.10 ff.

19. Plutarch, *Nicias,* 532A; cf. *The Oracles,* 403B.

20. Herodotus, *The Histories,* trans. de Sélincourt, 7:138–145.

21. See Herodotus, *The History,* 9.42.

22. Thucydides, *The Peloponneisan War,* 4:9.

23. Adapted from Pausanias, *Guide to Greece,* 4:9.

24. Ibid., 10.10.

25. Dionysius of Halicarnassus, 19:3.

26. Adapted from Dionysius of Halicarnassus, 8:23; 19:2.

27. Adapted from Apollodorus, *Epitome,* VI.18; cf. Podaleirius in Robert Graves, *The Greek Myths.*

28. Adapted from Herodotus, *The History,* 4:155–157.

29. Plutarch, *The Oracles,* 405C.

30. Adapted from Diodorus Siculus 8:17.

31. Adapted from Strabo, *Geography,* 6.2.4.

32. Adapted from Diodorus Siculus 15:18.

33. Adapted from Herodotus, *The History,* 1:165–67.

NOTES, CHAPTER 9

1. Ananda K. Coomaraswamy, *Manas,* vol. 1:259 (see n. 7, chapter 4).

2. Adapted from *Lyra Graeca,* 141–43, trans. J. M. Edwards (LCL, 1963), vol. 3.

3. Athenaeus, *The Deipnosophists,* 12:520 (LCL), vol. 5.

4. See Xenophon, *Memorabilia,* 1.3.1.

5. Plutarch, *Roman Questions,* 271C (LCL), vol. 4.

6. Athenaeus, *The Deipnosophists,* 13.606 (LCL), vol. 6.

7. Adapted from Apollodorus, 15.6; see also Plutarch, *Theseus, Plutarch's Lives* (LCL), vol. 1; and Pausanias, *Guide to Greece,* 1:20.

8. Adapted from Herodotus, *The History,* 6.86 and Pausanias, *Guide to Greece,* 8.7.

9. Pausanias, *Guide to Greece,* 8.7; see also Juvenal, *The Sixteen Satires,* trans. Peter Green, rev. ed. (Harmondsworth, Eng.: Penguin, 1974, Satire XIII), 256.

10. Herodotus, *The Histories,* trans. de Sélincourt, 9.93–94.

11. Adapted from Herodotus, *The History,* 5.92.

12. Guy Davenport, trans., *Archilochos, Sappho, Alkman: Three Lyric Poets of the Seventh Century* B.C. (Berkeley: University of California Press, 1980), 58.

13. Ibid., 24.

14. Adapted from sources cited in Parke and Wormell, *The Delphic Oracle,* vol. 2, 3–4, particularly Aelian, fr. 80, and Plutarch, *The Divine Vengeance,* 560.

15. Adapted from Emile Champry, ed. and trans., *Esope, Fables* (Paris: Belles Lettres, 1927), 24.

16. See Lloyd W. Daly, ed. and trans., *Aesop Without Morals* (New York and London: Yoseloff, 1961). The last days of Aesop, at Delphi, are memorably narrated on pp. 85–90.

17. Ibid., 85–86.

18. Plutarch, *Agis,* 11:3, trans. Bernadotte Perrin, *Plutarch's Lives* (LCL), vol. 10.

19. Adapted from Herodotus, *The History,* 6.52.

20. Plutarch, *The Oracles,* 403B–C.

21. Plutarch, *The Oracles,* 407C.

22. Grene, Herodotus, *The History,* 7.6.

23. See, for example, the wonderful description in Plutarch, *Obsolescence,* 421A–C.

24. Sophocles, *Oedipus Tyrannos,* ll: 284 ff., in *The Complete Greek Tragedies,* Grene/Lattimore.

25. Philostratus, 4.24.

26. Adapted from Plato (pseudo-Plato), *Hipparchus,* 228C–229B, trans. W. R. M. Lamb (LCL, 1927).

27. Aristophanes, *The Knights, Peace, Wealth,* trans. Alan H. Sommerstein, *The Birds, The Assemblywomen,* trans. David Barrett (Harmondsworth, Eng.: Penguin Books, 1978), 134 ff.

28. Ibid., pp. 186–87.

29. Ibid., p. 74.

30. Thucydides, *The Peloponnesian War,* 2.3.

31. Juvenal, Satire VI, ll. 510 ff.

32. Lucian, *Alexander the False Prophet,* 3–4, trans. A. M. Harmon (LCL, 1925), vol. 4.

33. Ibid., 8.

34. Ibid., 24.

35. Adapted from Philochoros, as cited by Zenobius, *Proverbiorum centuriae,* V:75, in P. Amandry, *La mantique,* 27, 252–53.

NOTES, CHAPTER 10

1. Euripides, *Andromache,* trans. John Frederick Nims, in *The Complete Greek Tragedies,* Grene/Lattimore, 1085 ff.

2. Plutarch, *The Oracles,* 399F.

3. Plutarch, *Alexander,* 74.6.

4. Plato, *Gorgias,* 447C–D.

5. Pausanias, *The Guide to Greece,* 10.8.7.

6. Pliny, *Natural History,* trans. H. Rackham (LCL, 1952), vol. 9:33.24.

7. Riginos, *Platonica,* 93.

8. Dio Chrysostom, "The Rhodion Oration," 37.29–30.

9. Pausanias, *Guide to Greece,* 10.14.4.

10. Dio Chrysostom, "The Rhodion Oration," 37.28.

11. Thucydides, *The Peloponnesian War,* 2.45.2.

12. Plutarch, *Bravery of Women,* trans. F. C. Babbitt, *Moralia* (LCL), vol. 3:243D.

13. Pliny, *Natural History,* trans. D. E. Eichholz (LCL, 1962), vol. 10:36.4.20.

14. Diogenes Laertius, *Diogenes,* 6:60.

15. Pausanias, *Guide to Greece,* 1:20.

16. On the status and life of women, see Eva C. Keuls, *The Reign of the Phallus: Sexual Politics in Ancient Greece* (New York: Harper, 1985).

17. Pausanias, *Guide to Greece,* 10.2.4.

18. Grene, Herodotus, *The History,* 9.80.

19. Hesiod, *Theogony,* 453–505; see also Pausanias, *Guide to Greece,* 10.24.6.

20. Pausanias, *Guide to Greece,* 10.9.

21. Thucydides, *The Peloponnesian War,* 1.1. Fragments of the monument survive.

22. Pausanias, *Guide to Greece,* 10.18.4.

23. Ibid., 10.9.3.

24. Ibid., 10.9.4.

25. Ibid., p. 428n, trans. Peter Levi.

26. Plutarch, *The Oracles,* 395B.

27. Adapted from Ibid., 401A–C.

28. Ibid., 402A.

29. Plutarch, *Nicias,* 13; Pausanias, *Guide to Greece,* 10.15.

30. Plutarch, *The Oracles,* 397F.

31. Ibid., 398A.

32. Ibid., 398B.

33. Plutarch, *The Oracles,* 401F.

34. Ibid., 402A.

35. Pausanias, *Guide to Greece,* 10.14; see also Aelian 12.40.

36. See Strabo, *Geography,* 9.3.7–8.

37. Pausanias, *Guide to Greece,* 10.18.3.

38. Plutarch, *The E,* 384F.

39. See Ananda K. Coomaraswamy, *Selected Papers,* vol. 2, "The E at Delphi," 43–45.

40. Plutarch, *The E,* 384F–385A.

41. Ibid., 392A.

42. Ibid., 392–394.

NOTES, CHAPTER 11

1. Clement of Alexandria, *An Exhortation to the Greeks,* trans. G. W. Butterworth (LCL, 1953), chap. 12:92. Readers will find in Robin Lane Fox, *Pagans and Christians* (New York: Alfred A. Knopf, 1986), an engaging extended history and creative restoration of the

centuries and issues covered by this chapter. A much shorter but equally vivid treatment is Pierre Chuvin, *A Chronicle of the Last Pagans*, trans. B. A. Archer (Cambridge and London: Harvard University Press, 1990).

2. "... The altar's fire surges up and the smoke of sacrifice purges the air ...," Libanius, a mid-fourth century pagan whom we will come upon again in this chapter, *Oration* XIII, trans. A. F. Norman (LCL, 1969), 1:47.

3. Plutarch, *Obsolescence*, 419B–D.

4. Eusebius, *Preparation for the Gospel*, trans. Edwin Hamilton Gifford (Oxford: Clarendon Press, 1903), 5.208a.

5. Thucydides, *The Peloponnesian War*, 2.5, Warner, p. 123.

6. Ibid., 5.3, Warner, p. 324; see also 5.7, Warner, p. 362, the Melian Debate, in the course of which the Athenians opportunistically demean oracles as "blind and vague."

7. Plato, *Charmides*, 173C.

8. Writing several generations after Cicero, Strabo reported: "Among the ancients both divination in general and oracles were held in greater honor, but now great neglect of them prevails, since the Roman are satisfied with the oracles of Sibylla, and with the Tyrrhenian prophecies obtained by means of the entrails of animals, flight of birds, and omens from the sky; and on this account ..., the oracle at Ammon has been almost abandoned, though it was held in honor in earlier times. ..." Strabo, *Geography*, 17.1.43.

9. Cicero, *The Nature of the Gods*, trans. Horace C. P. McGregor (Harmondsworth, Eng.: Penguin, 1972), I.71.

10. Cicero, *On Divination*, trans. William Armistead Falconer (LCL, 1923), vol. 20:1.1.

11. Ibid., 2.6.11.

12. Ibid., 1.18.37–38.

13. Cicero, *On Divination*, 2.55.115ff.

14. Ovid, *The Art of Love* 2.537 ff., in Ovid, *The Erotic Poems*, trans. Peter Green (Harmondsworth, Eng.: Penguin, 1982).

15. Ibid., 3.787 ff.

16. *The Poems of Sextus Propertius*, trans. J. P. McCulloch (Berkeley and Los Angeles: University of California Press, 1972), 1.9:29.

17. Ibid., 2.4:65.

18. Plutarch, *Obsolescence*, 412A.

19. Ibid., 411–18.

20. Plutarch, *The Oracles*, 398F–399B.

21. Ibid., 408D.

22. Epictetus, *Discourses*, 2.20.27.

23. Lucian, *The Lover of Lies*, trans. A. M. Harmon (LCL, 1921), vol. 3:38.

24. Lucian, *Zeus Rants*, trans. A. M. Harmon (LCL 1929), vol. 2:29–31.

25. Lucian, *The Double Indictment* (LCL), vol. 3:1.

26. Clement of Alexandria, *Exhortation to the Greeks,* 4P.

27. Ibid., 40P.

28. Ibid., 19P.

29. Ibid., 23P.

30. Ibid., 72–73P.

31. Ibid., 91P.

32. Ibid., 49P.

33. Ibid., 10–11P.

34. Ibid., 67P.

35. Ibid., 38P.

36. Ibid., 47P.

37. Celsus' arguments and Origen's responses are drawn from Origen, *Contra Celsum,* 8.45–46. Except where indicated, all translations from Origen are in *The Ante-Nicene Fathers: Translations of the Writings of the Fathers down to A.D. 325,* ed. Alexander Roberts and James Donaldson (Grand Rapids, Michigan: W. B. Eerdmanns, 1980), vol. 4.

38. This and the following passages, ibid., 7.3–5.

39. Saint Chrysostom, *Homilies on the Epistles of Paul to the Corinthians*, in *A Select Library of the Nicene and Post-Nicene Fathers of the Christian Church*, ed. and trans. Philip Schaff and Henry Wace (Grand Rapids, Michigan: W. B. Eerdmanns, 1978), vol. 12. This and the subsequent citation are from Homily XXIX.

40. Pindar, *Pythian,* 5, ll. 63–67.

41. Eusebius, *Preparation for the Gospel*, 140c, p. 153. Since the manuscript folio references (such as 140c) are somewhat difficult to follow in Gifford's edition, modern page numbers will also be noted for this text.

42. Ibid., 131c, p. 143.

43. Ibid., 132b–d, p. 144, and 136a–d, pp. 148–49.

44. Ibid., 178b, p. 195.

45. Ibid., 214a–215d, pp. 231–33.

46. Ibid., 215a–c, pp. 232–33.

47. Ibid., 213c, p. 231.

48. Ibid., 220d, p. 238.

49. Ibid., p. 235.

50. As noted earlier, readers will find full and engaging recent accounts of the era in Robin Lane Fox, *Pagans and Christians* and Pierre Chuvin *A Chronicle of the Last Pagans.*

51. Chuvin, *A Chronicle*, 25–26.

52. Eunapius, *Lives of the Philosophers,* 464, in Philostratus and Eunapius, *The Lives of the Sophists,* trans. Wilmer Cave Wright (LCL, 1921).

53. Julian, *Hymn to King Helios Dedicated to Sallust,* 130B–C (LCL, 1913), vol. 1.

54. Julian, *To the Cynic Heracleios,* 226C (LCL, 1913), vol. 2.

55. Ibid. 209B–C. In another essay, *To the Uneducated Cynics,* Julian describes Oenomaus as "shameless, impudent, a scorner of everything human and divine," unlike his Cynic forebear Diogenes who was "reverent toward sacred things. . . . For he obeyed the Pythian oracle nor did he repent of his obedience," ibid., 199B.

56. Libanius, *Oration XIII,* 47–48 (To Julian) (LCL), vol. 1.

57. Chuvin, *A Chronicle,* 39.

58. Julian, *Against the Galileans,* 198C–D (LCL, 1923), vol. 3.

59. Eunapius, *Lives of the Philosophers,* 504.

60. Chuvin, *A Chronicle,* 46.

61. Adapted from Fontenrose, *The Delphic Oracle,* 351.

62. Excerpted from "The Last Oracle," in *The Complete Works of Algernon Charles Swinburn,* ed. Sir Edmund Gosse and Thomas James Wise, vol. 3 (reprint, 1968) (New York: Russell and Russell, 1968), 1.

63. Libanius, *Oration XXIV* 2 (LCL), vol. 1.

64. Libanius, *To the Emperor Theodosius, For the Temples, Oration XXX* (LCL), vol. 2; excerpts from sections 2–31.

65. H. W. Parke, *The Delphic Oracle,* vol. 2, inquiry 475, p. 287.

66. Chuvin, *A Chronicle,* 65.

67. Ibid., 71, 75, 80.

68. Eunapius, *Lives of the Philosophers,* 473.

NOTES, CHAPTER 12

1. Xenophon, *Memorabilia* 4.2.24; cf. Pausanias, *Guide to Greece,* 10.24.1: "In the front of the temple at Delphi aids to human life have been inscribed, composed by the Seven Wise Men . . ."

2. Pliny, *Natural History,* 7.32.

3. Juvenal, Satire XI, l. 28.

4. From a lost work of Aristotle, cited in a lost work of Porphyry on "Know thyself," cited in turn by an anthologist of the early fifth century C.E., Johannes Stobeaus, in his *Florilegum,* XXI.26; yet again cited (p. 6) in a work of scholarship that will be centrally useful to anyone wishing to explore further this aspect of ancient thought: Eliza Gregory Wilkins, " 'Know Thyself' in Greek and Latin Literature," (Ph.D. diss. The University of Chicago Libraries, 1917). Referenced hereafter as Wilkins, diss. See also

Eliza Gregory Wilkins, *The Delphic Maxims in Literature* (Chicago: University of Chicago Press, 1929).

5. Diogenes Laertius, *Diogenes,* 1.36.

6. Cited in Plutarch, *A Letter to Appolonius,* 116D; Moralia (LCL), trans. F. C. Babbitt (LCL, 1928), vol. 2.

7. Iamblichus, *Life of Pythagoras,* 18; *Sourcebook,* p. 78; slight alteration in translation.

8. St. Basil of Caesarea, *The Hexameron,* 106, in *St. Basil: Letters and Select Works* (London: 1894); in *A Select Library of Nicene and Post-Nicene Fathers of the Christian Church,* 2nd Series.

9. Plato, *Protagoras,* trans. W. K. C. Guthrie, in *The Collected Dialogues,* Hamilton/Cairns, 343A–B.

10. Plutarch, *The Oracles,* 408B ff.

11. Plutarch, *The E,* 385D; cf. related thoughts in *idem, Concerning Talkativeness,* 511A–B, *Moralia* (LCL), vol. 6.

12. Dio Chrysostom, *The 72nd Discourse: On Personal Appearance,* 12.

13. Plato, *Protagoras,* 343B.

14. See Betty Radice, trans., *Seven Wise Men of Greece: The Sayings of the Seven Sages* (Verona: Officina Bodoni, 1976); and the related article by Louis Robert, "De Delphes à l'Oxus: Inscriptions grecques nouvelles de la Bactriane," *Comptes rendus de l'Académie des Inscriptions* (1968): 416–457.

15. Wheelwright, *Heraclitus,* fr. 1, p. 19.

16. Ibid., p. 21.

17. Ibid., fr. 3, p. 19: "Men who love wisdom should acquaint themselves with a great many particulars."

18. Ibid. respectively fr. 9, p. 19; fr. 8, p. 19; fr. 42, p. 58.

19. See for example Plato, *Charmides,* 164D–165E, and Diodorus Siculus, 9.10 ff. Plutarch, *A Letter to Apollonius,* 116B–E (trans. Wilkins, diss., p. 56), gives the taste: "These two of the Delphic inscriptions are exceedingly necessary for life—Know thyself and Nothing too much—for on these all else depends. They are in accord and harmony with each other, and through the one the force of the other seems to be revealed. For in knowing oneself there is included the Nothing too much and in Nothing too much the self-knowing. . . . He who has these in mind will be able to harmonize the experiences of life readily and to bear them successfully, while he looks to his own nature, and is neither exalted with undue arrogance in prosperity, nor dejected and given to wailing and lament through weakness of soul and the fear of death implanted in us."

20. Davenport, *Archilochos,* 36–37.

21. Aeschylus, *Prometheus,* 309, trans. David Grene, in *The Complete Greek Tragedies,* Grene/Lattimore.

22. Ibid., ll. 337–38.

23. This theme is richly investigated in Wilkins, diss.

24. Isocrates, *Panathenaicus* (LCL), vol. 2:513.

25. Plato, *Phaedrus,* 229A–230B, trans. R. Hackforth, in *The Collected Dialogues,* Hamilton/Cairns.

26. Plato, *Symposium,* 216A, trans. Michael Joyce, in *The Collected Dialogues,* Hamilton/Cairns.

27. Plato, *Philebus,* 48C–D, trans. R. Hackforth, in *The Collected Dialogues,* Hamilton/Cairns.

28. Plato, *Alcibiades I:*127E–128A.

29. Ibid., 129A.

30. Ibid., 132B–C.

31. Ibid., 133C.

32. Plato, *Symposium,* 220C–D.

33. Xenophon, *Memorabilia,* 4.2.24.

34. Xenophon, *Memoirs of Socrates,* 4.2.26–29, in Hugh Tredennick and Robin Waterfield, trans., *Conversations of Socrates* (London: Penguin Books, 1990). For more material on self-knowledge in Xenophon, see *Cyropaedia,* 8.2.16 ff., and *Hellenica,* 2.4.40–41 in the LCL editions. In *Cyropaedia,* Croesus is offered in an engaging dialogue as the very example of the ruler who does not know himself in the sense of misjudging his strength.

35. Menander, *Principal Fragments,* trans. Francis G. Allinson (LCL, 1964), 360–61.

36. *Magna Moralia,* trans. Wilkins, "Know Thyself," diss., 84.

37. Epictetus, *Fragments,* (LCL), vol. 2:331.

38. Plutarch, *How to Profit by One's Enemies,* trans. F. C. Babbitt, *Moralia* (LCL), vol. 2:89A–B.

39. Plutarch, *How to Tell a Flatterer From a Friend,* 267, trans. F. C. Babbitt, *Moralia,* (LCL, 1927), vol. 1.

40. Dio Chrysostom, "The Fourth Discourse on Kingship," trans. J. W. Cohoon (LCL), vol. 1:51–58.

41. Ovid, *The Art of Love,* 2, ll. 493 ff.; similarly Juvenal, Satire XI, ll. 27 ff.

42. Lucian, *The Dialogues of the Dead,* trans. M. D. MacLeod (LCL, 1961), vol. 7:19.

43. Lucian, *The Dance,* trans. A. M. Harmon (LCL), vol. 5:81.

44. Epictetus, *Discourses,* 3.14.1–3.

45. Ibid., 1.18.17–19.

46. Ibid., 3.22.53.

47. Ibid., 3.1.18.

48. See, for example, Cicero, *Tusculan Disputations,* 5.24, trans. J. E. King (LCL, 1927), vol. 18:5.24, and Philo Judaeus, *On Dreams,* 1.54–57, for the contrasting arguments.

49. Philo, *On Flight and Finding,* 46–47, commentating Genesis 27:44, trans. F. H. Colson and G. H. Whitaker (LCL, 1934), vol. 5.

50. Philo, *The Special Laws,* 1.44, commentating Exodus 33:13–24 (LCL), vol. 7.

51. See, for example, Julian, *To the Cynic Heracleios,* 211B–D (LCL), vol. 2.

52. Ibid., 225D.

53. Julian, *To the Uneducated Cynics,* (LCL), vol. 2:183–185A.

54. Plutarch, *Demosthenes,* 3.2.

55. Menander, fr. 538, trans. Wilkins, diss. "Know Thyself," p. 55.

56. Cicero, *Tusculan Disputations,* 5.24.

57. Plutarch, *The E,* 392, 394C.

58. Macrobius, *Commentary on Scipio's Dream,* 1.9.2–3, trans. Wilkins, diss., "Know Thyself," 75.

59. Proclus, *Commentary on Alcibiades, I,* vol. 1, p. 5, trans. Wilkins, diss., "Know Thyself," 74.

60. *Grégoire le Thaumaturge, Remerciement à Origène suivi de la lettre d'Origène à Grégoire*, ed. and trans. Henri Crouzel, trans. R. L. (Paris: Editions du Cerf, 1969) [*Sources Chrétiennes* 148], 153–54.

61. Philostratus, 7.14.

62. "Know Thyself," Wilkins, diss., p. 39, trans.; see note 60.

63. Pausanias, *Guide to Greece,* 5.14.9.

64. Pindar, *Pythian,* 9, ll. 77–78.

65. Pindar, *Isthmian,* 2, ll. 21–22.

66. Diogenes Laertius, *Diogenes,* 1.79.

67. Hippocrates, *Precepts,* 1, trans. W. H. S. James (LCL, 1923), vol. 1.

68. Greek Anthology, 12.197, trans. W. R. Paton (LCL), vol. 4.

69. Philostratus, 3.42, recalling the tale of Crow in chap. 9.

NOTES, AFTERWORD

1. René de Nebesky-Wojkowitz, *Oracles and Demons of Tibet: The Cult and Iconography of the Tibetan Protective Deities* (The Netherlands: Mouton and Co., 1956). Now available in a Taiwanese paperback edition (SMC Publishing Inc.).

2. On hearing this anecdote, a friend of mine called it a "shaggy oracle story."

Bibliographic Overview

It suits this book of tales simply to indicate where the trailhead begins for readers who wish to explore the Delphic oracle independently. The books noticed here offer scholarship central to the topic and, as well, extensive bibliographies. The four annual guides or indices, some of which are available online at larger libraries, offer access to recent scholarship. The notes for each chapter in the present work identify primary sources and much additional scholarly literature.

EXCAVATION REPORTS

École française d'Athènes. *Fouilles de Delphes*. Ed. Théophile Homolle and others. Paris: 1902–.

MONOGRAPHS

Amandry, Pierre. *La mantique Apollinienne à Delphes; Essai sur le fonctionnement de l'Oracle*. Paris: Boccard, 1950.

Defradas, Jean. *Les thèmes de la propagande delphique*. Paris: Kincksieck, 1954.

Delcourt, Marie. *L'Oracle de Delphes*. Paris: Payot, 1955.

Dodds, E. R. *The Greeks and the Irrational*. Berkeley: University of California Press, 1951.

Fontenrose, Joseph. *The Delphic Oracle: Its Responses and Operations, With a Catalogue of Responses*. Berkeley: University of California Press, 1978.

Parke, H. W., and D. E. W. Wormell. *The Delphic Oracle*. 2 vols. Oxford: Blackwell, 1956.

Roux, Georges. *Delphes: Son oracle et ses dieux*. Paris: Les Belles Lettres, 1976.

ARTICLES

Maurizio, L. "Anthropology and Spirit Possession: A Reconsideration of the Pythia's Role at Delphi." *Journal of Hellenic Studies*, vol. 115, 1995. Pp. 69–86.

GUIDES TO CURRENT BOOKS AND ARTICLES

L'Année philologique: bibliographie critique et analytique de l'antiquité graeco-latine. Paris: Les Belles Lettres, 1924–.

Art Index. New York: H. W. Wilson, 1932–.

Bibliography of the History of Art (BHA). = *Bibliographie d'histoire de l'art.* Vandoeuvre-lès-Nancy, France, and Santa Monica, Calif.: Centre national de la recherche scientifique, Institut de l'information scientifique et technique; J. Paul Getty Trust, Getty Art History Information Program, 1991–.

Humanities Index. New York: H. W. Wilson. 1974/75–.

Index